MESOAMERICA

The Evolution of a Civilization

Studies in Anthropology

CONSULTING EDITORS / MORTON H. FRIED and
MARVIN HARRIS
COLUMBIA UNIVERSITY

William T. Sanders
PENNSYLVANIA STATE UNIVERSITY

Barbara J. Price
COLUMBIA UNIVERSITY

MESOAMERICA

The Evolution of a
Civilization

RANDOM HOUSE / *New York*

9 8

Authors and Publisher gratefully acknowledge permission for the following:

Quotation from Eric R. Wolf, *Peasants*, © 1966. Reprinted by permission of Prentice-Hall, Inc., Englewood Cliffs, New Jersey.

Chart on p. 82, adapted from Marshall D. Sahlins, *Social Stratification in Polynesia* (Seattle: University of Washington Press, 1958), p. 132.

Figure 6. Ground Plan of La Venta. Adapted from Philip Drucker, Robert F. Heizer, and Robert J. Squier, *Excavations at La Venta, Tabasco, 1955,* Bureau of American Ethnology Bulletin 170.

Figure 7. Ground Plan of Tikal. Reproduced by permission of the University Museum, Philadelphia.

Figure 8. Ground Plan of Teotihuacán. From "Teotihuacán" by René Millon. Copyright © June 1967 by Scientific American, Inc. All rights reserved.

To
Carleton Stevens Coon

Foreword

This is a book on the theory of civilization. It deals with the factors and processes of growth that shaped culture history in Mexico and Guatemala long before the advent of the white man. But its intellectual significance transcends the geographical focus.

In the conceptual system of cultural evolutionism the term civilization has a precise meaning; it stands for a definite stage in the development of society and culture. The birth of any pristine civilization set a milestone in the evolutionary career of mankind, and this happened at different times in a few widely separated areas of the world. None of the human races has a monopoly on civilization. High cultures were developed in distant parts of the world by people whose skins had quite varied shades of pigmentation. Independent recurrence of the phenomenon—the crystallization of complex society and high culture in remarkably similar patterns resulting from distinct historical courses—begs scientific explanation in terms of relationships of cause and effect. Sanders' and Price's analysis of the conditions and forces that brought forth civilization and nurtured its growth in one of the hearths is an important contribution to the attainment of this aim.

The fact that this theoretical contribution is built on substantive data concerning one of the two aboriginal civilizations that took root in the New World attests to the coming of age of American archaeology. Though little known to outsiders, by default of the specialists to communicate the findings in assimilable form, the conceptual framework of prehistoric research has been developing fast on this side of the Atlantic Ocean since the early 1940s. The social science approach to the study of the pre-Columbian past has reached maturity. New World archaeology now has the capacity to make significant contributions to the methodology of retrospective study of complex societies and to the general theory of civilization.

To this end, the Americas present exceptional opportunities. Nowhere else in the world is the societal structure of pristine civilizations as well documented as in Mexico or Peru. This is due to the fact that the historical accident of European discovery and conquest, early in the sixteenth century, arrested the aboriginal American developments of civilization at a stage comparable to early phases of the most ancient civilizations of the Old World. The intellectual curiosity of the men of the Renaissance and practical requirements for the organization of the fast expanding Overseas Spanish Empire produced an unusual amount of information on native society and culture. The significance of this situation for the formulation of a general theory of the rise of civilization cannot be overestimated. The available written records on the structure of society in ancient Sumer, early Pharaonic Egypt, or Shang China are very fragmentary and often rather ambiguous; on the Harappan civilization this information is nil, as long as we cannot read the old Indus Valley script. By contrast, thanks to the full eyewitness accounts, inquests, and administrative reports left by the Spanish conquistadores, churchmen, and crown officials, we have vivid descriptions of the functional operation of the relatively youthful civilizations of the Aztecs, the Mayas, and the Incas.

It has become increasingly evident that long-standing formulations of the processes of growth of civilization must be reappraised in the light of the aboriginal American experiences. It seems fit to remind the reader that the concept of civilization was originally defined with reference to the Old World.

At the start of scientific research on ancient societies, Lewis H. Morgan, the great precursor of the theory of cultural evolution, barely sketched the idea of civilization; in fact, his only definite diagnostic criterion to mark the attainment of this stage was the invention of writing. It was his follower Friedrich Engels who gave the term its present technical meaning. Engels derived his definition of the concept from the analysis of societal structures in Classical Mediterranean antiquity which, as we well know now, represented in fact a relatively advanced and certainly late stage in the development of civilization. It could not be otherwise, for the discipline of archaeology was then in its infancy and little was really known of the most ancient Near East, not to speak of other original developments around the world.

In its modern form, the theory of cultural evolution fundamentally rests on analyses of inductive formulations of the processes of change, established on the bases of the sequences revealed by the testimony of the spade. V. Gordon Childe pioneered this approach when he undertook the formulation of the concept of civilization in the light of archaeological data pertaining to the developments in ancient Mesopotamia and Egypt. This was a great leap forward toward the aim of understanding the process in truly functional terms. But the scope was limited by the choice of only two instances of birth of civilization. In fact, Childe's identification of the attainment of civilization with the growth of urbanism represented by the earliest Sumerian cities may be a particular case of some more general law. The term "Urban Revolution" does not apply to all instances. Indeed, its validity seems questionable with reference to the rise of the other great ancient civilization of the Near East, insofar as nothing is known about Old Kingdom Egyptian cities.

In this book, Sanders and Price test the validity of these generalizations in the touchstone of the story of an independent development that took place in the New World. In the process they make significant contributions to the general definition of civilization and to methodology.

I think that the authors satisfactorily demonstrate that the rise of civilization can be seen as the outcome of a process of ecological adaptation. Consequently, the phenomenon must be analyzed, as they have done, in terms of autecology (with reference to environment) and synecology (community relationships). Each independent instance of civilization constitutes a unique ecosystem. This explains why the configurations of growth of the high cultures and complex polities appear to be diverse in the different hearths of pristine civilization.

In their analysis of the dynamic aspects of the ecosystem the authors have made a very important theoretical contribution. This is the formulation of the principle of critical population mass (size and concentration) as a condition of civilization. To forestall possible misinterpretations deriving from the current fashionable cult of the quantitative approach, the authors wisely make clear that the fundamental criterion of critical mass is not an absolute yardstick to be mechanically applied to any situation. They definitely state that population mass is only a relative factor: the minimal values vary for different ecosystems. And they add that numbers and density alone are not determinants of social structure. These qualifications lead to the consideration of the effects of circumscribed (in contrast to extended) ecological zones on the process of evolution and the achievement of critical levels of integration for the development of complex social systems. This concept completes the argument. I never saw this idea so precisely expressed and systematically applied to historical reconstruction.

The merits of this approach are brilliantly manifested by the ecological explanation of the structural differences between Highland Mexican and Lowland Mayan societies and by the authors' illuminating analysis of the effects of the conical structure of the old Mexican *calpulli* on the dynamics of urbanization and expansion. As Sanders and Price say, the variability and flexibility of this nucleus of social organization are features of adaptive significance.

Concerning the correlation between civilization and urbanism, the authors rightly point out that while urbanism implies civilization the reverse is not true. They make a fine distinction between the processes of population growth and socioeconomic differentiation, on the one hand, and nucleation, on the other. The first are characteristic of the development of civilization generally, but the last one is the particularly distinctive feature of the urban revolution. The concepts of civilization and urban revolution are not identical. American instances clearly show that high culture and the state type of political organization can develop with or without city life. Networks of integration can fulfill the functional requirements of complex societies, instead of nucleation. Urban-nucleated polities, however, possess greater evolutionary potential, as attested by the dominant role that the Mexican high plateau came to play in the development of Mesoamerican civilization after the arising of urban centers.

The foregoing remarks are but a few of the many reflections that this book stimulates. I trust the reader will find it as engrossing as I did.

Pedro Armillas
The University of Chicago
August 1967

Preface

        The enormous amount of archaeological research conducted during the past decade in Mesoamerica—work in which we have participated—has increased the need for an interpretive synthesis of a huge and ever-growing body of data. Just such a synthesis is presented in this volume, which views these data from the perspective of recent developments in general anthropological theory. Since field investigations show no sign of cessation—and perhaps this book will provide still further stimulus—many of our statements will undoubtedly require future modification or correction. Many of our conclusions are highly speculative, and will unquestionably provoke criticism and debate, which we consider desirable in the interest of the continued development of science. For there remain at least as many unsolved problems as questions to which we feel we can provide tentative answers. We believe, however, that an evolutionistic and ecological interpretation of cultural phenomena will remain valid and productive. This methodology, which regards the data of anthropology as essentially regular and subject to law, can provide a framework for answering old questions and raising new problems—ultimately perhaps rendering obsolete many of our present statements of fact.

    In recent years interest has grown on the part of many of our colleagues in the kind of phenomena presented here. One advantage of the ecological approach we employ is that ethnological and archaeological data can be encompassed by the same general theory, to what we regard as the mutual benefit of both subdisciplines. Facts alone are meaningless in the absence of theory and therefore cannot reveal what we consider the significant regularities in the development of human culture. We are concerned not merely with the what, but also with the why—both past and present. Our thinking, accordingly, has been stimulated by both archaeologists and ethnologists; our views favor and indeed necessitate consideration of both types of evidence within a unified, holistic conceptual matrix.

In any work whose purpose is synthesis, intellectual ancestry is necessarily long, varied, and not easily documented. This is especially true in a work of joint authorship, where each author brings to a given body of data a slightly different training and outlook; and where there is inevitable difficulty in distinguishing, so to speak, convergence from diffusion, and simultaneous independent invention from borrowing. Our bibliography is a partial recognition of our debt to many of our colleagues, past and present.

The influence of Pedro Armillas is evident throughout this book and represents a contribution to our thinking far beyond his own publications. He has, to our benefit and that of our common discipline, been a constant and provocative stimulus, not only to us, but indeed to an entire generation of scholars, both in the United States and beyond its borders. We are honored that he has provided the Foreword to this book.

In the course of the postwar return to anthropological thinking of large-scale problems of cause and effect, and of concern with general problems of development of culture and of civilization, Julian Steward has been a major standard-bearer. His formulation of the theory and methodology of cultural ecology and multilineal evolution is an invaluable intellectual basis for the present study. A second principal theoretical influence is the evolutionist position of Leslie White, Marshall Sahlins, and Elman Service. In particular, Service's *Primitive Social Organization* has stimulated our present treatment of the Mesoamerican archaeological sequence. A third approach to these problems that has strongly influenced our own has been that of Karl Wittfogel. His formulations of the relationship of irrigation systems to social organization are extraordinarily consonant with our data, and our debt to his thinking will be evident.

We cannot express the depth of our gratitude to Morton Fried and Marvin Harris, Consulting Editors of this series. Were it not for their good offices, far beyond the call of their editorial duties, this book would probably not exist in its present form. Originally a paper which insisted on outgrowing itself, it is published in the Random House Series in Anthropology at their suggestion and with their constant and much appreciated encouragement. Their warm enthusiasm and support have been of enormous assistance to us, and their advice and comments have benefited our work in many ways too numerous to mention.

Discussions and conversations with a number of friends and colleagues have proved stimulating and profitable. Many of them have read the book in manuscript, and have offered helpful suggestions and criticisms. While the authors retain full responsibility for the opinions expressed in this book, we would like to offer special thanks to Robert M. Adams, Paul T. Baker, Edward Calnek, Michael D. Coe, Kent V. Flannery, Richard S. MacNeish, Joseph Michels, René Millon, Angel Palerm, Gordon R. Willey, and Eric R. Wolf.

It would be inconceivable to write a book using the ecological approach without maps. Our heartfelt thanks, therefore, to Joseph Marino for his excellent maps and drawings. We also wish to thank Ilsa Schuster for preparing the index.

We dedicate this book to Carleton Stevens Coon, whose imaginativeness and intellectual daring, and whose great breadth of anthropological knowledge have stood as an example to us, his former students. His teaching—at Harvard and at the University of Pennsylvania—was instrumental in the intellectual formation of both the present authors. Largely on the basis of his early influence, we, like him, have been concerned with the question of cultural regularities resulting from similarity in level of complexity, and with the operation of causality in cultural development. Coon wrote in the Preface to his *Reader in General Anthropology* that the study of quantitative differences between cultures will help us to understand these problems. We can do no better than to quote him:

> . . . the study of the quantitative method is profitable because it is the method of systematic science which has proved fruitful in all other fields of learning in which it has been used. The essence of the quantitative approach in cultural anthropology lies in the thesis that the main stream or streams of human culture must have proceeded from simpler to more complex. The evidence of archaeology and of history supports this thesis, which in turn accords with all that we know of life in general. It must be equally apparent that the living cultures of the world vary in degrees of complexity, and that whole cultures can be listed and studied with greatest profit on the basis of such a progressive scheme—(COON 1948:vii).

William T. Sanders
University Park, Pennsylvania

Barbara J. Price
New York, New York

March 1967

Contents

Illustrations

MESOAMERICA

The Evolution of a Civilization

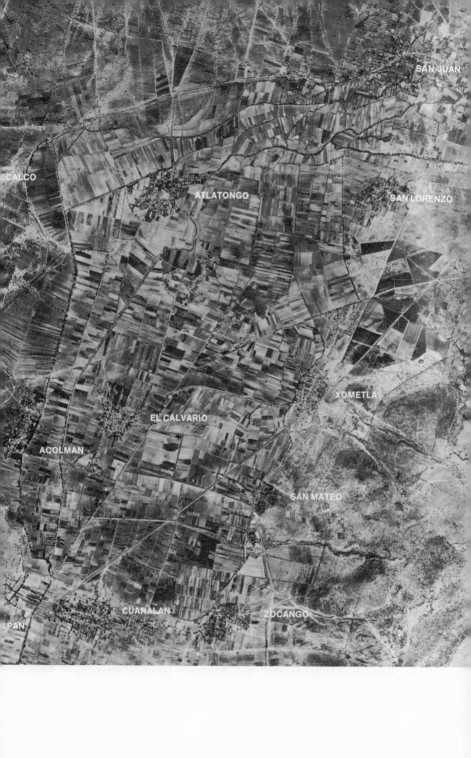

(Left Photo) Oblique view of central portion of the archaeological site of Teotihuacán, Mexico. The Camino de los Muertos, central axis of the city, runs approximately north-south, from the Pyramid of the Moon (left foreground), past the Pyramid of the Sun (center) and the Ciudadela (right center). The Patlachique Range (background) forms the southeastern boundary of Teotihuacán Valley. *Courtesy of Compañía Mexicana de Aerofoto, S.A.*

(Right Photo) Aerial photograph of Lower Teotihuacán Valley. Note density of modern settlement and the high concentration of contemporary population in nucleated communities in the permanently irrigated plain. San Juan Teotihuacán, the source of the springs for irrigation water, is at upper right; Patlachique Range at lower right. *Courtesy of Compañía Mexicana de Aerofoto, S.A.*

INTRODUCTION

Mesoamerica as a Culture Area

This town of Chiurtecal stands in a fertile plain, and inside its walls are twenty thousand houses built of stone and lime, and as many more in the suburbs. It was formerly a republic; but Montezuma had conquered and reduced it to a state of vassalage. Chiurtecal and Tascalteca readily obeyed the Spaniards. The inhabitants of the first of these towns are richer and better dressed than their Tascaltecan neighbors. They irrigate a large part of the country by a system of trenches. The walls of the town are solidly built and furnished with towers. Cortes writes that from the summit of a lofty temple he counted four hundred of these towers and an even greater number on the highways of the city; the latter being attached to temples. There are traces of land in the country admirably adapted for cattle raising; for everywhere else the population is so dense that there is hardly room in the country for the crops (Peter Martyr 1912 ed.:83).

This quotation from a letter written by Peter Martyr, historian of the court of Charles V of Spain to Pope Leo X, is a contemporary description of the city of Cholula in Central Mexico in the sixteenth century. It is an apt introduction to this study: the evolution of civilized society in Mesoamerica, with an explanation of the factors and processes responsible for this development. Cholula, Tenochtitlán–Tlatelolco, Texcoco, and other such sites represent the end product of millennia of cultural development, the crystallization of cultural patterns of greater or lesser degrees of antiquity, the solution by man of problems posed by his environment, both physical and social.

Explorations by the Spanish, Portuguese, French, English, and Dutch during the fifteenth, sixteenth, and seventeenth centuries revealed a huge double continent populated by millions of people whose existence had been unknown and unaccounted for within the religious and philosophical traditions of contemporary Europe. Thousands of organized native societies—diverse in size, complexity, language, and customs—greeted the new conquerors in bewildering welter. The impact upon European societies of the discovery and incorporation of the new lands and peoples has been amply documented. As the extraordinary economic, political, and social consequences of the Age of Exploration reverberated through Europe, scientific and philosophical systems were virtually forced to change concomitantly. Almost from the moment of Columbus' first landfall, Europeans were faced with the problem of accounting for the presence of this native population and attempting to determine its biological and cultural origins. What modern archaeologists term "civilizations"—the unusually large, complex societies of Mexico–Guatemala and Peru–Bolivia—posed special problems because their organizations so closely paralleled those of Europe.

In this book we will be concerned primarily with the development of one of these two centers of native New World civilization, the area referred to by twentieth century anthropologists as Mesoamerica. Geographically it includes Mexico south of the Pánuco–Lerma drainage, Guatemala, Salvador, British Honduras, and western Honduras to an approximate boundary formed by the Ulúa River and Lake Yojoa. The area is one of enormous geographical variability. At the time of the Conquest it was occupied by a great number of linguistic and ethnic groups, and displayed striking regionalism in cultural characteristics; yet in spite of the diversity, all these component groups participated in a single great tradition. Considered strictly synchronically, such a phenomenon constitutes a culture area. Diachronically, we shall use the term "co-tradition" (Bennett 1948; Armillas 1948). (Cf. Figure 1.)

The presence over wide areas of certain culture traits, some of greater diagnostic significance than others, permits us to classify the cultures of the region as a unit. Our definition of a culture area is therefore based as much upon the characteristics of the component cultures as upon the geographical characteristics of the region they inhabit. As Kroeber (1947) has observed for North America, geographical and cultural similarities tend to be closely correlated; we feel that there is a clearly causal relationship obtaining here. The bulk of the succeeding discussion represents an attempt to clarify the nature of this cause-effect relationship for one culture area of the New World.

Most of our knowledge of the Mesoamerican area has been derived from archaeological methods. In spite of the fact that the presence of native writing systems has been taken as diagnostic in this area (Kirchhoff 1943), and that traditions of historiography were well-developed, outright acceptance of these data would be naïve and ill-advised. The methodological problems of reliability that would ensue from uncritical acceptance of this evidence are immediately apparent to a historian. Where myth, legend, political propaganda, and so forth, are interlaced inextricably with actual history, it is impossible to separate fact from fiction without independent evidence from another source. That source has been archaeology, which has in fact revealed the general overall Mesoamerican cultural pattern and the diversity within it, and provided a fairly clear picture of the overall trends in historical development. Most archaeological data are, however, essentially technological, providing an outline of regional styles of artifacts and the history of technology. Within archaeology comparatively little emphasis has existed on the

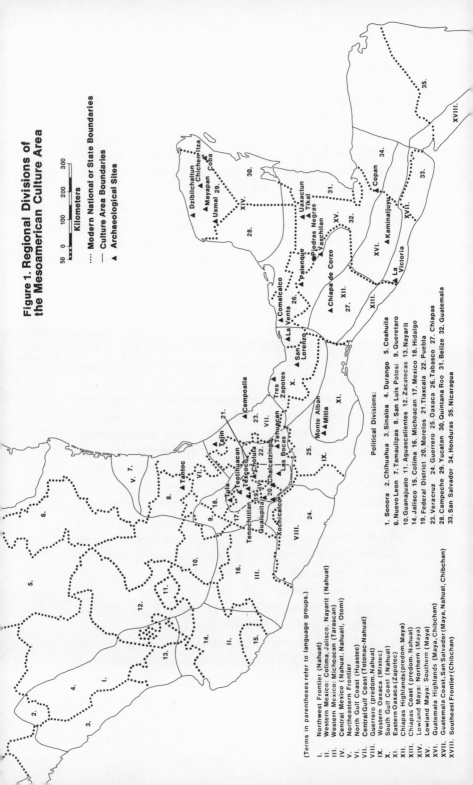

Figure 1. Regional Divisions of the Mesoamerican Culture Area

Kilometers
50 0 100 200 300

······· Modern National or State Boundaries
——— Culture Area Boundaries
▲ Archaeological Sites

(Terms in parentheses refer to language groups.)

I. Northwest Frontier (Nahuat)
II. Western Mexico: Colima, Jalisco, Nayarit (Nahuat)
III. Western Mexico: Michoacan (Tarascan)
IV. Central Mexico (Nahuat, Nahuatl, Otomi)
V. Northeastern Frontier
VI. North Gulf Coast (Huastec)
VII. Central Gulf Coast (Totonac-Nahuat)
VIII. Guerrero (predom. Nahuat)
IX. Western Oaxaca (Mixtec)
X. South Gulf Coast (Nahuat)
XI. Eastern Oaxaca (Zapotec)
XII. Chiapas Highlands (predom. Maya)
XIII. Chiapas Coast (predom. Nahuat)
XIV. Lowland Maya: Northern (Maya)
XV. Lowland Maya: Southern (Maya)
XVI. Guatemala Highlands (Maya, Chibchan)
XVII. Guatemala Coast, San Salvador (Maya, Nahuat, Chibchan)
XVIII. Southeast Frontier (Chibchan)

Political Divisions:

1. Sonora 2. Chihuahua 3. Sinaloa 4. Durango 5. Coahuila
6. Nuevo Leon 7. Tamaulipas 8. San Luis Potosi 9. Queretaro
10. Guanajuato 11. Aguascalientes 12. Zacatecas 13. Nayarit
14. Jalisco 15. Colima 16. Michoacan 17. Mexico 18. Hidalgo
19. Federal District 20. Morelos 21. Tlaxcala 22. Puebla
23. Veracruz 24. Guerrero 25. Oaxaca 26. Tabasco 27. Chiapas
28. Campeche 29. Yucatan 30. Quintana Roo 31. Belize 32. Guatemala
33. San Salvador 34. Honduras 35. Nicaragua

nonmaterial aspects of culture—the sociological, economic, religious patterns. It is precisely these which are, in Mesoamerica, so striking.

Theoretically one can easily show, as White (1949) has done, that nonmaterial aspects of culture have evolved as adaptations to technological revolutions. Such an approach, however, oversimplifies the problems of the causal relationships involved. Technological change as a basic causal factor is, we feel, significant only where such change results in a *substantial increase in the numbers and densities of human beings, or in the markedly increased efficiency of the individual human producer.* The development of agriculture, for example, or of irrigation represented such an impetus in the development of new institutions and modes of organization. Much of what is generally considered under the rubric of "technology" by anthropologists seems rather to be the effect, the product, of types of societies, rather than their cause. Monumental public architecture, a traditional hallmark of what is termed civilization, is clearly the result of a particular institutional order whose techno-economic causal bases lie elsewhere. Some aspects of technology are, in other words, more important than others for the purposes of analyzing the evolution of culture. One of our major problems will be to clarify these and their operations, and to present a theoretical justification of our selection.

In spite of the regional diversity of the various Mesoamerican cultures in the sixteenth century, the area as a whole was characterized by a basic and widespread cultural complex. Most important was a subsistence base of highly developed cereal agriculture with maize as the staple crop. Beans, squashes, and a great variety of minor crops were also of importance; but animal domestication was poorly developed, to a great extent because of the absence of potentially domesticable wild species. Therefore, although the dog and the turkey served as sources of food, land transportation remained undeveloped.

Two fundamentally distinct agricultural systems correlate

well with basic geographical divisions. In the tropical lowland areas, slash-and-burn or swidden agriculture was—and is—predominant. Of necessity this system tends toward relatively low population density per unit of land and, in a region such as Mesoamerica where transportation and communication systems remained primitive, development of markets and of militarism tended also to be limited. Large macro-states and empires, and true cities did not evolve. Rather, the settlement pattern consisted of ceremonial centers or elite residence centers on the one hand, and scattered rural hamlets containing the bulk of the population, on the other.

In the arid highlands such intensive techniques of agriculture as irrigation and terracing supported considerably higher population densities. Correspondingly, markets and local craft specialization assumed greater importance than was the case in the Lowland pattern. The social stratification was more complex, with more distinct levels in more complex interrelations with each other, and religion and religious specialists relatively less important. Warfare was more highly developed and of greater economic significance, and huge macro-states and empires were formed. True cities evolved, and a settlement pattern of city-village rather than ceremonial center-hamlet was the rule.

Given the agricultural economic base, many crafts were highly developed, with two overall patterns of specialization of production. The first of these, correlated with geographical diversity and localization of resources, is local specialization, much of it part-time; the second professional and usually full-time. Metallurgy in gold, silver, and copper, although present, was restricted to ornamental and votive functions, primarily for the ruling class and for the gods. Full-time specialization was a result, with considerable implications for social complexity even where metallurgy did not substantially affect the basic techniques of production. Most of the principal cutting tools were stone: chipped obsidian for scrapers, knives, drills, projectile points; ground stone tools for woodworking and the grinding of grain. Yet in terms of social complexity, it is more apt to compare sixteenth-century Mesoamerica not to the Neolithic of the Old World, but to its Bronze Age.

The high level of craft development is seen further when we consider for example weaving (in cotton and maguey fiber); ceramics (a rich variety of utility and ceremonial vessels, ornaments, figurines, and musical instruments, employing a great repertoire of technological skills and decorative techniques); feather mosaic; lapidary work in jade, turquoise, opal, crystal; paper-making; mural painting; and monumental sculpture. Architectural construction and planning were undoubtedly professional skills, as is evidenced by the monumental platform-plaza groups, built of earth and stone and faced with lime stucco and plaster, that required the coordination of unskilled labor and a number of different kinds of professional craftsmen. Besides the high level of technical skill, a further index of economic specialization is the widespread occurrence of markets, special institutions for exchange. Such institutions themselves require specialists in trade and administration to assure their continued operation. In the absence of draft animals, organized caravans of human porters would carry out widespread long-distance trade in luxury goods.

Throughout the area in the sixteenth century there was a social organization of states with populations in at least the tens of thousands, often in military competition with each other. Conquest and collection of tribute, often from areas quite distant from the major centers, formed the basis of macro-states and even empires, which in the course of time arose and declined and in some cases were re-formed; at least three such empires are known to have been based in Central Mexico. Society was highly stratified, with at least two fundamental levels throughout, and in some regions, a still more elaborate system of social differentiation. At the top was a landed nobility with control of production and distribution of goods by means of the market and taxation systems. At the bottom was a peasantry that provided agricultural produce, many of the craft goods, and the labor requisite for warfare, construction, and other state enterprises. In Central Mexico clearly defined strata of professional warriors, merchants, and craftsmen were found between the nobility and peasantry, and depressed classes of serfs and slaves formed the bottom of the social pyramid. Although in marginal areas peoples with simpler social institutions existed (and continue in some cases to do so), their numbers were small, and their societies of necessity influenced and modified by the institutions of the numerically and politically more powerful and complex states within whose orbits they existed.

As society was hierarchical in its organization, so too was religion—a unifying, recurrent, dominant theme of Mesoamerican civilization. The religious system involved a highly complex pantheon of gods with specialized functions, the most important of which were agricultural in nature, especially the rain gods. To establish a stable relationship between man and his world, these deities had to be constantly propitiated, nourished, and sustained, an idea which reached its climax in human sacrifice. Monumental temples were built and much fine craftsmanship devoted to religion. The various calendrical systems served as much to order the elaborate ceremonial and to predict divine behavior as to predict the cycle of the seasons. A professional priesthood, with formal schools for novices and an elaborate rank system, existed, apart from the laity, to minister to the various cults; as a concomitant was an intellectual tradition with writing and a highly developed astronomy-astrology.

We have mentioned the geographical and ethnic diversity of Mesoamerica at the time of the Conquest, and there is in fact considerable correlation between these two. In the sixteenth century through most of Guatemala, Yucatán, and adjacent Tabasco and Chiapas, British Honduras, and western Honduras was a belt of closely related Maya languages. Culturally, two provinces may be recognized: a lowland tropical province to the north, with relatively great cultural, linguistic, and geographic uniformity; and a considerably more heterogeneous southern highland one. Along the Gulf Coast lowland plain three linguistic groups were found; in the south, the Náhuat-speaking Olmec, the Totonac in the central plain, and the Huastec (a distant relative of Maya which separated before the evolution of the distinctive Lowland Maya culture) in the north.

In the heart of Mexico lies a clearly defined zone of arid tableland over 2,240 m. in elevation, separated by high mountain masses from adjacent areas and divided internally into a series of basins by mountains. The eastern and central basins of this Central Plateau, plus the adjacent southern escarpment comprised a distinct cultural province occupied primarily by Náhuatl-speakers, with the Otomí a minority group on the northern fringes and in marginal interstices. The centrally located Basin of Mexico was the home of the Aztec, with the western sector of the Plateau (Michoacán) occupied by Tarascans.

The low mountain area and adjacent Pacific coast of the modern state of Guerrero was occupied primarily by Náhuat-speakers, close relatives of the historical Olmec of the South Gulf Coast and more distantly related to the Náhuatl of the Central Plateau. Zacatecas, Nayarít, Jalisco, Durango, Aguascalientes, and Sinaloa were also occupied by members of this far-flung language group. This northern area, however, was characterized by intense social and cultural fragmentation; geographically it was a frontier zone, a clinal area of increasing aridity and therefore increasing precariousness of settled life. Historically and culturally also it was a barbarian frontier to the more advanced cultures to the south.

To the east of Guerrero is the arid mountainous state of Oaxaca, one of the scenes of climactic development of Mesoamerican civilization. The western part is Mixtec-, the eastern Zapotec-speaking. Between the states of Oaxaca and Veracruz, mountain barriers form a cultural as well as a geographical internal frontier area, occupied by a number of small, distinctive groups. The Pacific coast of Chiapas and Guatemala were culturally distinctive, occupied by Náhuat-speakers. Enclaves of these latter are found deep into Central America, minorities surrounded by speakers of other languages.

Archaeological research has demonstrated that the regional patterns observed in the sixteenth century have considerable time depth. Household and rural technology, as well as the more dramatic remains of the ceremonial or urban centers, reflect this differentiation, variation on the more general Mesoamerican patterns. Because of the intense regionalism, it is difficult to summarize the culture history of the area as a whole; not only the final stages, but also the rates of cultural evolution from one subregion to another were enormously varied. It is not the purpose of the present volume to analyze each of these archaeological sequences in detail. Rather, we shall outline the major trends quite briefly for the convenience of the reader. Proliferation of terminology, often confusingly applied, has complicated the situation still further. We therefore refer the reader to Figure 2, which will attempt to correlate the various kinds of terms with each other.

An Outline of Mesoamerican Cultural Development

The intense regional and local variation that characterizes Mesoamerica has made summation of its culture history a difficult task. Methodologically, two approaches are possible, each with its own advantages and drawbacks, depending upon the problem at hand and the purposes of the inquiry. As is the case with any classification—for such an outline of Mesoamerican prehistory is, in effect, a classification of culture types—no one approach is ever inherent in the body of data. Rather, it is imposed by the classifier to solve a particular problem or to clarify for purposes of presentation a large mass of information. Given the essentially arbitrary nature of the process, it then follows that any scheme is valuable insofar as it sheds light upon the

Mesoamerica as a Whole		North Gulf Coast	Central Gulf Coast	South Gulf Coast	Central Plateau	Oaxaca		Chiapas Highland Central Valley	Guatemala	Lowland Maya	Northwest Frontier	Civilization
Post-classic	Late — 1500 A.D.	Panuco	Cempoalla	Soncuautla	Aztec	V	M o n t e	Urbina / Tuxtla	Chinautla	Mayapan	N u m e r o u s	zation
	— 1200 A.D. Early	Las Flores	Tajin III	Upper Cerro de las Mesas	Toltec (Mazapan)	IV		Suchiapa / Ruiz	Tohil	Chichen Toltec		Chief-dom
	— 900 A.D.				Coyotlatelco	III b	A l b a n	Maravillas	Pamplona Amatle	Tepeu	L o c a l	
Classic	Late — 600 A.D.	Zaquil	Tajin II	Upper Tres	Metepec / Xolalpan	III a		Laguna	Esperanza	Tzakol		
	Early — 300 A.D.	Pithaya	Upper Remojadas II	Zapotes	Tlamimilolpa / Miccaotli / Tzacualli	II		Jiquipilas / Istmo	Aurora / Santa Clara	Chicanel	C u l t	
	Terminal (Protoclassic) — B.C./ A.D.	El Prisco	Upper Remojadas I	Middle Tres Zapotes	Patlachique / Chimalhuacan	I		Horcones / Guanacaste	Arenal / Miraflores		u r e s	Tribe
Form-ative	Late — 600 B.C.	Chila / Aguilar	Lower Remojadas	La Venta	Ticoman / Tlatilco Amacusac	?		Francesca / Escalera / Dili	Providencia / Majadas / Las Charcas	Mamom		
	Middle — 1500 B.C.	Ponce / Pavon	Trapiche / ?	La Venta Pre-Complex A / San Lorenzo / ?	Early Zacatenco			Cotorra	Arevalo Ocos			
	Early — 2500 B.C.			Coatepec / Purron								
Archaic	— 7200 B.C.			Abejas / Coxcatlan / El Riego								
Early Hunters–Gatherers				Tepexpan—Ixtapan								

Figure 2. Stages and Periods in Mesoamerica

materials dealt with. Our evaluation of any particular system is therefore heuristic.

The two principal methods of classification of entire culture histories are summary by period and summary by developmental stage (cf. Rowe 1962). Each is in good measure arbitrary and designed to facilitate comparison in time and space. The two, however, differ according to the kind of classificatory criteria employed. Confusions both of terminology and of concept have resulted, in that often the same terms—Formative, Classic, Postclassic, and their various synonyms—are used to denote both chronological period and developmental stage. In brief, a chronological period is an arbitrarily defined block of time, irrespective of cultural developments taking place within the designated span. As such, it is by definition universal. A developmental stage, on the other hand, is defined on the basis of the presence or absence of particular cultural traits or configurations, irrespective of absolute time. Any chronological period may include many levels of cultural development, on the basis that all are found within the given time span; conversely, developmental stages need not occur at the same time or rate, or even at all throughout the world. Accordingly, the different purposes of these two approaches to cultural classification are evident; often data presented according to one scheme may be difficult to correlate with the alternate presentation of the same facts. Despite overlapping terminology, the two represent distinct classificatory operations.

So long as it is recognized, the arbitrary nature of both stages and periods need in no way limit their usefulness in interpretation. Period classification is advantageous for comparison of contemporary cultures of whatever type; its arbitrariness is based on the selection of particular events, not necessarily universal ones, as chronological cutoff points that are used as universals. Stage classification enables comparison of similar culture types of whatever time period. Its arbitrariness lies in the selection of traits designated as characteristic of the stage in question. Willey and Phillips state that

> We are under no illusion that this is anything resembling a *natural* system. There is nothing inevitable about five stages. . . . Nor can we accept the criticism that ours are not the "right" stages, if such criticism carries the implication that "right" stages are to be found (1958:77).

The only "rightness" in stage formulation lies in its applicability, and this is not, strictly speaking, rightness at all.

Willey and Phillips (1958) define five stages. Krieger (1953) for North America has postulated a series of four: Paleo-Indian, Food-Gathering, Food-Producing, Urban Life. Strong (1948) divides the Peruvian sequence into six: Pre-Agricultural, Developmental, Formative, Florescent, Fusion, Imperial. In Strong's sequence there is nothing really comparable to Krieger's Paleo-Indian, and Strong draws finer distinctions higher up in the sequence. But Krieger is working in the United States, north of the high cultures of Nuclear America; he draws the distinctions he needs where he needs them to order data completely different from Strong's.

Further examples of the possible variation in formulating developmental stages is shown by a comparison of several sequences for the same area, Peru (Bennett 1948; Steward 1948; Strong 1948; Collier 1955; Mason 1957). One is immediately struck by the differences, not only in nomenclature but also in the way the entire sequence is subdivided in terms of content.

Classification by developmental stages has been practiced by both archaeologists and ethnologists. Probably the most famous, and one of the most influential, of these was that of Morgan (1877) which, though formulated by an ethnologist with no background whatsoever in archaeology, depended on almost exclusively technological criteria. Those subsequently postulated by archaeologists tend also to be heavily weighted, not unexpectedly, in this same direction. Childe (1951) feels that the advantage of this kind of criterion lies especially in the ease of recognition of the relevant materials in the archaeological record, but warns also against the a priori assumption that particular technological features necessarily have the same significance in all contexts. Insofar as the technological determinism of White (1949) is accepted, there is theoretical substantiation of this procedure beyond the sour grapes of "That's all there is. There isn't any more." Criteria commonly used for the formulation of stages in the New World have been based on such factors as excellence of technology, monumental art, and so forth, in much of which a frequently strong and usually unstated bias is perceptible.

More recent stages suggested in ethnology represent increased reliance upon economic, sociological, and political criteria. That of Fried (1960) is an example. So too is that of Service (1962). The bulk of this book will be in effect an attempt to correlate the levels of cultural development recognized by Service with archaeological materials in the sequence of Mesoamerican cultural evolution. At this point, we will merely trace some of the recent influences of ethnology in American archaeology, in the building of a more general and inclusive theory of culture. Strong's Peruvian classification, for example, is based explicitly in part upon political criteria:

> The seventh, or Colonial epoch represents the loss of continental authority in favor of invaders from overseas who had brought in gunpowder and the iron age. The sixth, or Imperial, epoch, indicates the loss of regional native autonomy in favor of wider coastal and, later, pan-Peruvian military conquests. . . . The epoch of Fusion represents the downfall of local valley, or valley-group, autonomy, as well as local artistic individuality, due to regional cultural or military conquests (1948:101).

Our position very strongly favors the view that sound and reliable inference is not only possible but necessary in archaeology, a position we will amplify and clarify in a later chapter. Steward has presented this view succinctly:

> The need to reconstruct culture sequences has necessarily centered attention on art styles, but in so doing it has also stressed the distinctiveness of each local sequence. There is, however, little doubt that agricultural proficiency, population density, settlement patterns, sociological complexity, and craft technologies were functionally interrelated in some manner, and it appears that there may have been certain regularities in the development of these features in the different areas of native American high cultures. The present need, therefore, is a sequential scheme and corresponding terminology that takes into account basic technologies and associated socio-religious patterns rather than stylistic peculiarities (1948: 103).

It is perhaps not insignificant that both Strong and Steward were trained in both ethnology and archaeology. At any rate, the preceding quotation from Steward serves very aptly as an introduction to the plan of the present volume.

We shall present at this point a very brief summary of Meso-american culture history for the convenience of the reader. Fuller documentation of the archaeological sequences of the area, in greater detail, are available in Coe (1962, 1966), Wolf (1959), and Covarrubias (1957). It is not our purpose in the present volume to treat these data in full, and our presentation is of necessity abbreviated. As will be seen in subsequent chapters, our major concern in this book will be with developmental problems, including the questions of regional precocity or retardation. Our summary here will be presented in terms of chronological periods rather than stages; however, we have some reservations about this method of presentation, and will therefore deal also with the problem of correlations of stages and periods.

Between approximately 300 and 900 A.D. (Goodman–Martínez–Thompson correlation) one of the regional groups in Mesoamerica, the Lowland Maya, erected a series of dated commemorative stelae inscribed in a system of calendrical notation called the Long Count or Initial Series. Following Coe (1962), among others, we designate this period, in this area and in all others irrespective of particular local profiles of culture history, as Classic. In the Petén lowlands this was also the period of local climax of artistic development, but for purely chronological classification by periods this fact is irrelevant. What is relevant is rather the fact that dated monuments establish and demarcate a clear block of time. Dates prior to 300 A.D. and post-2500 B.C. are therefore considered Formative, and those subsequent to 900 A.D. but before the Spanish Conquest of 1519 A.D. Postclassic. The selection of the date 2500 B.C. for the inception of the Formative is in effect arbitrary. In developmental terms, the principal characteristic of a Formative stage is the adoption of settled agriculture as the dominant mode of subsistence, along with the diagnostic use of ceramics.

In several areas of Mesoamerica this pattern seems clearly established at circa 1500 B.C., a date which has become almost traditional in most of the recent literature. The absolute chronology presented in this volume, however, is based upon recent research that indicates that the developments in question have considerably more time depth than had formerly been thought. In the Tehuacán Valley and probably also in the Valley of Oaxaca, the Formative, in a developmental sense, seems well established about a millennium prior to the more traditional date. Although the developmental criteria are quite distinct from the use of any particular date to mark a chronological period, we nonetheless consider it advisable to recognize this new evidence even in a period terminology. Our internal subphasing of the Formative will also reflect this expanded time scale for the period as a whole, and is based also on recent evidence suggesting that the diagnostic criteria for Middle and Late Formative occur earlier than the established chronology would indicate. Research of the past twenty years has resulted in the definition of two earlier periods prior to the Formative, which we begin at 2500

B.C.; and for this reason we consider the term Formative preferable to Preclassic.

Coe (1962), following a more traditional absolute chronology, calls these two earlier periods Early Hunters (?–7200 B.C.) and Archaic (7200–1500 B.C.), with absolute chronology based largely on radiocarbon evidence. In practice, therefore, we recognize five periods within the various archaeological sequences in Mesoamerica, which we use to organize the summary immediately following. In this section, we will attempt to clarify the relation of chronological periods with commonly used developmental-sequence subdivisions of this body of data.

1. Early Hunters (?–7200 B.C.). During the Wisconsin glaciation of the terminal Pleistocene, man invaded the New World, taking advantage, presumably, of a land bridge across Bering Strait resulting from lowered sea levels. The date of man's entry into Mesoamerica is unknown, but was almost certainly prior to 11,000 B.C. (Aveleyra 1965), the tentative date of the Tequixquiac complex. Between this time and 7200 B.C. the area was occupied by a number of groups, small in size, nomadic in settlement pattern, and dependent for subsistence upon the hunting and gathering of the wild resources of their environment. Coe (1962) suggests a total population of perhaps 30,000 for all of Mexico. A variety of chipped stone tools are known. There have been recent attempts to establish two phases, an earlier one dating from 11,000–8000 B.C. (Diablo complex of Tamaulipas, for example), characterized by crude percussion-flaked tools, and a generalized hunting-and-gathering economy. The succeeding later phase, 8000–7200 B.C., was characterized by a pressure-flaked tool industry and an emphasis on big-game hunting (Lerma complex in Tamaulipas, Tepexpan-Ixtápan of the Valley of Mexico).

We feel that this picture is overly simplistic, and that the subdivision of this long period on this basis is inadequate. The term "Early Hunters" is first of all misleading, and in developmental terms we would question the validity of its separation from the earlier levels of the succeeding Archaic period. Since we discuss the problems of the Archaic in more detail below, at this point we merely characterize it as that stage in which experiments with plant domestication took place, ultimately leading to the establishment of a Formative pattern. An independent "Hunters" substage or subperiod, distinct culturally or chronologically from one of "Gatherers" is highly questionable. Service (1966) observes that modern groups of hunting peoples obtain by far the bulk of their diet from gathered vegetable foods, an observation parallel to that of MacNeish (1964), questioning the importance of big-game hunting at any period of Mesoamerican prehistory: the man who did bag a mammoth probably never stopped talking about it.

It would be unrealistic to expect a uniform subsistence base at any time in the history of an area where geographical variability is so striking, and particularly odd to find such uniformity at a time level when man depended exclusively upon the resources of nature for his subsistence. Much of the supposedly sharp distinction would be more probably ecological and local, rather than chronological or cultural. The approximate cutoff date of 7200 B.C. distinguishing Early Hunters from Archaic has been justified by the geological fact that at about this time the Pleistocene macrofauna—mammoth, horse, cameloids, and so forth—had become extinct in Mesoamerica and therefore could not have comprised a part of the subsistence base. Our point is that their mere existence, along with the considerable evidence that they were at least occasionally used for food, is no proof that any group ever derived even a substantial part, let alone all, of its diet from this food source. The question to us is one of significance. We would prefer to regard this early period as one of hunting-gathering, and to begin the Archaic, in developmental terms, somewhat later, with the El Riego phase of the Tehuacán Valley as the earliest known incipient cultivation. In other words, we would draw the dividing line at a somewhat different point.

In regard to the preceding argument, we may return to the problem of internal subphasing of this Early Hunters-Gatherers period. Again, much of the difference between the generalized food gatherers and the specialized big-game hunters seems to us an artifact of research. Most of the finds of specialized hunters have been reported from the arid areas of central and northern Mexico; no definite site is yet known from the tropical lowlands. This fact may be significant in view of our suggestion that the distinction of hunters from gatherers might be in large measure ecological and quantitative, one of emphasis merely. Equally, the absence of this kind of remains in the lowlands may be only the product of insufficient research. More specifically, however, we observe that the specialized hunters have been reported only from kill sites. No representative habitation sites are known or recognized. We suggest that the evident differences in artifact assemblages represent a functional, rather than chronological or cultural, difference. Hunters, in other words, would in all probability take only their hunting equipment—not their entire cultural inventory—out on the chase. The preponderance of specialized weapons and butchering implements at kill sites would be fully expectable.

In summary, we prefer to view this long early period as one of hunting and gathering of wild food resources, with the relative emphasis of one or the other dependent upon ecological factors. The handicap of comparatively meager data limits more complete analysis. Populations were small, nomadic, and, we feel, more or less generalized in terms of subsistence base. Technological changes visible in artifact types did not appear to have significantly affected the nature of subsistence or of society.

2. Archaic Period (7200–2500 B.C.). The hallmark of this period, if we temporarily regard it as a developmental stage, is what is generally called in the literature the "food-producing revolution": the gradual shift in subsistence from hunting-gathering to agriculture. The transformations of this period provided the basis for development in subsequent periods of in-

creasingly elaborate cultural forms. It was agriculture that provided the surplus production, population capacity, and residential stability required for the support of complex societies.

Archaeological research has demonstrated conclusively that Mesoamerican agriculture was a local development based on gradual domestication of native wild plants. In view of the excruciatingly slow pace of this process (which seems also to have been rather slower in the Near East than once thought), the "revolution" is perhaps more properly regarded as an "evolution," one which was in terms of its implications for cultural development, however, truly revolutionary. Evidence of the process of domestication during this stage of incipient cultivation comes primarily from two areas: Tamaulipas on the northern frontier of the area (MacNeish 1958) and the Tehuacán Valley in the modern state of Puebla in Central Mexico (Mac-Neish 1964). The basic social community appears to have been the nomadic band, and subsistence was in large measure still dependent on wild food resources. Such dependence, however, declined steadily from the Coxcatlán phase of Tehuacán, with its earliest domesticated maize, through the Purrón phase, when agricultural produce comprised some 70 percent of the diet (MacNeish 1964). Given the absence of large domesticable animals in Mesoamerica in comparison to the Old World, the continued, if limited, dependence upon wild foods is more understandable. By the Purrón phase also, perhaps as early as 2500 B.C., pottery—apparently a local development from stone prototypes—appears in the Tehuacán Valley. In terms of developmental stages, we strongly prefer to consider Purrón Early Formative. Accordingly, we have begun our Formative—used as both stage and period—with this date.

The principal domesticates known historically for Mesoamerica came under cultivation during this Archaic period. At various points in the sequence maize, beans, squash, avocado, chile, pumpkin, amaranth, cotton, tobacco, and probably also tomato, maguey, nopal and other economically significant plants came under human control. It is highly likely that the foci of domestication were multiple; in other words, domestication occurred, probably at more or less the same time, wherever potential domesticates existed as wild plants. We shall explore more fully the problems of where and why in a later chapter.

3. Formative Period (2500 B.C.–300 A.D.). This period begins with the inception of settled agricultural villages in at least some areas of Mesoamerica, and ends with the Long Count dated monuments in the Maya Lowlands. When the term is used as a developmental stage it is terminated with the emergence of the climactic art styles of the Classic in various regions of Mesoamerica at different times: Teotihuacán on the Central Plateau; the Classic Maya; Monte Albán or Classic Zapotec in Oaxaca; Tajín or Classic Totonac on the Gulf Coast. Just as the beginnings of these manifestations occur at different absolute dates (perhaps B.C./A.D. for Teotihuacán, post-600 A.D. for Tajín), so too must the end of the Formative, considered as stage, be regarded as highly variable. It is primarily with the Formative and post-Formative developments that the terminological confusion becomes most acute. In dealing with the literature, therefore, the cautions applicable to the Formative as a whole (as distinct from the Archaic on the one hand and the Classic on the other) are equally relevant to the problem of determining the subphasing of the period.

Coe (1962), for example, divides the period into three phases: Early (1500–1000 B.C.), Middle (1000–300 B.C.), and Late (300 B.C.–300 A.D.). He correlates local sequences primarily on the basis of the similarity of ceramic modes in various regions, plus a fundamental assumption of little or no time lag in their appearance in different regions. We seriously question his assumption, however, particularly in reference to a period in which large political entities were absent and the overall population of only moderate size. Coe's reliance on this assumption leads him to reject many radiocarbon dates from Central Mexico as too early. Early Zacatenco for example has ceramic traits—notably an incised cream-slipped ware—that do not appear until the Middle Formative (Dili phase or Chiapa II) in Chiapas. Yet C-14 dates place Early Zacatenco well prior to 1000 B.C. Ticomán, another example, is typologically Late Formative as this term is used to refer to a developmental stage. Radiocarbon dates have placed Ticomán at 600–400 B.C., chronologically Middle Formative. Some C-14 dates from Cuicuilco, which had a Ticomán phase occupation, are much later, falling well into Coe's Late Formative; but recent evidence indicates a post-Ticomán, Late Formative occupation at the site (Chimalhuacán phase) (Bennyhoff and Heizer 1965). Unpublished obsidian dates (calculated by Joseph Michels) from the Teotihuacán Valley Project, directed by Sanders, indicate that Chimalhuacán replaces Ticomán in that portion of the Basin of Mexico, and dates from 300 to 100 B.C. This evidence supports the earlier dating of Ticomán.

Although, as we have indicated, the absolute chronology and subphasing of the Formative are very much in debate, and although we are doubtful of the assumption of contemporaneity of specific ceramic modes over all of Mesoamerica, we will proceed with a general summary of the period as a whole. In the Early Formative (2500–1500 B.C.) sedentary village life became established over the central and southern portions of the area. This pattern probably had its inception much later in the northwest, perhaps as late as the chronological Late Formative. Sites are small villages or hamlets, lacking civic architecture. Yet in artifact inventory they do not differ strikingly from rural Aztec sites. Pottery was well made, more restricted in form and decoration than that of later periods; figurines hand-made rather than made in molds as in later times. The stone industries included chipped obsidian projectile points, knives, drills, scrapers, and rectangular blades; and ground stone manos, metates, and woodworking tools. Cloth was woven of maguey and cotton fiber; even the basic Aztec garments were present. Houses were built of split stone and adobe in the highlands, and of pole-and-thatch in the lowlands. Probably the full agricultural complex was present, but hunting and gathering were still of some significance to the subsistence pattern, as they were in historic times. We can characterize this phase as the one in which the basic Mesoamerican rural technology was fully evolved.

The Middle Formative (1500–600 B.C.) was characterized by the appearance in some areas of monumental sculpture, jade carving, civic architecture, and social differentiation between religious centers with a professional priesthood on the one hand, and the agricultural supporting settlements on the other. These developments are most typical of a crescent of tropical lowlands extending from southern Veracruz across the Isthmus of Tehuantepec and up the Pacific Coast of Guatemala. Recent evidence suggests, however, the possibility that these characteristics appeared earlier in the highlands. In other words, many of the elements that are distinctively Mesoamerican appear at this time. The complex of traits in question reached its greatest elaboration in a small, compact lowland zone of southern Veracruz and western Tabasco, with three centers at La Venta, Tres Zapotes, and San Lorenzo. This local complex has been termed Olmec, after the sixteenth-century inhabitants of this zone; but the term has been used by extension for the specific art style of this region occurring in portable objects of clay or stone (masks, figurines, carved celts) and found over an area including Guerrero, the Central Plateau, and the central Gulf Coast. More dubious examples of "Olmec influence" in local art have been reported from Oaxaca, Chiapas, the Guatemala Highlands and Pacific Coast, and from as far away as Salvador. In a few cases this influence occurs in the form of monumental sculpture or cliff carvings as well as in portable objects.

In the Olmec area proper, however, the distinctive art style occurs characteristically on objects of monumental size. The center of La Venta (Drucker 1952; Drucker, Heizer, and Squier 1959) included earth pyramid-plaza complexes, tombs, and platforms with fence-like enclosures of basalt columns. Massive relief-carved altars and stelae, and in-the-round sculptures of human heads are present, as well as caches and burial offerings of smaller objects carved in typical Olmec style in jade and serpentine. Especially characteristic of this style is a distinctive iconography dominated by an anthropomorphic feline rain god, represented in both monumental and portable art. The size and complexity of these three Olmec centers implies the presence of a well-organized social system with some professional administrative and craft personnel.

We terminate the Middle Formative at 600 B.C., with the emergence of Monte Albán I in Oaxaca, Cuicuilco-Ticomán in the Central Plateau, Miraflores at Kaminaljuyú. Although radiocarbon evidence points to the persistence of Olmec style in the Gulf Coastal Plain until perhaps 400 B.C., this fact alone is insufficient to warrant the extension of the Middle Formative period to this date, a practice commonly adopted by most published chronologies. In terms of cultural content, to revert temporarily to a developmental-stage terminology, the Late Formative represents a spread and intensification of patterns established in some areas during the Middle Formative—including the increasing diversity of content and the divergence of the overall patterns of Lowlands and Highlands that remains even today a striking feature of Mesoamerican culture.

By Late Formative times (600 B.C.–B.C./A.D.), the basic dichotomy between center and hinterland became widespread and in many cases intensified, except in the Northwest. A number of regional styles and regional centers assumed dominance: Cuicuilco in the Central Highlands, Monte Albán in Oaxaca, Kaminaljuyú in the Guatemala Highlands, Tikal in the Petén, Chiapa de Corzo in the Central Depression, Tres Zapotes in the Olmec area. There is no evidence of unusual artistic precocity in any area, and no horizon style is present. The distinctive Mesoamerican calendar and writing seem to appear in this phase, with evidence from Monte Albán and Long Count dates from Tres Zapotes (Stela C).

Our chronology departs once more from most of those established in the literature in the recognition of the period B.C./A.D.–300 A.D. as distinctive from what we are calling Late Formative. We refer to this period as either Terminal Formative or Protoclassic. In terms of its content, the term "Protoclassic" is perhaps preferable, since the various Classic regional traditions emerge. As in the case of the boundary between Middle and Late Formative, that between Late Formative and Protoclassic is often indistinct, in that in developmental terms there is a substantial and fully expectable continuity, with difference more often quantitative than qualitative. On the Meseta Central, Teotihuacán replaced Cuicuilco as the dominant center—a position of power the former would retain throughout much of the succeeding Classic period.

In summary, the chronological period we term Formative witnessed the transformation of Mesoamerican peoples from simple village agriculturists through the emergence of stratified society and the state. The agricultural subsistence base became, in many areas, progressively more intensive; and a continuous and rapid population growth took place, as is evidenced by the greater numbers of sites, their larger size, and the increasing evidence of socioeconomic complexity within and between them.

4. Classic Period (300–900 A.D.). As a chronological period, the Classic is that span of time demarcated by Long Count dates in the Maya Lowlands, where stage and period terminologies in fact coincide. As a developmental stage, the Classic is characterized by the spectacular development of art in stone, painting, clay, cloth, mosaic, and particularly in architecture. The regional Mesoamerican traditions known from the sixteenth century emerged as distinctive. If the term is used as a stage, the regional variations in the absolute chronology of development are thrown into sharp relief. Teotihuacán, in the Central Plateau, was typologically Classic by about B.C./A.D., and declined at about 700 A.D. as a major center, well before the end of the Maya—and chronological—Classic. Still more paradoxically, Te-

otihuacán at its height (Xolalpan phase) was, according to the typology of Willey and Phillips (1958), very likely Postclassic. So too were the centers which rose in the Central Highlands to fill the power vacuum resulting from the collapse of Teotihuacán —Xochicalco in Morelos, Cholula in Puebla, and a nascent Tula in Hidalgo—in spite of the Classic date of these last three centers. In order to correlate stage and period insofar as possible, we refer to the span 700–900 A.D. in the Central Plateau as Terminal Classic, with the understanding that we consider the cultural developments there to have been typologically Postclassic. Again, developmental stage terminology would regard Tajín as Classic in characteristics in spite of its partly Postclassic date florescence.

Although much monumental and portable art of the Formative period is equal in quality to the best of the Classic, the latter far surpasses the former in the scale, quantity, and spatial distribution of craft products, and in the number of media used. Particularly distinctive of the Classic, in contrast to the Formative, was the emergence of truly massive architectural centers, with pyramid temples, plazas, priests' dormitories, shrines, ballcourts, adoratorios, ritual chambers. Construction was of earth, stone, lime concrete, and plaster. Buildings were grouped in planned complexes around plazas and were elaborately ornamented with stone sculpture, painting, stucco, and clay modeling. Centers included Teotihuacán, Xochicalco, and Cholula in Central Mexico; Tajín in Veracruz; Monte Albán in Oaxaca; and in the Lowland Maya area Tikal, Copán, Palenque, Uxmal, and Piedras Negras. The spectacular development of writing and particularly of calendrics in the Maya Lowlands is diagnostic of the Classic as a chronological period.

Among these various regional centers of civilizations, however, one—Teotihuacán—emerged as the dominant polity, with a stylistic influence felt all over Mesoamerica with the exception of the northern frontier and northern Yucatán. Unlike the Classic Maya centers, Teotihuacán was fully urban, with a zone of at least 19 km² and a population of perhaps 85,000 persons (Millon 1966a, b). In our opinion, it represents the first cyclical-conquest macro-state in Mesoamerica, and it is in this sense that for certain purposes we may well regard it as typologically Postclassic. Earlier syntheses of Mesoamerican archaeology date the florescence of Teotihuacán as approximately contemporaneous with the Maya Classic. More recent research, however, demonstrates that its style was well-developed between B.C./A.D.–300 A.D., and that its destruction occurred in the seventh century A.D., two centuries prior to the end of the Maya Classic. A series of local centers—principally Xochicalco, Cholula, and Tula, evidently in competition with each other for supremacy in the Central Plateau—replaced it during the phase we call Terminal Classic. By what we feel is probably rather more significant than mere accident, most other typologically Classic regional centers reached their maximal development subsequent to the fall of Teotihuacán. In view of the widespread dominance of the latter in the fifth and sixth centuries A.D., we see in fact a functional interrelation among these events which we will subsequently consider in more detail.

Regarded as both period and as stage, the Classic has often been characterized in the literature as peaceful, theocratic, intensely religious, nonurban, and nonimperialistic. We question these generalizations on many grounds, and later on present our arguments concerning the supposed sharp contrast between Classic and Postclassic.

5. Postclassic Period (900–1519 A.D.). Within a century or two of the year 900 A.D., most of the great Classic centers were abandoned. The cessation of Long Count dates in the Maya Lowlands is diagnostic of the Postclassic as chronological period, whose termination is marked by the Spanish Conquest. As a stage, it has been characterized as militaristic, imperialistic, urban, and secular with a corresponding decline of religious art. How these traits are presumed to have developed out of the conceptually diametrically opposite Classic is unclear.

Numerous hypotheses have been offered for the supposed sudden abandonment of so many major centers and their replacement by new ones. The factors responsible probably did vary from area to area, just as the "abandonments" themselves seem to have followed different patterns. The heart of the Maya Lowlands, for example, appears to have suffered massive population loss equivalent to the sixteenth-century depopulation of the Gulf Coast (the latter the product of foreign diseases); in Central Mexico, however, "abandonment" involved simply the replacement of one focus of power by another. Among the more defensible explanations of the upheavals that terminated the Classic have been the following: (1) agricultural failure due to overcycling in swidden areas and erosion in the highlands; (2) climatic deterioration; (3) peasant revolts against the elite as a result of overtaxation; (4) southward migrations from the northern frontier resulting in southward and eastward population displacements. If one regards the Classic as a developmental stage, these abandonments spanned about five centuries, beginning with that of Teotihuacán at circa 700 A.D., and ending perhaps as late as 1200 A.D. at Tajín. Clearly no single explanation of so complex a series of events is possible; rather, a number of causal factors, interrelated over some 500 years, must be invoked.

The Postclassic period is customarily divided into two phases, an early and a late, which equate with the rise of two dominant polities in Central Mexico, the Toltec at Tula or Tollán, and the Aztec of Tenochtitlán. In the Maya area, the demographic center of the lowland province shifted to northern Yucatán; in the highland province, a number of petty states existed in constant competition with each other. The Postclassic (like the Central Mexican Classic) was characterized by large imperialist states, intensive development of urbanism, and widespread trading networks. Within such a socioeconomic setting, specific pottery types (Plumbate, Fine Orange), horizon styles (Mixteca–Puebla), and religious symbols, especially those of human sacrifice, were widely diffused. Technologically the only really notable innovation is metallurgy, apparently imported from Central or South America.

Tula and its empire, unlike Teotihuacán which preceded it, seems to have had a northward and westward orientation, at least initially; only later did it expand to the south, the traditional direction of expansion of the states focused on the Central Plateau. The northwest frontier of Mesoamerica was well-populated, but during the chronological Classic the cultures were lacking in the elaboration of their southern neighbors, most of them being at a typologically Formative level of development. During the final phase of the Classic and particularly during the early Postclassic, there seems to have been rapid demographic growth and northward expansion of the frontier of sedentary life into this climatically clinal zone. Concomitantly, there was apparently the emergence of polities of Mesoamerican type that made conquest by an expansionist Toltec state not only economically profitable but probably a virtual strategic necessity as well. The heart of the Toltec domain was centered in the Central Plateau and the Northwest, but its influence was widespread throughout Mesoamerica, with administrative-warrior-merchant colonies established at considerable distances to the south and east, analogous to the earlier Teotihuacán colonization of Kaminaljuyú in the Guatemala Highlands. Probably the most notable example of such a Toltec colony was Chichén Itzá in northern Yucatán, where a civic center in pure Toltec style was constructed.

The Toltec seat of power fell in the twelfth century A.D. Documentary sources ascribe its fall to a series of invasions from the northern frontier. Armillas (1964a) has correlated these events with a southward shift of climatic zones resulting in disastrous droughts in the expanded frontier zone. In a region where sedentary agriculture is at best precarious, the climatic situation would have been of crisis proportions and could in fact have triggered population movements southward to destroy the Toltec state. After the collapse of Tula, an interregnum, two centuries of local retrenchment and competition for supremacy on the Central Plateau, paralleled to a striking degree the political situation of power vacuum following the fall of Teotihuacán five centuries earlier. Aztec hegemony was established in the fifteenth and sixteenth centuries, and this empire had undoubtedly not attained its full growth before the Spanish Conquest of Mesoamerica cut short its development.

Part ONE

Civilization as
an Ecological
System

I / THE EVOLUTION OF SOCIAL SYSTEMS

Introduction

      *One of the major problems of archaeological re-*search is that of elucidating the factors and processes leading to the evolution of civilization. Archaeologists generally define civilizations in terms of excellence of technology and particularly by the presence of monumental architecture. These traits have been used as criteria for obvious reasons, particularly because they present an enduring archaeological record. More significant are the social and economic implications of these technological achievements. They are always the product of a large, formally organized society with marked social differentiation based on occupation, wealth, and control of power. The political structure involves a pyramid of statuses with well-defined delineation of authority, rights, and duties and offers a striking contrast to tribally organized political systems. The social coalitions, in Wolf's terms (1966), that integrate the system are primarily vertical rather than horizontal; communities are linked by a network of obligations and rights based on stratification and economic specialization, rather than marriage or kinship ties alone.

The social and economic system defined above as civilization is obviously the product of a long process of growth and elaboration that transformed a small, socially homogeneous society into a large heterogeneous one. To define the factors involved in this process we utilize an evolutionary and ecological approach. Our objective is to trace the development of Mesoamerican civilization step by step with particular emphasis on the ecological system as the primary matrix of change.

Elman Service in his book *Primitive Social Organization* classifies culture into four basic evolutionary levels based on qualitative differences in social and economic structure. He states as follows:

> The evolution of culture as measured by changes in social structure consists of a movement in the direction of greater size and density of the social body, an increase in the number of groups, greater specialization in the function of groups, and new means of integrating the groups (1962:111).

These levels he calls bands, tribes, chiefdoms, and primitive states in ascending order of sociocultural integration. Though there are a number of difficulties in application of these levels to archaeological complexes, this system does provide a useful tool for measuring the evolution of Mesoamerican society.

It is readily granted that in addition to the practical problems of applying this typology, it can be criticized on more general methodological grounds. Since such criticisms are ultimately of greater importance, we should point out that we are cognizant of the limitations of taxonomy in general and of this one in particular. There is an overall question concerning the nature of the phenomena being classified. In a certain very real sense, the differences are as frequently quantitative as qualitative, and any classification distorts when dealing with a continuum by breaking it into discrete pigeonholes. We do not feel that this limitation is so serious an obstacle if it is recognized that such pigeonholes are arbitrary, imposed by the classifier upon a body of data and dependent not upon the nature of the data but instead on the nature of the problem. Typologies are an aid to science; they impede it only when they are in themselves regarded as sacrosanct. Service's classification of social levels need not serve all purposes; he may lump where others, with other aims, prefer not to lump, and vice versa. In subsequent sections, we take issue with specific points raised by this system; we will, therefore, not deal with them in detail here. For our purposes, however, the advantages outweigh the drawbacks.

In addition to the limitations inherent in any typology, that of Service in particular is subject to more specific criticisms as well, criticisms of which we are fully cognizant. Levels of cultural development—band, tribe, chiefdom, state—are used by Service to represent unilineal or universalist categories, types occurring in the evolution of world culture, with, presumably, the same kinds of implications wherever they occur. Regarded as such, they are of course open to the theoretical and methodological limitations germane to any sequence of this kind, such as those of Morgan and of Marx. Our use of the Service terminology, however, is not wholesale; rather, in many important ways we are modifying and adapting his original scheme. Our approach is more compatible with what Steward calls multilineal evolution, and our use of Service's taxonomy reflects this important difference.

Our concern is primarily with one major problem, that of the origin of civilization, and with one area of the world, Mesoamerica. Just as there are of course other problems in Mesoamerican anthropology, so too are there other areas of the world (though few in number) where the problem we discuss is also a critical and outstanding one. The limited worldwide distribution of what Fried (1960) calls the pristine state—Mesoamerica, the Central Andes, the Tigris–Euphrates, the Nile Valley, the Indus Valley, China—is itself a significant regularity, one requiring explanation. The similarities in development in these regions have long been noted, but overall resemblance need not imply a priori similarity in detail in such factors as rates of change and duration of phases relative to each other. These to us are essentially empirical questions, a view which in no way militates against the solution of more general problems of causality. Similarity in principle, in other words, need not imply identity in detail. There is a problem in identification of what Steward calls core and superstructural features and the question of whether a single trait necessarily pertains to the cultural core in all instances of its occurrence.

Our acceptance, therefore, albeit with reservations, of Service's stages does not imply a position concerning the general nature, or reality, of these stages in a universal evolutionary sequence. Universal questions of stability, duration, and structural implications of one stage for another do not concern us. We are merely taking this classification as convenient for our purposes, in the observation and clarification of processes noted for a single sequence. The universalistic aspects of the stages themselves, and their nature, is a problem tangential to the major concerns of this volume. For example, the tribal stage, in Central Mexico at least, appears to be a relatively ephemeral one, difficult to delineate archaeologically and of brief duration. It is not our problem to proceed from this fact to a general statement concerning the nature of the tribal stage *qua* stage, or its role in the development of world culture. Further research in those areas of the world where essentially autochthonous civilizations did develop may reveal this stage as equally fleeting in these other sequences as well. Data, similarly, from areas which did not witness the developments with which we are here concerned may also indicate this—or something quite different. We regard these as problems that can legitimately and profitably be investigated, and prefer therefore not to build their solutions into the terminology at the outset. The problems of cause and effect in cultural development are too complex to be relegated to simple definition, especially if the universalistic view of cultural evolution is adopted initially.

Although, therefore, we use Service's classificatory system, we are using it for purposes rather different from Service's own. This being the case, our system has been modified accordingly. In our sense, it has become a developmental sequence, analogous to the more traditional ones long familiar in American archaeological terminology. The statement of Willey and Phillips (1958:70–71) is relevant in this context:

> Cultures A and B are classified as Archaic because they possess certain common denominators that we have chosen as criteria for that stage. Their common possession of these features may be the result of historical contact, environmental determination, homotaxis in a truly evolutionary sense, or any two or all three of these. In other words, the system, if it can be called a system, is not rigged to exclude any particular kind of explanation . . . it cannot claim to operate on the explanatory level.

Having therefore discussed our use of Service's cultural stages, we shall proceed to a brief summary of those stages. The bulk of this volume will, we feel, put the flesh of explanation onto the bare bones of the typology.

Levels of Integration

BANDS

Bands are small (30 to 100 people) territorial, hunting-and-gathering groups characterized by local exogamy and unilocal residence. Because of these two rules, bands tend to be kin groups made up of a group of related men or women and their spouses and unmarried children. Service argues that all bands, before contact with Western civilization and consequent social disorganization, were virilocal in residence. Bands vary in size, degree of nomadism, and seasonal changes in membership according to the character of food resources, their quantity, and seasonal occurrence. They may be characterized as associations of related nuclear families who claim a given territory and reside together wnen subsistence circumstances permit. Formal political organization, rank (other than age and sex status differentiation), and economic specialization are absent (some slight local specialization and trade may, however, occur). Rarely present are social techniques for integrating local groups into larger aggregations.

Tribes

Tribal social structures, from an evolutionary point of view, may be considered as an outgrowth of band social structure in which new techniques are developed to integrate local groups into a larger society. Band-like patterns of exogamy and marital residence, Service argues, cannot hold such large societies together, since affinal alliances become increasingly diffuse as the number of residential groups increases. Tribes are not organized, however, by hierarchical or political techniques. Instead the local groups are integrated by sodalities which crosscut them such as clans or sibs, age-grade associations, secret societies, warrior and religious societies. Tribal society evolves from band social structure and, therefore, remains egalitarian and with an essentially horizontal integrative network. Tribal society, as conceived by Service, is usually associated with an agricultural economy, but such economic institutions as markets, organized trade, and craft-specialized groups are lacking.

Chiefdoms

At the chiefdom level we are dealing with what Fried (1960) calls "ranked society." Local groups are organized into a cone-shaped hierarchical social system in which variation in rank, with the associated privileges and obligations, is the primary technique of social integration. This hierarchical system centers on a single status position, that of the chief. Since commonly the entire society is believed to be descended from a single ancestor, and the occupant of the position of chief is chosen on the basis of descent from this original postulated ancestor, it follows that everyone else in the network is ranked according to his degree of relationship to the chief. There are, in Fried's words, "fewer status positions than personnel qualified to fill them," and consequently a selection procedure, usually either primogenitive or ultimogenitive, is employed to fill the positions. Service's model is based on the essentially bilateral systems of Polynesia and therefore tends to emphasize primarily individual rankings. In Africa, however, we note the presence of this approximate level of complexity associated with unilineal descent groups; here entire groups are ranked, again on the basis of kinship proximity to and seniority vis-à-vis the group from which the chief is selected (cf. Fallers 1965 on the Basoga). In either case the result is great variation in rank throughout the society but without sharply defined social classes.

Local specialization of production and a concomitant need for distribution of goods and services throughout the society is characteristic of chiefdoms. The rank positions are, therefore, associated with the various levels on which redistribution of local surpluses takes place; as such they have definite economic functions and are not merely based on relative prestige. Yet despite the position of the chief in the redistributive network, he lacks for the most part the true differential access to and control of strategic resources that would constitute social stratification.

As a consequence of this fact, the position of chief also lacks formal delineation of power and coercive techniques of political control that would be provided by professional police or courts. His authority is based in large part on the existence of sumptuary rules providing for elaborate ritualistic isolation by regulations of dress, ornamentation, food, mobility—rules which are extended in varying degrees to other individuals and groups according to their relationship to the chief. The role of the personality of the occupant of the position may also be significant to the authority of the position (cf. Mead 1930). Service feels that sumptuary rules become increasingly elaborate as chiefdoms increase in size, and serve as a method of social control. They may persist into the next level of integration, the state level, along with the true political techniques; in chiefdoms, however, such rules constitute the basic mechanism of social control.

Chiefdoms, as compared with tribes, have considerably greater capacity for the incorporation of new groups. In contrast to the essentially egalitarian tribe, they are distinguished by the presence of a center for the coordination of economic, social, and religious activities. In the case of larger and more elaborate chiefdoms, these centers may include not only the resident chief, but also a greater or lesser number of administrative assistants (usually drawn from close kinsmen of the chief), service personnel, and even full-time craftsmen.

STATES

Many of the features of social structure present in chiefdoms carry over into this level: hierarchical relationships between units, sumptuary rules, specialized economic functions of the constituent groups. What Service calls states, however, are larger societies, more complex in organization. Following Service, a state

. . . is integrated by a special mechanism involving legitimatized force. It constitutes itself legally; it makes explicit the manner and circumstances of its use of force and forbids other use of force by lawfully interfering in disputes between individuals and between corporate parts of the society (1962:173–174).

Commonly associated with state levels of political organization are sharply defined social classes or castes (Fried 1960), markets as distribution systems, and more intensive patterns of economic and social differentiation. Since the term state is generally understood to have political meaning only, the term civilization will be used here to identify this higher level of economic and social organization.

Urbanism

A major problem, distinct from but often confused and identified with that of the growth of civilization, is that of the origin and development of urbanism. The terms "urban," "urbanism," "city," and "town" have been used with extreme looseness in the history of archaeology. In the Near East, where the two developments do, in fact, occur synchronously, the term urbanism has been used synonymously with civilization. The term urban as used by Childe (1950) refers to a unique economic system in which full-time occupational specialization is a characteristic trait. In the Near East these specialists lived in large, compact, tightly nucleated communities focused around temple-palace precincts. The size of such communities, it is argued, required state-like political systems to regulate human behavior and integrate such a big society.

The variations of economic roles and control of power result in a wide range of rank that ultimately evolves into a well-defined system of social classes. Specialization, plus the demands of a wealthy upper class and the pantheon of gods, is dependent upon and results in the further development of a highly skilled technology that archaeologists call fine art and monumental architecture. There has been a strong tendency to see all of these processes and traits as being functionally interrelated.

The major problem in the definition of urban and urbanism has arisen as the product of research in the New World, particularly Mesoamerica. Maya culture, for example, included monumental architecture; extraordinary skill in sculpture, painting, ceramic and stucco modeling, and woodworking—indicating the existence of large social systems and professional craftsmen at least for the elite crafts (including also the most advanced system of writing in the New World—a trait that

many archaeologists include in the definition of urbanism).
Large, nucleated communities were, however, rare. Other writers have considered as significant only the presence of nucleated
centers and have called such cultures as the Anasazi urban
(Rowe 1963)—yet the latter lacks the intensive social differentiation based on occupation that is the critical point in
Childe's definition.

The definition of urbanism here is borrowed primarily from
sociology. Urbanism may be defined as the process by which
physical communities emerge with large populations that are
concentrated in a small, continuous, compact area and are characterized by intense internal differentiation based on variations
in wealth, economic specialization, and power. These characteristics—population growth, nucleation, and social differentiation
—may be conveniently analyzed as separate but interrelated
processes. This means that in any area where urbanism is a historical process one would expect a continuum of development of
these characteristics from community to community. For this
reason it is difficult to establish completely objective criteria to
determine the precise point at which a community is to be
classed as urban. An important point is that there is a functional
relationship between these three processes—particularly in preindustrial urban centers. The tendency toward nucleation is directly related to the level of development of transportation on
the one hand and need of craftsmen and merchants to be close
to markets on the other. Land values in an urban community
are, therefore, characteristically high and as a result, very little
unused space is expected. The degree to which the interrelationships referred to operate would seem to be a function of the
significance of nonagricultural activities in the economic life of
the residents. The size of the population is functionally related
to the degree of internal differentiation. We would, therefore,
make a distinction between towns, urban communities with
populations in the thousands, and cities in the tens of thousands. Generally, cities are more densely nucleated than towns

and have a higher percentage of non-food-producing specialists. It is probable, however, that all preindustrial cities had a sizable population of food producers residing within the physical community. In contemporary Mesoamerica all physical communities possessing the type of socioeconomic differentiation we have called urbanism have population densities exceeding 2,000 persons per square kilometer (5,000 per square mile). Correlatively, we know of no communities with populations exceeding that density and with total populations above 5,000 to 6,000 inhabitants without socioeconomic differentiation of the urban type.

These guidelines then may be used to measure urbanism and its development. In discussing the history of urbanism in a prehistoric area it is useful to think of urbanism as a set of interrelated processes occurring in a continuum of development. A major objection to the foregoing discussion may be voiced by our archaeological colleagues that such criteria are difficult to measure archaeologically. We agree, but the point is that the term urban is already in the sociological literature, has a definite meaning, and refers to economic, demographic, and social processes—not to architecture and craft products. If we must use it at all then our obligation is to correlate such processes in some way with archaeological data, not use strictly technological definitions that may or may not correlate with nonmaterial institutions.

Both survey and excavation can reveal data on population growth and nucleation in the history of an archaeological site. The detection of variations in wealth and economic status within a prehistoric community requires more intensive application of both survey and excavation methods but can be done. In many urban communities social differentiation may be accompanied by spatial segregation of status groups within the city.

There seems to be a tendency in preindustrial urban centers for a concentric zoning of status levels, with the upper levels residing near the center in proximity to religious or secular centers, and the lower levels in the peripheries (a direct reverse of Burgess' [1925] concentric zoning principle in industrial urban centers). Furthermore, residents in the peripheries of preindustrial cities tend to be more rural, less urban in mode of life. In many urban centers, social differentiation may be so formally recognized as to result in physical segregation of craftsmen or social classes in wards; in some cases such units may even be defined by avenues, streets, or walls and possess secondary civic centers. However, regardless of the degree to which such segregation is characteristic, variations in the distribution of artifacts and workshops and in the size and quality of housing would indicate, in an archaeological setting, the kind of social differentiation we are calling urban. In summary, there are adequate archaeological techniques for measuring urbanism using the sociological definition.

Distribution of Civilizations

Civilizations, whether urban or not, had an extremely limited spatial distribution prior to the use of iron tools. In the Old World they were limited to two areas, one a large continuous region that extended from the Indus Valley across southwest Asia and into southeastern Europe and northeastern Africa; the other, a much smaller area, was located in north China. In the New World they were limited to the Central Andes and Mesoamerica.

The reasons for the limited distribution, which we elaborate below, probably involve a variety of factors. From a negative point of view civilizations are expensive systems in terms of restriction of behavior of individuals and of small communities, involving a considerable sacrifice of social and economic freedoms. In his study of peasant society, Wolf (1966) discusses in detail the problems of survival of people and communities in their highly circumscribed social and economic worlds and cites cases of tribal groups rejecting a peasant role in a national culture. On the other hand, civilizations do offer certain advantages over noncivilized societies, such as protection from enemies and famine (since the state frequently acts as a storage and distribution agency of surpluses). Furthermore, the state provides a systematic distribution of resources through markets and craft specialization, and, unless society is characterized by an unusually rigid system of social stratification, permits individuals to select a variety of modes of life. The nature of their organization makes them, furthermore, more efficient in the competition for strategic resources that underlies expansionism.

Social Levels and the New World

Native cultures corresponding to each of Service's four types along the continuum from "bands" to "states," which we have redefined here as civilization, were encountered by Europeans at the time of their discovery of the New World. What he calls the state was achieved only in Mesoamerica and the Central Andes. Chiefdoms were found in the southern Andes, some areas of the Eastern Woodlands, on the Northwest Coast, and in the West Indies; but the largest continuous area of chiefdom level of organization and the most complexly organized chiefdoms occurred in the Intermediate Area (that is, Central America south and east of Guatemala and northwestern South America). Groups on the tribal level resided in the American Southwest, Central Chile, much of the Eastern Woodlands, and the Amazon Basin; bands were found on the northern and western peripheries of North America and the southern periphery of South America. (Cf. Figure 3.)

In this volume Mesoamerica, the Central Andes, and the Intermediate Area are grouped into a cultural-historical unit that will be referred to as Nuclear America.[1] We use the term "nu-

[1] This term has been in common usage in American archaeology. It was probably first used by A. L. Kroeber in the 1948 edition of his *Anthropology*.

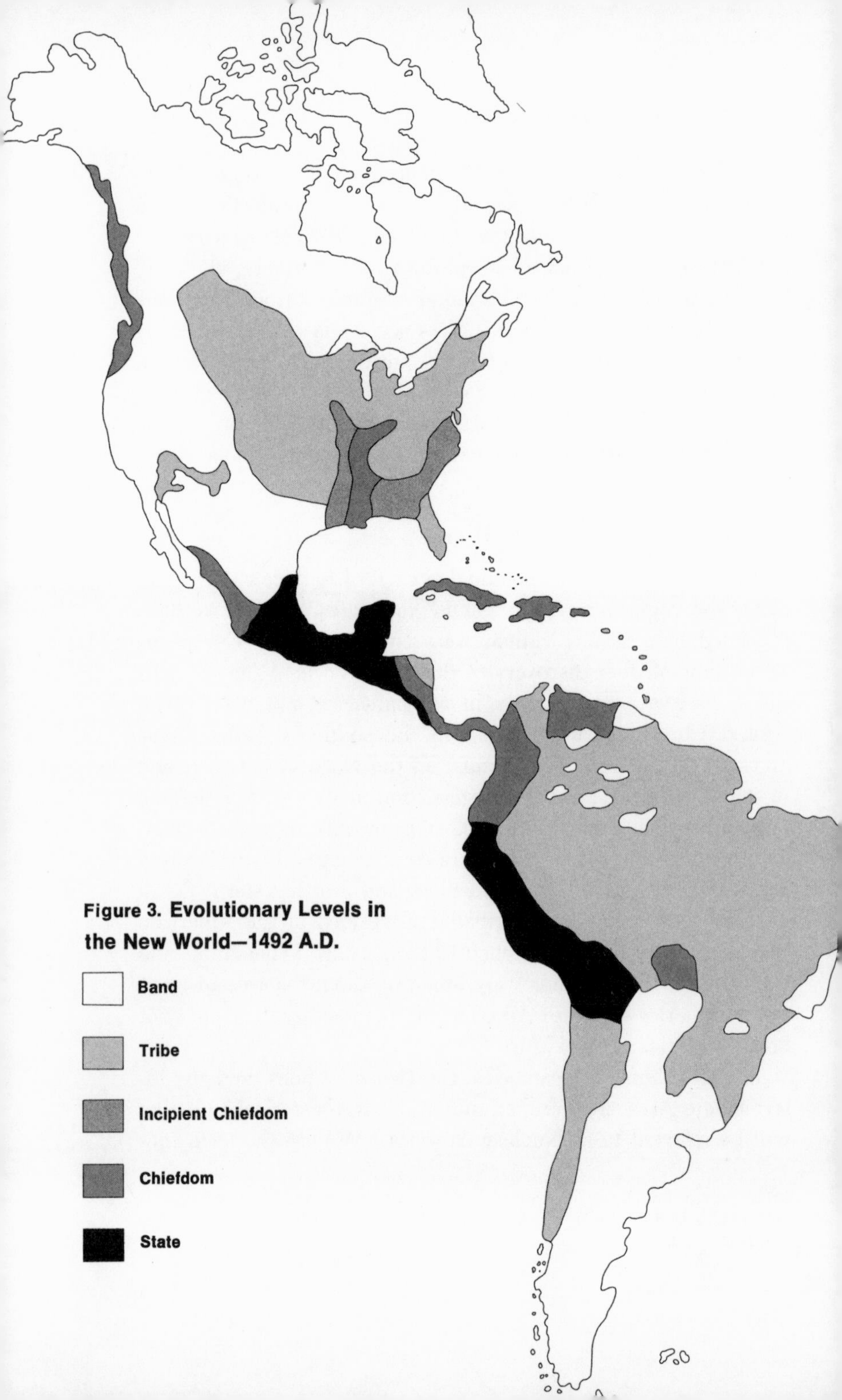

Figure 3. Evolutionary Levels in the New World—1492 A.D.

Band

Tribe

Incipient Chiefdom

Chiefdom

State

clear" in a variety of contexts. Generally, it refers to areas that were particularly vigorous foci of culture change and where, furthermore, such change had strong extra-local repercussions. Although local cultural processes have undoubtedly been of primary significance in the patterning of all cultures, throughout history there have been exceptionally dynamic cultures that have exerted considerable influence on others. The concept of a nuclear area is a flexible one; one can conceive of nuclear areas within nuclear areas. With respect to the New World as a whole the area noted above is nuclear. Within Mesoamerica the Basin of Mexico was one of several nuclear areas, and within the latter several small areas played nuclear roles from one period to another.

There is considerable historical utility in the concept of a nuclear area for the New World as a whole. The evolution of agriculture has undoubtedly been one of the primary processes in the development of New World chiefdoms and civilizations. Nearly all of the cultigens apparently originated in the defined nuclear area. Three primary centers have been suggested for plant domestication: Highland Mexico, Western Venezuela, and the Central Andean altiplano, along with numerous secondary centers. The distribution of domestic plants and other associated culture traits suggests that this enormous area was a sphere of intensive and continuous diffusion, the details of which are just beginning to be understood. Finally, at the time of discovery it was a huge, nearly continuous area of distribution of societies on the chiefdom-state levels of sociocultural integration.

II / Archaeology and
Social Systems

A major problem in delineation of the history of Service's levels in Mesoamerica is one of methodology, that is, how to identify them in an archaeological setting. The problem is one of ascertaining the kinds of material data that provide clues concerning the size of a prehistoric society and the degree and nature of internal differentiation. Housing, dress, and burial furniture may provide clues as to the social status of individuals. Community size, degree of nucleation, density of refuse deposits, plan, internal variations in housing, and functions of areas and structures—what Sanders (1956) has referred to elsewhere as "community settlement patterns"—and spatial relationships of communities, variation in community type based on size, plan, and function within an ecological unit—what he terms "zonal settlement patterns"—all provide pertinent data on the size, structure, and internal differentiation of whole societies.

Particularly pertinent is evidence of what may be called "site stratification." By this term is meant indications of differences in rank among a number of contemporary communities located within a restricted geographical area. By definition bands and tribes should lack such evidence; chiefdoms and civilizations possess it. The relative size of settlements or civic centers would be clear evidence of intercommunity and intracommunity specialization as well. This would be attested to by variations in the quality of craft products, housing and burial furniture, and by indications of spatial segregation of craftsmen.

A major problem is attempting to infer reliably the distinction between chiefdoms and civilizations from the archaeological evidence. Where cultural remains indicate an urban civilization the problem hardly exists. The difficulties lie in seeing the distinction between unusually large chiefdoms and nonurban civilizations in the archaeological picture. To a great extent many of the ethnographic differences are quantitative, and in theory large chiefdoms should have organizational characteristics approaching those of civilizations. The difference lies essentially in the distinction between ranking and stratification—in the presence at the state level of true social stratification and existence of classes and the absence of this phenomenon at the chiefdom level.

In theory this distinction is clear and is made with facility. However, in any sorting out and ordering of a large number of ethnographically well-defined societies from simple to complex, many of those which fall within categories of chiefdoms and civilizations will be found to lie along a continuum from large and complex chiefdoms to relatively simple states. The distinction between the two kinds of societies, so easy to draw in theory, is extremely difficult to infer reliably from archaeological materials, which generally bring more quantitative than qualitative evidence to bear upon the problem. Certainly, however, if the largest centers of a given period can be determined to represent a given proportion of the labor and skill that can be mobilized by the total society, this proportion may be compared with that of preceding and succeeding periods, and the comparison may in turn reflect differences in size and complexity of the societies that built these centers.

Several papers have been published recently that challenge

two of the primary assumptions made above regarding the social and economic significance of monumental architecture (Kaplan 1963; Erasmus 1965) and the restricted distribution of civilization in the New World (Meggers 1963). Both Kaplan and Erasmus attempt to show that the construction of civic buildings in major Mesoamerican centers (Teotihuacán, Uxmal) could have been carried out by organized groups of relatively small size and do not necessarily imply the existence of large states. Erasmus, for example, suggests that a population of 1,200 families could have built Uxmal over a period of 250 years.

To support his contention that civic architecture of monumental size can be the product of a relatively small society Erasmus uses as illustrations the well-documented cases of Colonial and contemporary communities in Latin America. In the fervor of religious conversion in the sixteenth century there was an enormous building program organized by the Spanish priesthood; one does have the impression that the size of religious buildings in Latin American communities today is disproportionate to the size of the community. Actually, we know of no community of 1,200 families in post-Hispanic Mesoamerica with a civic center comparable in size and investment of labor to Late Classic Uxmal. (Furthermore, it must be emphasized that Uxmal was constructed with Neolithic technology, thus demanding a much larger labor force than if constructed with iron tools.)

The example, moreover, of church construction in Colonial Latin America is, in fact, one of the most dramatic illustrations of the relationship between population size, architectural monumentality, and the civilized level of society. With the exception of communities that have suffered a significant reduction of status since the construction of their churches (the most striking example would be Cholula), one could demonstrate a very close correlation between the size of the church, quality of its ornamental art, and sophistication of architectural engineering in a Colonial Mexican community and that community's ecclesiastic rank in a graded series from sujeto (dependent community) to cabecera (parish center) to obispado (diocese) to arzobispado (archdiocese).

Furthermore, as Kubler has pointed out (1948), the Spanish ecclesiastic orders based their construction projects on populations available for corvée labor. He demonstrates in fact a close correlation between the size and quality of ecclesiastic architecture and the size of the population available for its construction.

Kubler also points out that the Franciscan order was first on the scene, tended to take over the more densely populated areas, and was able to maintain a much more consistent and workable program of construction. The Augustinians and Dominicans, on the other hand, arrived late and were either allotted districts of lesser populations or given portions of former Franciscan territory. Both of these orders attempted to duplicate the architectural feats of the Franciscans on a deficient population base. The result was strong Indian resistance, in some cases rebellion, and further population loss through overwork.

Still another critical issue: Although the construction of a village church was primarily the product of village labor, it was organized and directed within the administrative setting of a state church, and the skilled labor derived from the kinds of economic institutions we are identifying as civilizations. The studies of Erasmus and Kaplan are of considerable value in that they do provide a picture of the amount of labor demanded in the construction of civic centers. However, these studies in no way demonstrate the probability or even the possibility that civic centers of the size of Uxmal or Teotihuacán were in fact dependent upon the labor of so small a population. The question is not what *can* be done, but what is *normally* done by organized groups of humans in the way of cooperative building projects. We know of no ethnographic parallel of a center of the size of Uxmal being constructed by an organized society of only 1,200 families. Carrying such calculations to absurdity, one could say that the Sun Pyramid of Teotihuacán could have been built by a labor force of one man and a society of one family if a single worker and his descendants labored 365 days a year for 9,000 years! Such calculations can be manipulated at the will of the researcher to "prove" that societies of almost any size are capable of building any structure or group of structures. Since civic buildings and centers are built by societies intending to use them within a reasonable amount of time, the availability of large labor forces, particularly with a neolithic technology, is a necessary prerequisite. There is probably a close correlation between the size of civic centers and the size of the supporting population—holding the level of technology constant.

Furthermore, the archaeological reconstruction of large social systems is based also on apparent stratification of sites by size. When one very large and several considerably smaller civic centers, all contemporaneous, are located within an area of say, several thousand square miles, it may be assumed that the construction of the large center depended upon a labor force drawn from the population tributary to the smaller centers as well. There is, we feel, undeniable evidence of such site stratification in the two areas of New World civilization in the periods prior to the final pre-Hispanic period. For the final period, of course, there is abundant documentation of such large and complex sociopolitical systems. In Mesoamerica such sites as Teotihuacán, Tula, Cholula, Xochicalco, Monte Albán, Tajín, Tikal, and Copán; and in the Central Andes, Moche, Wari, Chan Chan, Pachacamac, and Tiahuanaco were certainly centers for large social systems of the type defined here as civilization.

The second point, raised by Meggers (1963), is whether the supposed difference in level of sociocultural integration between the Intermediate Area on one hand, and Mesoamerica and the Central Andes on the other, is, in fact, merely the product of archaeological preservation or vagaries of research history rather than of real cultural differences. She suggests that scholars may have been unduly biased by the use of permanent building materials in the construction of civic centers in the latter two areas and that equally imposing centers of perishable materials may have been constructed in the Intermediate Area. Assumptions of the simpler level of socioeconomic organization in the Intermediate Area, however, are based on the sixteenth-century Spanish descriptions of native culture as well as on archaeological data. Furthermore, it is doubtful that archaeologists would not be able to detect major civic centers regardless of the construction materials used. This factor certainly has not hampered archaeological methods in areas like Nigeria or Uganda where large palaces were constructed of perishable materials. A more pertinent question would be not whether archaeologists have failed to detect such sites but whether large organized societies always construct monumental buildings. We believe that they do so. Very large societies must be integrated by means of correspondingly large-scale institutions whose personnel and services must be housed. The absence, therefore, of such a trait in an archaeological setting would, in fact, indicate an absence of civilization.

To recapitulate, we have defined civilization as a type of socioeconomic system and urbanism as a special kind of civilization, discussed the distribution of civilizations in the New World, and briefly stated some of the advantages and disadvantages of such systems. It now remains to discuss the causal factors underlying their origin and distribution in the New World—in other words, the dynamic aspects of civilization.

III / THE DIFFUSION-
EVOLUTION
CONTROVERSY

Diffusion and New World Civilization

Culture change is a result either of factors engendered by internal processes or in response to the stimulus of contact with other cultures. The former may be referred to as "cultural evolution"; the latter is referred to in the literature as "diffusion." In either case new customs must be integrated with the existing culture in such a way that the continued functioning of the whole cultural system is possible. As a result new customs, whether the product of diffusion or evolution, undergo a selective process. From Morgan to the present day the subject of the relative significance of the two processes in the culture history of man as a whole or that of any particular culture has been hotly debated.

Since all archaeologists agree that the American Indian was an immigrant from eastern Asia, this debate has profound implications for the study of the history and origin of native New World cultures. The question revolves around the place and time of the emigration and the kinds of cultures that the immigrants introduced.

Some archaeologists have felt that most or all of the immigrants were primitive hunters and gatherers originating in northeastern Asia who introduced a relatively simple culture with a band level of social organization. The hundreds of native cultures described by the European explorers are understood as the product of local evolutions within the New World. Others feel that the origins of the New World population were more complex and diverse; that the Pacific was a major route of immigration as well; and that much of the variation in native culture, including the characteristics of civilization, were direct imports from Asia (Ekholm 1962, 1964). Since the emphasis is on major processes of change rather than on the origins of particular traits, it matters little to the present formulation whether one or the other has been the dominant factor. We do wish, however, to summarize our position on the "diffusion versus evolution" argument as it relates to the origin and growth of native civilizations in the New World.

Within culture areas the sharing of specific customs by different social or linguistic groups is likely to have been the product of diffusion. New customs invented by one group are much more likely to be copied by neighboring groups than to be reinvented by these groups simply because of the relative facility of communication and the factor of time. Furthermore, the invention is accepted by the first group because it is easily integrated into the existing cultural system and well adapted to the particular area; neighboring groups would, therefore, find the trait equally useful since they live in a similar environment and face approximately similar problems. The term "primary diffusion" was used by Dixon (1928) for diffusion within a single culture area and seems a useful term to retain. He used the term "secondary diffusion" in reference to diffusion between culture areas.

The greater the distance between groups in time and space, the more unlikely it is that diffusion would take place. There is first the problem of establishing or maintaining contact over great distances with primitive transportation, and second, the fact that much of the culture of one area would not necessarily be useful in, or adaptable to, another. We believe, therefore, that the archaeologist has the right to demand more conclusive evidence of such contacts than in the case of primary diffusion. We would unhesitatingly accept as proof of diffusion between Illinois and Ohio the presence of cord-marked pottery in both states but would be extremely reluctant to postulate contact between Neolithic Europe and Illinois on that basis. Assumption of diffusion between widely spaced culture areas in the New World and particularly between the New World and the Old should be very critically examined. Similarity in culture traits between two groups can be the product of convergence as well as diffusion. The reasons for convergence, or the independent invention of custom in different cultures, are numerous. Some traits are directly linked to the use of particular types of environment; thus groups living in the tropical forests of the Congo and Amazon basin will share some customs simply because they have similar geographical resources which they exploit in similar fashion. Examples of convergence on this level would be slash-and-burn agriculture, dispersed settlement pattern, and pole-and-thatch dwellings. Such inventions as ceramics, weaving, and metallurgy are so useful and generalized that the probability of their multiple reinvention would be high. Arguments that pottery making and metallurgy are such complex crafts that they could not have been reinvented independently seem highly illogical: If they are so complex that duplicate invention is improbable how were they ever invented in the first place? Such assertions ignore the well-documented cases of duplicate invention of at least equally complex traits and trait complexes cited by White (1949) and Kroeber (1948) (for example, theory of organic evolution, discovery of sunspots, explanation of respiration, calculus, rediscovery of Mendelian inheritance, law of conservation of energy, cellular theory in biology, telescope, thermometer, telephone). Anthropologists have reported numerous cases of cultural similarities, not well documented, but because of their peculiar spatial distribution explicable only as parallel inventions. Examples are sibs, the couvade, the various types of descent, kinship terminologies, preferential marriage patterns. Some of these are internally complex, certainly as much so as metallurgy and pottery making.

Other kinds of examples of similar traits in widely separated cultures, in a sense harder to explain by convergence, are those unrelated to either environmental resources or function, for example, stylistic features in artifacts. Meggers, Evans, and Estrada (1965) have postulated trans-Pacific contacts between Middle Jomon phase fishermen in Japan and the Valdivia phase population of the Ecuadorean coast on the basis of close resemblances in pottery vessel form, decorative techniques and motifs along with stylistic resemblances in other artifacts. These ideas may be correct, but stylistic convergence can and does occur. Although clay is highly plastic and capable, therefore, of enormous variability, there are limits to the variability of style within any ceramic technology. It would be puzzling if duplication of style did not occur simply by chance. In this connection Rands (1961) cites the curious reappearance of ceramic modes in Late Classic Tabasco and Chiapas that occur first in the Late Preclassic period. The incised collared rims found in Middle Jomon could be reproduced in Iroquois pottery in New York State!

One of the curious stylistic phenomena that seems to recur repeatedly in numerous cultural-historical sequences is what we might call divergence. Mesoamerica, for example, is a huge area and in the sixteenth century was occupied by a great number of ethnic groups, each with its own regional styles in ceramics. This regionalism extended back through the Postclassic and Classic periods. Proceeding backward in time, one finds the Formative ceramics of the various areas looking increasingly alike—so much so that archaeologists have reconstructed the history of the total area in terms of an initial phase of widespread population movement followed by relative stability of population and local entrenchment (cf. Spinden 1928; Piña Chan 1960; Coe 1962). Recent research, as we have indicated, carries the argument even further and postulates widespread population movements between the various New World culture areas in the early phases of ceramic development. We have always been suspicious of this interpretation of stylistic divergence, particularly so of the population movement aspect. Migrations undoubtedly have occurred in human history and there are, of course, well-documented cases. But why should such movements be the major vehicle of culture change precisely in those periods when populations were small and demographic pressure minimal? If anything, one would expect convergences at the ends of cultural sequences when population was dense, competition more intense, and contacts more extensive within the setting of more complex and efficient institutions.

We suggest another explanation for stylistic divergence. In the earlier phases of New World history generally and Mesoamerican history in particular techniques of decoration and uses of pottery were much fewer than in later times, expectedly so in a nascent craft. A commonly noted characteristic of ceramics from the earlier phases is a restriction of decoration to plastic techniques like punctation, incision, and stamping. There is consequently greater restriction of choice and motifs. How much variety of design is really possible using punctation as a technique? If it is the basic method of decoration, then it seems to us that the design capabilities of a ceramic complex would be exhausted within a few generations of potters. Continuing the argument, the restricted uses of pottery would lead to a reduction in variety of form. We believe that this argument is particularly pertinent to the Valdivia–Jomon situation where decoration was restricted to plastic techniques.

One of the puzzling aspects of the claim of a Jomon–Valdivia relationship is the fact that Meggers herself presents a chart and discussion illustrating an extraordinary case of cultural convergence, that between the Anasazi of the American Southwest and the Belén–Santamaria complex of northwestern Argentina (Meggers 1964). The resemblances in style of a great variety of artifacts, including pottery, are much more striking than the Jomon–Valdivia resemblances; yet she explains the former similarities as the product of convergence. Apparently she found unacceptable the possibility of direct contact over such a huge distance. Furthermore, the developmental phases of both have been well defined, and each case seems to have been a local development out of local antecedents. The primary argument in favor of a Jomon origin for the Valdivia complex is the lack of developmental stages in Ecuador and their presence in Japan. But do we really know the archaeology of northwestern South America as a whole or of Ecuador in particular that well? Five years ago we had no Valdivia either.

Linguists have long noted examples of apparent convergence of sound and meaning in widely separated and genetically unrelated languages, which they attribute in fact to the operation of chance. Such instances are not taken as proof of genetic relationship unless they occur demonstrably in regular and patterned systemic contexts; only then are they termed true cognates. We suggest, additionally, that a methodological analogy with the linguistic technique known as mass comparison could be adaptable to the analysis of archaeological material in such problematical situations. In brief, this approach maintains that it is illegitimate to compare isolated features of widely separated languages (archaeological cultures) without first drawing comparisons with those languages (cultures) most closely related, or potentially so. What this method provides is, in a sense, precisely a control for chance convergences, which can be revealed as what they are. The analogy with language breaks down somewhat, in that cultural systems are in many ways more "open" than linguistic ones; the adoption of a diffused type of pot need have fewer repercussions throughout the total culture than will the adoption of a borrowed phoneme, generally speaking, upon a language. But these methods, or analogies of them, serve to warn against placing undue emphasis upon single traits in, say, ceramic decoration, regardless of the nature of the entire assemblage and changes in it through the course of time.

We are not suggesting that diffusion between New World culture areas or contacts across the Pacific did not occur. But it is doubtful that they were of major significance in the origin and growth of either the Andean or Mesoamerican civilizations, and the hypothesis of such contacts must be very critically evaluated.

A higher level of criticism of diffusion theories concerns the origin of the two New World civilizations, and the relative probabilities of the dynamics responsible for those origins. Contacts between Mesoamerica and the Andes, or between Asia and either of the New World nuclear areas, are generally assumed to have been the products of small-scale migration or of sporadic visits. In the case of the suggested Jomon–Valdivia relationship, the assumption is that a boatload of Japanese fishermen were blown off course and shipwrecked on the coast of Ecuador. Several questions arise, germane to the possibilities of interpreting such a phenomenon. In the first place, assuming the origin of the migrants from a complex civilization (which Jomon was not), what sort of repertoire would they be likely to have with them? Given the fact that specialization of labor tends to be a highly significant aspect of complex civilization, these migrants would not be in possession of the total range of techniques and skills of their parent culture and would hence be able to transmit little more than their own specialty. Were their arrival accidental, it would be improbable that even a small fraction of the original cultural repertoire would be represented among the migrants. Even with deliberate missionization this generalization would hold; professional priests generally do not themselves control great numbers of craft skills, although they may exert political control over craftsmen.

Further, we would question the ability of a small group of

migrants to transform a native tribal society. Rowe (1966) treats this problem in considerable detail. Although early diffusionists suggested that the prestige of the migrants would be higher the greater was the gap in cultural level between them and the beneficiaries of their superior knowledge, the step between prestige and success of diffusion cannot logically be taken. In this context, Rowe suggests analysis of documented instances of successful and unsuccessful diffusion. When this is done, it appears that success is correlated to a greater degree with similarity between the two peoples in cultural level.

To illustrate, we may note the comparative success of the Spanish attempt at the conversion of the Indians of Mexico and Peru to Catholicism and their concomitant incorporation into the Spanish Colonial economic and political systems. This success stands in striking contrast to the notable failures of the conquerors in these respects in the Amazon Basin and in the American Southwest. The case of the acculturation of the native Mesoamerican and Peruvian populations by Spain was based, furthermore, on continuous, regularized contact over several centuries—contact which involved several hundred thousand Spanish immigrants, thoroughly organized religious conversion, and at least equally well-organized economic exploitation. Numerous writers have emphasized that the Spanish success in Mexico was due in great measure to the relative ease with which Spanish institutions and symbols could be equated with native ones. More to the point is that these native institutions were organized in ways which made them exploitable by techniques amply available to sixteenth-century Spain, and were of sufficient wealth to merit considerable time and effort devoted to such exploitation (cf. Harris 1964).

Even today where nations like Peru and Guatemala have a national educational system, modern communication and transportation, and organized programs of directed cultural change, a huge segment of the population continues to speak Quechua or Maya and maintain a style of life that has changed little since the end of the sixteenth century. Yet some archaeologists would have us believe that a few boatloads of merchants, missionaries, or shipwrecked sailors were catalysts of major revolutions in the native culture of the New World.

Perhaps a better documented parallel to the supposed Jomon–Valdivia situation, however, lies in the shipwreck of the two Spanish soldiers Guerrero and Aguilár on Cozumel prior to the Cortés expedition. Although Aguilár subsequently joined Cortés, Guerrero had become, in effect, a Maya, and his impact on Maya culture was negligible. In the case of neither Spaniards nor Maya are we dealing with a tribal society, but the probabilities support this model as more applicable to the situation of Jomon fishermen or Buddhist missionaries. As Rowe puts it: "No sound basis has ever been established for the romantic theory that occasional castaways will be listened to, like the Connecticut Yankee at King Arthur's court, rather than knocked on the head or put to work cleaning fish" (1966:336).

One questions whether the ecclesiastics of the Conquest itself would have been listened to had it not been for the power of the Spanish state hovering in the background.

The questions involve problems of an essentially empirical kind regarding the natures of both donor and recipient cultures, and of the patterning of relations between them. Not only are complex symbols easily grasped only by people living in a complex society (in which case the question of origins is not answered by postulating diffusion), but in general, such symbols require a rationale of some sort on the part of the donor culture to diffuse in the first place. It is unwise to regard diffusion as a sort of mechanical process, like osmosis; it occurs within a patterned, systematic context which must be specified if sound conclusions are to be drawn. (Cf. Foster 1960.)

A number of recent papers have stressed diffusion between Mesoamerica and the Central Andes on the Chavín–Olmec horizon (800–500 B.C.) and continuing sporadically thereafter throughout the culture history of the two areas (Coe 1962,

1963, Kidder *et al.* 1963; Estrada and Evans 1963). In such papers the Olmecs are viewed somewhat as a wandering missionary group, spreading the doctrine of civilization and the jaguar god—in effect, as culture bearers similar to the Aztec view of Quetzalcóatl. This mechanism has been used to explain the origin of the various regional variants of Mesoamerican civilization. It is not always clear in the reconstructions whether the Olmecs actually settle in the Andean areas, or simply convert and then return home. If the reconstruction involves actual settlement, it is difficult to understand why a people would leave the tropical jungles of Mexico and settle in Peru either on a desert coast or at an elevation of 3,177 meters above sea level. Migrant groups usually attempt to settle in areas whose geographical characteristics are comparable to those from which they come and to which their subsistence system may be easily adapted. In the case of missionaries, they would tend to settle where population and potential converts were most densely settled already. Such being the case, it is evident that to invoke diffusion is but to beg the question once again: Why were the strategic resources, from the point of view of the missionaries —the population—concentrated where they in fact were found? The purpose of the migrants, in summary, must be taken into account.

A documented instance of immigration and settlement may accordingly be analyzed at this point: the Spanish predilection for settlement in the Central Plateau of Mexico. In part, the geographic similarities between the Central Plateau and the conquerors' native Spain may be responsible. It is clear also that the population, the principal resource of Mesoamerica from the point of view of the Spaniards, was already concentrated here. The Spanish government had previously developed techniques of dealing with the resources—natural, in terms of subsistence potential, and human, in terms of a population organized in a particular way. The influence of geography is, therefore, both direct and indirect in this instance.

The archaeological record itself tends to render unlikely the assertion of an Olmec origin of Central Andean civilization. Recent C-14 dates provided by the Japanese excavations at Kotosh near Huanuco (Horkheimer 1964)—1800 B.C. for a preceramic temple—and by Lanning (1965) in the Chillon Valley for a contemporary ceremonial precinct certainly do not justify the postulated Olmec origins.

Olmec influence is, however, another problem, distinct from that of origins. Chavín art is frequently cited as a case of the diffusion of Olmec religious tradition to the Central Andes. The two art styles are, however, strikingly different. It is true that both contain within their respective repertoires of basic motifs the feline, the serpent, the raptorial bird (but these occur commonly throughout the Americas), as well as certain specialized techniques of rendering, such as the eye with eccentric pupil. The presence of equivalent motifs is not surprising. What is not demonstrable is that these motifs, although similar in type, maintain equivalent or even similar meanings within the respective Olmec and Chavín systems of iconography, equivalences which might be expected had the religious tradition of the Olmec been transplanted to highland Peru. Rather than posit an Olmec migration (other serious objections to which are developed below), we suggest that in regard to the partial sharing of motifs found in the two art styles, it makes much more sense to regard these two distinctive cultures as exchanging ideas in much the way that Egypt and Sumeria did two thousand years earlier.

A final major point remains to be emphasized: Civilization and urbanism are not traits or complexes that can be readily diffused by casual or even prolonged contact between groups. They belong, unlike art motifs and specific techniques of style, to what Julian Steward (1955a) calls "core features" of culture, and as such, the growth of civilization can be understood only in terms of evolutionary processes. The place of origin of each of the components is irrelevant; what concerns us is the function and configuration of the entire socioeconomic system. The outward symbols, on which many archaeologists dote, are in effect superficial features, highly variable in contrast to the underlying structure. The parasol and the litter as symbols of rank may, for example, have been ideas introduced by Buddhist missionaries—but only a society already stratified would have accepted these traits and assigned to them the same meaning and the same position in a total cultural system as they had possessed in Southeast Asia. Where core features resemble each other, we are likely to find such convergence in the superstructure as well.

This does not imply that foreign influence upon a given culture never occurs, nor that it is in all cases negligible. In a subsequent section of this volume, we deal in greater detail with this problem in regard to the regional variants of Mesoamerican civilization. However, for us to attribute major causal significance to this factor, it is necessary first to adopt a more sophisticated analysis of the nature of that influence.

The Ecological Approach

The term ecology, in current use in anthropology, was borrowed from the biological sciences. It was first coined by Ernest Haeckel, a German zoologist, in 1870 and defined as the "total relations of the animal both to his organic and inorganic environment." The concept has, therefore, two levels of meaning: It refers, first, to the dependence of plants and animals on their inanimate environment, second, to the mutual interdependence of the various species of plants and animals who live together in a local area. The local population of interdependent organisms is called a biotic community, which, like a human community, has a structure. The interdependence between the various species of plants and animals is referred to as symbiosis. Several types of symbiosis are defined: parasitism, in which one animal or plant derives advantages from the relationship to the disadvantage of the other; commensalism, in which one derives a benefit but without conferring either harm or benefit on the other; and mutualism, used to describe a relationship in which both derive benefit.

The living organisms of a biotic community are structured into what is referred to as a pyramid of life. At the bottom of the pyramid are the plants, the food producers who convert solar energy into primary energy for the whole community. The type of vegetation in a biotic community depends upon the inorganic environment—soils, topography, hydrography, precipitation, and temperature. On the next level are the herbivores who eat the plants and convert them into a new form of energy. Above these are the first level of carnivores who depend on the herbivores for food and above them the top carnivores who prey on both the first level of carnivores and on the herbivores. There is a fascinating similarity between the life pyramid and pyramids of social stratification in preindustrial civilizations. In both cases there is a sharp decrease of population as we move upward. In summary, the local biotic community, under normal conditions, comprises a balanced population pyramid with considerable interdependence of its members based on specialization of subsistence activities.

As used in cultural anthropology the term ecology refers to three levels of relationships of man to his environment. As in the case of the biotic community it refers, first, to the relationship of a human community to its inorganic environment and, second, to the plants and animals that it depends on, both wild and domestic. A third level, however, is uniquely pertinent to human ecology—the interrelationships between human beings (in other words animals of the same species) within an organized local community and between human communities. Since human behavior is primarily learned behavior or, as anthropologists call it, cultural behavior, we refer to the use of ecology in cultural anthropology as cultural ecology.

We believe that the relatively new and rapidly developing ecological approach in anthropology offers a more creative explanation of the growth of civilizations. Briefly, the cultural ecologist sees the culture of a given people as a subsystem in interaction with other subsystems. He argues that the key to understanding the developmental processes of the cultural subsystem lies in this interactive relationship. The total network of relationships between subsystems has been called the "ecological system" or "ecosystem." It includes three subsystems—culture, biota, and physical environment.

By the way of warning, we wish to emphasize that we hold no brief for nineteenth- and twentieth-century concepts of environmental determinism. Neither, however, shall we reject the powerful influence of the biological and physical environments on the development of man's diverse cultural systems. As stated above, the cultural, biological, and physical environments are all components in a single higher-order system. Furthermore, all three subsystems interact mutually in a three-way process. Cultural systems modify the biological and physical environment and vice versa. Perhaps Toynbee (1947) in his "challenge-and-response" theory comes closest to a formal presentation of the ecological approach as it relates to the evolution of civilization. Sanders (1965) has stated the ecological position by way of the following postulates:

a. Each biological and physical environment offers particular problems to human utilization.

b. Diverse environments offer different problems; therefore, the response by man (that is, the development of a cultural subsystem) will be different.

c. There is an almost unlimited number of possibilities but a limited number of probabilities in the way in which a people may adapt to a given environment. It is in part for this reason that groups with quite distinctive cultures may occupy the same or similar environments. The level of technology and the degree of productivity of the subsistence pattern of a group affects the degree to which variation in response in other aspects of culture is possible. Some geographical environments with a given level of technology are inherently less productive than others. This factor limits population growth, which in turn restricts the variability of response in other aspects of culture.

d. Response to environmental challenges may be technological, social, or ideational. The adaptation of a group is achieved primarily by technological and subsistence techniques but always involves economic, social, or even ideational processes as well. Social organization generally may be regarded as an adaptive system since organized human groups can always exploit their landscape more effectively than isolated individuals or inchoate mobs.

Other aspects of culture such as religious beliefs and practices have as a primary function the integration of the social group. If this argument is correct, then all aspects of culture have adaptive significance.

Some aspects of culture, however, are more directly related to the use of the physical environment—therefore, it is methodologically more simple to discover the interactive pattern. Steward (1955a) refers to these aspects of a culture as the culture core.

e. In a broad sense men living in similar environments solve the problem of adaptation in similar ways; in differing environments, in different ways. This is essentially what Steward demonstrates in his concept of multilineal evolution. Furthermore, although a number of alternative solutions may be possible, certain kinds of responses are more likely to occur than others and are repeated throughout the culture history of a given area.

f. There is some overlapping of responses and solutions even in cases of strikingly dissimilar environments; for example, the Mesoamerican cultural configuration occurred in arid mountain valleys and lush tropical lowlands.

g. Cultures, as are all of the components of an ecological system, are dynamic, and the degree of integration of a cultural subsystem to the total ecological system will vary. This integration may be a function of time, of external disturbances that temporarily disrupt the integrative processes, or because the initial course was an alternate one to that leading to the most efficient adjustment.

h. The culture of a given people, therefore, can be considered essentially as a complex of techniques adaptive to the problems of survival in a particular geographical region. Human cultural evolution generally is a superorganic process that grew out of organic evolution. The culture of man is, in an ecological sense, a means by which humans successfully compete with other animals, with plants, and particularly with other humans. The product of plant and animal evolution is more effective utilization of the landscape in competition with individuals of the same and other species. This effectiveness is usually expressed in population growth, and this growth can therefore be taken as a measure of success in a given area at any given point.

The physical and biological environments play a restrictive, permissive, and (in the sense that they restrict choice) a directive role in the evolution of culture.

IV / THE DYNAMIC ASPECTS OF THE ECOSYSTEM

*Proceeding to the dynamic aspects of the eco-*logical system, or ecosystem, we cite three basic processes which have played a major role in the evolution of New World civilizations: population growth, competition, and cooperation.

Population and Civilization

Population growth may be considered as a primary process in the cause-and-effect network, with competition and cooperation as derivative processes. Civilizations by definition are large social systems characterized by intense social stratification and economic specialization. Based upon comparative data from Bronze Age Mesopotamia and sixteenth-century Mesoamerica, our estimate is that such systems require a minimum of 10,000 individuals to function. The stage we are calling civilization was probably reached in Mesopotamia by 3000 B.C. Braidwood and Reed (1957) estimate an average population of the Sumerian states at 17,000 at that time. Although much larger states occurred in Central Mexico and in Mesopotamia in various areas and time periods, the most stable political units involved 12,000 to 30,000 persons. This population, for several reasons, must be concentrated in a relatively small area. To function effectively, large social systems require a reasonably efficient system of communication and transportation, the former to maintain durable patterns of interaction between constituent subgroupings, the latter to supply the non-food-producing center. As a general rule, the more primitive the system of communication and transportation, the smaller the physical area that can be effectively integrated. Really large, complex socioeconomic systems under such limitations, such as were particularly characteristic of the native New World civilizations, therefore, require a high population density.

A gross relationship between the distribution of civilizations in the New World and population density is easily demonstrated. Approximately two-thirds of the population of the New World in 1492 lived in Mesoamerica and the Central Andes, in an area embracing only 6.2 percent of the total land surface of the double continent. The major theoretical problem is determination of the minimal and maximal population density for each of Service's various levels of socioeconomic integration.

In some environments population density may be quite high but the small size and relative isolation of the settled areas act to limit the total size of an organized population to such a level that civilizations cannot function. This may occur on small islands or in deserts where tiny oases of population are so widely spaced that supra-community social structures are not feasible. In the case of the American Southwest the size of each of the individual settled zones in the Anasazi areas was so small and the total number of such zones so few that the regional population density in the sixteenth century was but .757 per square kilometer and the total population only 33,800 persons (Kroeber 1947). Sahlins (1958) has demonstrated a close correlation between degrees of social stratification and island size and geographical complexity in Polynesia. The population density in Polynesia at the time of European contact (excluding New Zealand) was some 40 persons per km², considerably higher than in the American nuclear area. The Polynesian population, however, was distributed in tiny oases of land scattered over millions of square miles of ocean. The evolution of civilization was aborted by the small total population capacities of islands or groups of islands. The largest population cluster was in the Hawaiian group with an estimated population of 240,000 in an area of 15,000 km².

Aside from the requirements of localized, densely settled populations numbering in the tens of thousands, civilizations apparently require large overall territories and the existence of considerable numbers of such population units to function. The civilization of Mesoamerica, for example, was spread over an area of nearly 1.25 million square kilometers, and the Central Andean area is approximately two-thirds as large. The essential demographic requirements seem to be a large area with a moderately high overall population density within which are a great number of fairly extensive, much more densely settled zones.

A major theoretical problem is that of determining the minimal population density of the region as a whole and of the intensively settled local areas required for the maintenance and growth of a civilization. Both of the New World civilizations occur in large territories in which the overall population density was only light to moderate. Rowe (1946) estimated a population of 6 million for the Inca Empire on the eve of the Spanish Conquest. Steward and Faron have (1959) estimated 3½ million for the Central Andes—a considerably smaller area, with an overall density of 4 persons per km² (10 per square mile). These writers emphasize that a very high percentage of the area is uncultivable due to elevation, aridity, or topography and estimate that the 2 percent under cultivation today is probably close to the arable maximum. (The population today, excluding Lima, is approximately three times that for 1531.) When only arable land is used, the population density ascends to 200 per km^2—a striking testimony to the intensiveness of land use. Willey in his Virú Valley Project, an archaeological study of one of the small, densely settled oases on the coast, suggests a peak population in the past of 25,000 persons using 170 km^2 of irrigated land or a local density of approximately 150 per km^2 (Willey 1953). Kosok (1965) estimates a total area under irrigation on the Peruvian coast of 6,000 to 7,000 km^2, and a total population of 1,000,000 persons or a corresponding density of 143 to 167 per km^2.

The situation in Mesoamerica is more complex, and the overall agricultural situation much more favorable. The population in 1519 could not have been less than 12 million, with 15 million a more probable estimate, in an area of approximately 1.25 million square kilometers. This total yields an overall density of at least 10 persons and more probably 12 per km^2 —still only a moderate population density. The Mesoamerican highlands had a demographic pattern similar to that of the Central Andes. The Teotihuacán Valley for example had a population of approximately 100,000 and a density of 200 persons per km^2 at the time of the apogee of Teotihuacán and again in 1519. In both the Virú and Teotihuacán Valleys civilization was accompanied by urbanism. Urbanism was generally characteristic of the arid portions of the Mesoamerican highlands and everywhere correlated with unusually high population densities. The tropical lowlands, on the other hand, were the scene of a number of vigorous regional civilizations but lacked cities. The lowland environment, in sharp contrast to the microgeographic complexity of the highlands, was much more uniform in those characteristics that affect agriculture (cf. Coe 1961a). The population density of the lowlands in 1519 varied between 5 to 30 persons per km^2. The overall population density of the arid highlands, with the exception of a core area of 20,000 km^2 in the Central Plateau, was comparable to that of the lowlands but with considerable difference in distribution. Much of the population was concentrated in small, densely settled mountain valleys. In highland areas of heavier rainfall the demographic pattern was similar to that in the lowlands.

Braidwood and Reed (1957) in their discussion of the demographic characteristics of third millenium B.C. Sumeria suggest a total population of 500,000 in an area of 25,000 km² or an overall density of 20 persons per km²—again, with urbanism as a trait. The actual distribution of population was very similar to that along the Central Andean coast during the Urbanist Period. In each area there was a series of twenty to thirty well-spaced towns and small cities each with its intensively cultivated irrigated hinterland and each separated from the others by deserts and marshes. The spacing of densely settled areas in Peru was determined by the topographic and hydrographic peculiarities of the area (some thirty small streams separated by hilly ranges and desert), whereas in Mesopotamia it was the result of the factor of time and level of population growth. The subsequent history of civilized Sumeria was one of a gradual filling-in of the intervening spaces with irrigated land, and increasing size of communities and states to reach a peak in population, urbanism, and political complexity during the Abassid Caliphate. During the third millenium B.C., however, the demographic pattern was very similar to that of the Andean coast. Braidwood and Reed do not state explicitly but imply strongly that the density of population within the oases was approximately 170 persons per km² (100 km² per state).

Steward and Faron (1959) comment on the unusually low overall population density of the Central Andes. Even within the New World the population density of the Central Andes was only slightly higher than that achieved by the chiefdoms of the Intermediate Area (2.5 persons per km² in Ecuador and Colombia, 2.0 in Central America).

In summarizing the foregoing discussion one can make the following generalizations:

a. If the demographic pattern is one of dense clusters of populations separated from one another and distributed over a very large region, then civilization can be maintained with an unusually low overall population density. The figure of 4 persons per km^2 for the Central Andes is probably the minimum. In such a demographic pattern, however, the local clusters must be large enough to support populations in the tens of thousands, must have unusually high population densities, and must be numerous and not too isolated from each other.

b. In a setting of large areas of relatively uniform agricultural potential and distribution of population, the overall population density must be considerably higher. The data suggest a minimum close to the overall Mesoamerican average of 10 to 12 persons per km^2. Detailed settlement pattern studies in the Mesoamerican lowlands are needed to confirm this point. The absence of civilization in the Andean montaña (population density, .4) and presence of it in the Mesoamerican lowlands is in part the product of the failure of the former area to attain this minimal density and the success of the latter in so doing.

c. For urban civilizations the data suggest a minimal local density of 100 persons per km^2 with primitive transportation.

d. There is no magic about population numbers and densities as determinants of social structure, but there is certainly a gross correlation between population size and density and Service's levels of social structure. Increasing population densities from band through tribal and chiefdom to state levels with critical minimum and maximum population densities and sizes could be established for the New World and probably the Old World as well. The following discussion is not intended as an exhaustive study of native New World demography but is offered as an illustration to support this generalization.

The population density of bands and tribes in native North America (cf. Kroeber 1947) ranged from .002 to 2.72 persons per km^2 with a tendency for bands to have densities at the lower end of the range and tribes at the upper. The entire range was strikingly lower than the densities of Nuclear America; but there was considerable overlapping of density between bands and tribes, depending on variations in wild food resources, agricultural systems, and probably on the time depth of agriculture in particular areas.

The distinction between bands and tribes in size of society was much sharper than in population density, suggesting a closer functional relationship. Local bands (that is, the permanently interactive group) rarely exceeded forty to fifty persons. In most areas there was a loosely structured supra-local group, the macro-band, that ranged in size between 300 and 600 inhabitants. It lacked a formal structure and functioned primarily as an interactive association of local bands. The macro-band occasionally resided together for short periods to engage in communal food collection and religious, ceremonial, or social activities.

Tribes, on the other hand, were permanently organized societies ranging in population from the size of a macro-band up to several thousand. Local communities within the tribes ranged from the size of local bands up to such cases as the Pueblos of the Southwest where entire tribes resided in single nucleated settlements. The Pueblos also had the highest population density of North American tribes. Both this density and the nucleated plan of Pueblo settlements resulted from their need for defense against nomadic predators, their unusually high dependence on agriculture, and their intensive use of limited land and water resources in a desert environment.

In considering the population density of North American tribes and bands, a strong case could be made for a correlation between tribes and agriculture on the one hand, and bands and hunting and gathering on the other, rather than a correlation between structural level and absolute differences in density. The highest population densities for North America were achieved among the acorn gatherers of California and the sedentary Pueblo farmers of the Southwest. Yet tribes, if present at all in California, were only incipiently developed. All that really seems to happen in the history of rich environments occupied by a hunting-and-gathering people is a multiplication of the number of bands and a consequent reduction of territory size, with some increase in the size of the local band— up to Steward's (1955a) maximum for bands of 150—but with no significant development of sodalities or a supra-local social structure.

There is, however, one exception to this rule, the fishing Indians of the Northwest Coast. Their food resources were rich but could be obtained only in a few highly localized places, and so a division of labor was required for effective utilization of the resources. The result was the development of a rank system based on centralized collection and redistribution of those resources—a simple chiefdom level of social structure.

Chiefdoms were most highly developed in the Intermediate Area. We have cited figures on the population density of the area from Steward and Faron, which, however, provide us with very little data on the sizes of the chiefdoms. The native population of the island of Puerto Rico is estimated at 50,000, divided into eighteen chiefdoms for an average of 2,800 persons in each. Hispaniola is estimated as having a population of 100,000 persons divided into six chiefdoms with an average of 16,500. General statements about the demography of the area as a whole suggest that population size generally remained at this level, with one interesting exception. The five Chibcha chiefdoms are estimated to have had an average population of 60,000 per chiefdom. Of all the groups in the Intermediate Area it was the Chibcha that the Spaniards equated in level of political development with the Aztec and Inca. Possibly something closer to our definition of the state characterized Chibcha political organization. The lack of architectural remains comparable to those of Mesoamerica and the Central Andes, however, would rather suggest an unusually large chiefdom.

Sahlins' demographic data (1958) on chiefdoms from Polynesia are much more detailed and offer a fascinating parallel to the rather scanty New World demographic figures. We have modified his chart somewhat in the following table:

Population sizes of chiefdoms and complexity of stratification

Islands	Permanently Organized Chiefdom	Occasional Extensions of Chiefdoms	Types of Stratification
Hawaiian Islands	Aver. 30,000	up to 100,000	Type I
Tongan Islands	20,000– 25,000—entire group	. . . .	Three levels
Society Islands	8,250	up to 68,000	
Samoan Islands	5,000	up to 48,000 (entire group)	
Mangareva	4,000		Type 2A
Easter	3,000–4,000		Two basic levels;
Uvea	3,000–4,000		incipient develop-
Mangaia	2,000–3,000		ment of a third.
Marquesas	1,500		Type 2B
Futuna	2,000		Two levels
Tikopia	1,250		
Ontong Java	?–2,000		Type 3
Pukapuka	435–632		Two levels but
Tokelau	500–?		rank of little economic significance.

The chart shows a very close correlation between number of levels of stratification and size of the society; the range is much like the few examples of chiefdoms in the Intermediate Area. As in the case of the Chibcha, the unusually large Hawaiian chiefdoms had structural features approximating those of states and civilizations characterized by a system of coercive authority backed by economic sanctions, some full-time occupational specialties, despotism, and elaborate court protocol. The lowest level, Type 3, might be characterized as an incipient chiefdom comparable to those on the Northwest Coast of North America.

One final note of caution and defense is necessary here. Dumond (1965) and Fortes and Evans-Pritchard (1940) cited cases of unusually high population densities in association with very simple social structures and in fact, have challenged our assumption that there is a close correlation between population density and complexity of social structure.

All of the illustrations or exceptions, however, involved contemporary or recent cases of tribal or chiefdom societies that have maintained some ethnic identity but have been incorporated within the institutional structure of a national state. We contend that the high population densities are the product of the same factors which have led to the enormous world-wide expansion of population that has occurred since 1800 and do not reflect aboriginal situations at all, and that the kind of societal evolution from tribes to chiefdoms to states that Service has defined is aborted and controlled by the presence of the external states. The Philippines will serve as an example. With the exception of a few Muslim states in Mindanao and hunting-and-gathering pygmies in the mountains, the population in the sixteenth century was organized into tribes or tiny chiefdoms. The surface area of the islands is approximately 287,000 km², and the population in 1948 19,234,182. Many of the groups are still identifiable as ethnic and linguistic entities. We doubt, however, that their social structure has not been modified substantially by their contact first with the Spanish Colonial institutions, and subsequently with the national state. We argue, furthermore, that the high population density (67 persons per km²) is recent. There are a number of population estimates available for the islands in the sixteenth and seventeenth centuries when contact with large societies by local groups was relatively light. These estimates vary between 500,000 and

667,612 with a density at the time of Spanish contact of only 1.7 persons per km^2, and a maximal Colonial density of 2.3— directly comparable to the density of chiefdoms in the Intermediate Area (Zaide 1949:28).[2]

In summary, organizational stresses occur as a society increases in size; size is broadly limited by population density, and such stresses stimulate the development of more effective systems of social control. Considered in this sense, social systems are adaptive systems that may be viewed as both causes and effects of population growth.

If the preceding generalizations are valid, then population growth is a major stimulus toward the evolution of social systems to each of the levels cited by Service. There is probably a close correlation between the rapidity of population growth and culture change. Whether chiefdoms, civilizations, and cities evolve seems to depend in part upon the level at which population growth stabilizes. In some cultural sequences this plateau was achieved early and at a relatively low level—the rates of evolutionary development were, therefore, considerably slowed down. In some of the most extreme cases the evolutionary process appears to have been frozen at these relatively low levels, though even in these cases no culture remains completely static. The native culture of central California is a

[2] We are aware of the great range of opinion concerning the size of the population of the New World at the time of discovery. We have preferred to take a conservative position. Hemispheric totals range from Kroeber's (1947) 8 million to 9 million up to a recent estimate by Dobyns (1966) of between 90 million and 112 million. We have accepted Kroeber's estimates for North America, north of Mesoamerica and Steward and Faron's calculations for Central and South America (south of Mesoamerica). For Mesoamerica Cook and Simpson (1948), Cook and Borah (1960), and Borah and Cook (1960, 1963) have treated the subject of the sixteenth-century population in exhaustive detail. Sanders feels that their estimates are much too high and is preparing a full critique of their methodology and the underlying assumptions of their studies. Although these wide ranges of opinion do not alter the picture of relative population density within the Americas, they would certainly affect any effort to establish a world-wide pattern of population density-societal level interrelationship.

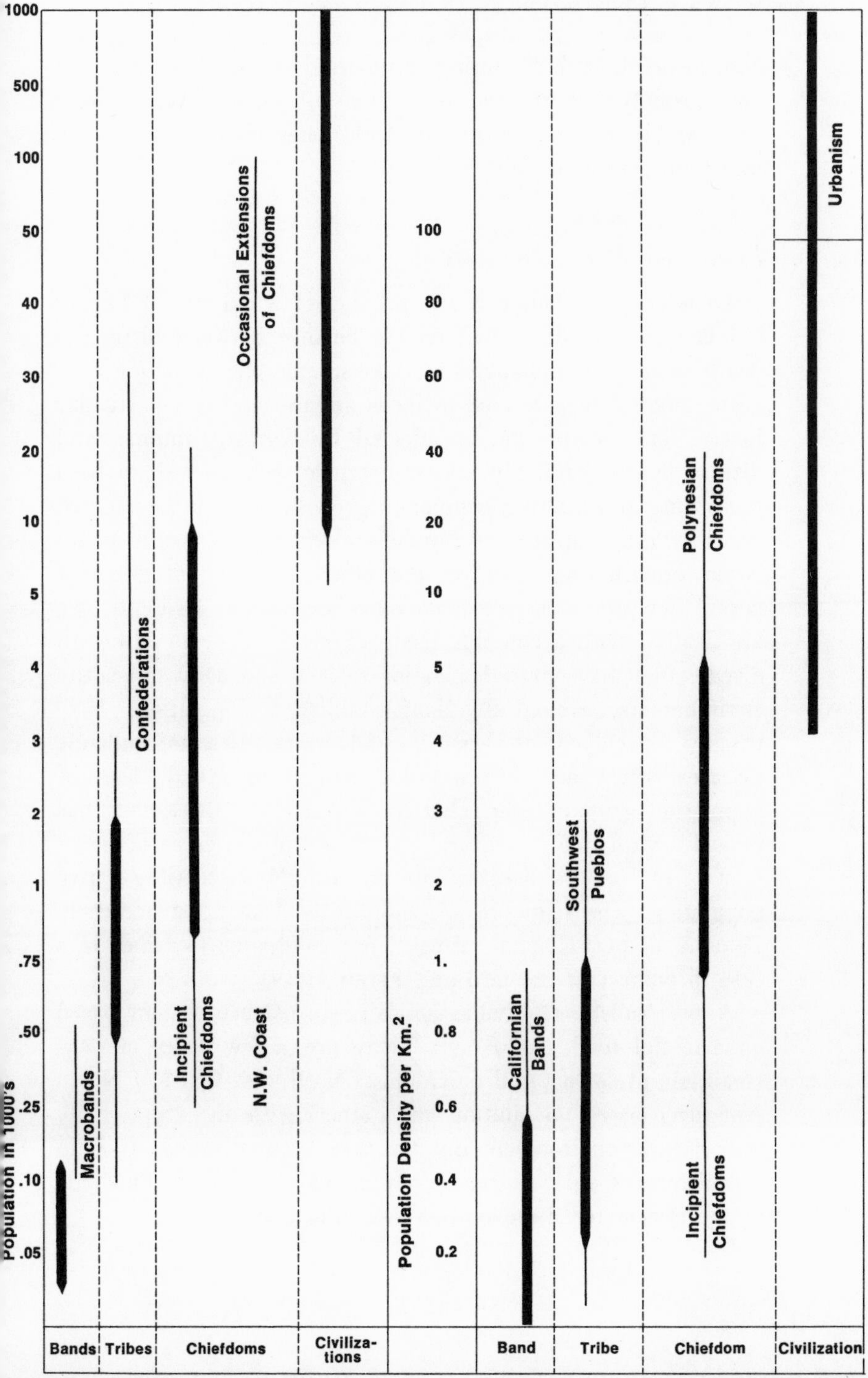

Figure 4.   Societal Level—Population Size—Population Density

case in point, with a hunting-and-gathering subsistence base in an unusually rich environment. This culture achieved ecological stability around 2000 B.C., and later changes were primarily in artifact style.

Population and Agriculture

Demographic change is the product of a number of factors but is primarily dependent on the balance between birth and death rates. Since changes in food supply play a major role, archaeologists have tended to focus attention on this particular factor. The death rate, as affected by warfare, famine, and disease has undoubtedly played a crucial role as well in both permitting and limiting population growth. It might be argued, however, that warfare and famine are really responses to population growth—one positive, the other negative—products of population pressures generated by other factors. Evidently we are dealing with a complex feedback situation here. Although disease may have played a major role in unusually unhealthy environments, ecologically long-established populations have usually developed at least partial immunities to endemic diseases; there are few well-documented historical cases of population growth being aborted primarily by disease. It has played a vital role in cultural processes only in cases of introduction of foreign diseases into an entirely susceptible native population. The reduction of complexity of social structure in Panama in post-Hispanic times from chiefdoms to tribes is a case in point (cf. Steward and Faron 1959).

A prerequisite of civilization is a subsistence system based on artificial food production. There are a few cases of very small, simply structured chiefdoms (Northwest Coast of North America) based on hunting and gathering in an exceptionally rich natural environment but no cases of civilization. It is in the history of agriculture, therefore, that we look to find part of the reason for the evolution of civilizations.

There is an enormous variation, however, in population density among agricultural peoples, and a great number of societies that possessed agriculture have failed to develop civilizations. In view of our assumptions about the relationships between civilization and population size and density a major historical problem may be posed. Why did agriculture lead to dense populations in some areas and not in others?

All nonwestern farming societies tend to emphasize a particular crop as a staple—usually a cereal (wheat, barley, maize, rice, millet, sorghum), in some areas a root (potatoes, sweet potatoes, manioc, yams, taro), and occasionally a fruit (plantains). A very high percentage of land under cultivation is devoted to the staple crop which is characterized by a very high caloric production (in the form of carbohydrates) per unit of land planted. For this reason most archaeologists have evaluated demographic capacities of agricultural systems in terms of estimates of caloric yields of the staple crop. This is undoubtedly a critical factor affecting size but may not be the only one or even the most significant one. The productivity of the staple crop per unit of land cultivated must be considered in relationship to several other major factors summarized as follows.

Some agricultural systems necessarily involve a pattern of field rotation and fallowing. Wolf classified agricultural systems into five basic types based essentially on this factor. He defined these five types as follows:

1. *Long-term fallowing systems*, associated with clearing by fire and cultivation with the hoe. These systems are called *swidden systems*, after an English dialect word for "burned clearing." Fields are cleared by firing the vegetation cover—grass, bush, or forest; planted to the point of decreasing yields; and abandoned to regain fertility for a stipulated number of years. Then other plots are similarly opened up for cultivation, and reoccupied after the critical period of regeneration is past. Swidden systems are found in both the Old and New World.

As we shall see below, such systems have supported peasantry only under exceptional circumstances.

2. *Sectorial fallowing systems*, in which cultivable land is divided into two or more sectors which are planted for two to three years and then left to fallow for three or four. The dominant tool is the hoe or the digging stick. Such systems are also found in both Old and New Worlds, for instance, in West Africa and highland Mexico.

3. *Short-term fallowing systems*, in which land cultivated for one or two years is reoccupied after a year of regeneration. The dominant tool is the plow, drawn by draft animals. Such systems are usually associated with the cultivation of cereals and are primarily found in Europe and Central Asia. Hence they may also be called *Eurasian grainfarming*.

4. *Permanent cultivation*, associated with techniques for assuring a *permanent water supply* for the growing crops. Such systems have been called *hydraulic systems* because they depend upon the construction of waterworks. They occur in the dry lands of both the New and Old World where rivers can be tapped for irrigation, and in the tropical areas of the Old World where cultivators have succeeded in substituting a man-made landscape for the original forest cover and in tapping water resources to insure the production of their crops. There are no parallel systems in the tropical lowlands in the New World.

5. *Permanent cultivation of favored plots*, combined with a fringe of sporadically utilized hinterland. Such systems have been called *infield-outfield systems* where they occur along the Atlantic fringe of Western Europe. They are, however, also found in the Sudan, in highland Mexico, and elsewhere. The ability to cultivate permanently a given set of plots depends either upon special qualities of the soil, as in Atlantic Europe (where the limited areas of good soil on deltaic fans or fluvial and marine terraces are further supplemented by careful manuring), or upon the ability to irrigate permanently some portion of an otherwise unpromising landscape, as in parts of the Sudan and Mexico (1966:20–21).

Factors affecting the specific cycling of land in cultivation versus land in rest are soil fertility, soil humidity, rainfall, topography, absence or presence of specialized techniques of soil restoration, competition of natural vegetation, demographic pressure, ratio of man-hours of labor to production, pressures from nonfarming groups within the total social system, and market values of various crops. Though we have not gone into the distinction between the several kinds of factors (primary factors and those deriving from these) enumerated above, it may be seen that the mere list of factors underscores the complexities of determining cause and effect in the evolution of agricultural systems.

Calculations of the demographic capacity of a functioning system of agriculture cannot be applied to a total area without careful assessment of microgeographical variations within it. In any geographical area there are always sectors that are unusable for agriculture; even within those portions that are usable there are variations in productivity. If the population has not yet reached stability in terms of the existing agricultural system it may select only the better lands for use. Calculations for the entire area based solely upon those portions actually cultivated without taking into account the proportion of the total area which they constitute are, therefore, likely to be misleading. Some of the unusually high estimates of the demographic capacities of swidden agriculture result from this type of error (cf. Allan 1965 for a revealing discussion of African swidden systems).

Although high-caloric staples dominate the diet of nonwestern farming societies, a nutritional balance must be achieved to provide minimal requirements for growth and health of its members. This means that carbohydrates must be supplemented by protein-rich foods and by the minimal requirements of vitamins and minerals. The vitamin-mineral requirements are usually easily met by the use of a variety of minor crop products. The protein supply seems to be the most critical variable. There is an extraordinary correlation between cereals, dense populations, and complex social systems. In part this may be related to ease of storage, as many archaeologists have observed; but even more significant, we believe, is the fact that cereals have a protein content that is relatively high compared to most vegetal foods. A comparison of the nutritive value of various staple foods per one hundred grams of weight (INCAP–ICNND) is presented below:

Nutritive value of various foods per 100 grams weight

Cereals	Food Energy (Calories)	Protein (Grams)
Amaranth	358	12.9
Barley	348	9.7
Maize (yellow)	361	9.4
Quinoa	351	12.3
Rice (brown)	357	7.2
Sorghum	342	8.8
Wheat (hard red spring)	330	14.0
Roots and Fruits		
Taro	92	1.6
Manioc-bitter	148	.8
Manioc-sweet	132	1.0
White potato	79	2.8
Sweet potato (orange)	116	1.3
Yam	100	2.0
Yellow plantain	122	1.0

It is difficult to establish an absolute scale of nutritional requirements that would apply to all populations as Mazess and Baker (1964) point out. They suggest fifty-seven grams as a desirable minimal daily protein intake for highland Peruvian Indians. The average daily maize consumption of a contemporary Maya peasant (cf. Stadelman 1940; Steggerda 1941) is approximately 700 grams. This means that he receives a daily protein intake from maize alone of 65.8 grams. The same amount of sweet manioc would yield but 7 grams, sweet potatoes 9.1 grams, and bitter manioc 5.6 grams. Root crop consumers however, because of the lower caloric yield of these staples, consume two to three times the weight of food that cereal cultivators do (cf. May 1965). This would increase the daily protein intake to 14 to 21 grams from sweet manioc, 18 to 27 from sweet potatoes and 11 to 17 from bitter manioc, still far below the recommended minimum. Thus if a cereal is the staple, then a sizable amount of the necessary protein in the diet can be derived from eating the food that makes up a high percentage of the diet. Some writers (Carneiro 1961; Oliver 1955) have demonstrated that such tropical root crops as manioc, taro, and yams have an extraordinarily high caloric productivity per unit of sown land, considerably higher than cereals; yet, with the exception of small tropical islands (where marine products are important in the diet), the use of root crops as staples is correlated with light population densities, small settlements, and simple social systems. The crucial factor here may be the low protein content of root crops, so low that proteins must be derived entirely from nonstaple foods. Aggravating the situation in tropical forest areas is the paucity of game and the difficulty of raising domestic animals (in most cases food for the latter must be provided from agricultural produce).

Much of the variation in population density among the farming groups of native South America probably derives from this factor. The tropical lowlands of Colombia and Venezuela were much more densely settled than Brazil, the Guianas, and eastern Peru and Ecuador. In the case of the former, maize was the staple; in the latter, manioc. The preference for riverine or coastal settlement in the Amazon Basin, noted by many writers, may well relate to the need of a protein-rich food resource, where the only one available in abundance is fish. The supply of fish rather than the productivity of manioc would be the critical limiting factor in population growth.[3]

Cereals by themselves do not provide an adequate protein source and must be supplemented with other foods. However, unlike the root crops, they do make it possible for a group to complete their protein requirements primarily from vegetal sources. In Mesoamerica beans, combined with maize, plus a minimal amount of animal proteins, made up a nutritional complex that resolved this problem. Added to these staples, of course, was a great variety of minor crops that provided the

[3] In a recent article Bronson (1966) has challenged the assumption of the superiority of cereals over root crops as staple foods for swidden cultivators and has suggested that the spectacular development of the Lowland Maya civilization involved a population density equivalent to that achieved in hydraulic agriculture. This, he argues, was possible because of the much higher caloric yields of root crops.

We agree that the various field studies do show a higher caloric yield for root crops as contrasted to cereals with swidden agriculture, but he has greatly overstated the case. First he makes the incorrect statement that the caloric yield per weight of root crop is equivalent to that of cereals. As our chart demonstrates, 100 grams of sweet manioc yields but 36 percent of the calories produced by 100 grams of maize; for sweet potatoes and bitter manioc the percentage is 32 and 41 respectively. This means that 6 to 8 tons of root crops per hectare (the modal yield in contemporary Africa according to May 1965; Allan 1965) is equivalent to 2 to 3 tons of maize in caloric yield. Maize yields in the tropical lowlands of Mesoamerica with swidden agriculture range from area to area between 1 to 3 tons per hectare. The ratio in caloric yield therefore between native New World root crops and maize is approximately 2:1, not 10:1 as Bronson asserts.

Furthermore, he assigns no significance to the protein value of cereal crops and therefore misses a critical point. In root crop areas of Middle Africa today kwashiorkor (a nutritional disease resulting from protein deficiencies) is endemic (cf. May 1965). May also reports stature depression as the product of dietary deficiencies.

Bronson cites cases of swidden root crop agriculture supporting densities up to 600 persons per square mile in Nigeria. He completely ignores several significant facts about Nigerian demography and national economy. It should be stressed that the overall density of population in 1948–1949 was but 24 persons per square kilometer. Nigeria is divided into three administrative regions—Northern (regional density 20), Western (density 38), and Eastern (density 45). Within each region was a major population cluster: the Kano area in the North, Ibo in the East, and Ibadan in the West. In those areas were concentrated one-

necessary minerals and vitamins to round out the nutritional system (chile peppers were particularly important). Once this balance is achieved, and if it is based almost entirely upon artificial food production, then dense population could and did result. For this reason in Mesoamerica the gauge of potential population density may be taken from the index of productivity of maize alone. In the Central Andes several equally productive nutritional complexes were present. In the highlands the complex included potatoes, quinoa, cañahua, and an unusually rich domestic animal protein resource (guinea pigs, llamas), with maize and beans added in those areas below 3,600 m. altitude.

---

seventh of the population of Nigeria; each had densities exceeding 40 per square kilometer. In those small sectors where densities exceeded 100, each such cluster was associated with a highly developed commercial economy—cacao in the West, palm nut in the East, and groundnut-cotton in the North. Areas with densities exceeding 100 per square kilometer were rare, highly localized, and supported in part by importation of staples from areas of lesser density, particularly from the Middle Belt (the southern half of the Northern Region) (cf. Buchanan and Pugh [1966] for an excellent statement of the internal and external economy of Nigeria).

The economy of Nigeria is characterized by intensive interregional trade in foodstuffs based on a modern highway-railway transportation system. The unusually high densities he cites are in areas of intensive commercial agriculture involving cocoa and oil palm, areas which are not self-supporting in foodstuffs and that import foods from other areas of lesser density. The high densities are made possible only by the development of international and national trade and transportation. Densities exceeding 50 persons per square kilometer for self-sufficient swidden areas are exceedingly rare in Africa, whether root crops or cereals are staples.

Finally there is no good evidence from either documentary or archaeological sources that roots were ever staples anywhere in Mesoamerica! It is possible that, as the product of population pressure, the Lowland Maya gradually shifted to root crop staples as a short-range solution to food shortages. A process similar to this is taking place in Nigeria today. If so, then a serious nutritional problem would have resulted, comparable to recent Nigerian trends. In connection with this possibility, Haviland (personal communication) reports a 10-cm. stature reduction between Early and Late Classic Maya skeletons. Frank Saul (personal communication) feels that he has evidence of frequent nutritional illnesses in a sample of Maya skeletons from Altar de Sacrificios—including calcium deficiency (which would be inconceivable with the maize tortilla as a staple food). (Cf. Haviland 1967; Saul 1967.)

On the coast maize and beans plus an extraordinarily rich fishing resource provided a well-balanced nutritional system.

The relationship between nutrition and population growth may be summarized in the following way: If a balanced nutritional system can be designed that is based upon artificial techniques of food production, then the productivity of the staple crop in a given environment is the permissive or restrictive factor in population growth. If, however, one or more of the critical nutritional elements is based on natural resources, then the population must stabilize at a much lower level, a level determined by the available quantities of that wild food resource.

Competition and Cooperation

The second ecological process that we believe is significant in the evolution of civilization is competition. Diagnostic of contemporary peasant society is a strong competitive relationship between families and communities over land. A number of authors, particularly Foster (1965) and Lewis (1951), have emphasized the competitive quality of personal interaction in peasant societies and the general suspicion of outsiders—on one level of those outside the immediate family, and on a higher level of those outside the local community. This is characteristically true in areas of dense population, as is the case in the contemporary Mesoamerican highlands. This social atmosphere seems to be the product of (a) a relatively static system of food production; (b) a system confined to areas definitely limited geographically; and (c) a population that has completely occupied a geographical niche in terms of existing patterns of land use. The economic problems are frequently aggravated by socioeconomic systems in which the land is owned by a small ruling class who extract rent from the peasant population; but even in areas where land reform has occurred, population growth catches up to land availability within a few generations of the reform.

Today national governments are more or less effective in regulating aggression within their territories; competition as a dynamic factor of culture change is thus considerably reduced. We will now analyze competition as an ecological process within the social setting of ancient civilizations, prior to and during the periods in which small territorial groupings were the largest stable units.

Competition for economically useful resources probably occurs as a factor affecting culture change in virtually all human societies. The assumption of many anthropologists that population pressure and conflict over resources would occur only in later phases of occupation when respectably dense populations would be present seems to us overly simplistic. Not only absolute size of population, but also population size considered in relation to total productivity of an area under any given exploitative system, in addition to such factors as resource distribution and allocation, must be taken into account. Population pressure is, in a real sense, relative rather than absolute; and many factors in addition to sheer numbers of people must be considered in evaluating it.

Subsistence systems are as resistant to change as any other aspect of culture, in some ways perhaps even more so. Food preferences, local variations in soil and topography with consequent selective patterns of land use, and inequalities of tenure may be important factors in promoting stability. Hockett and Ascher (1964) cite what they call "Romer's Rule" in discussing the question of stability and change: The initial survival value of a favorable innovation is conservative in that it renders possible the maintenance of a traditional way of life in the face of changed circumstances.

One factor that promotes competition is the ratio between man-hours of work and crop production. In this critical ratio swidden agriculture is actually more productive than most labor-intensive systems of agriculture. Exceptions would be unusually productive systems of wet rice agriculture in exceptionally favorable environmental conditions. Only extreme population pressure, in terms of the capacity of each system, will force farmers to shift from swidden to more intensive patterns of land use. Since pressure depends upon the system of exploitation as well as on absolute numbers of people, conflict and competition over resources can, therefore, occur at any stage in the occupation of an area. A further example is reported by Vayda (1961) for a New Guinea setting with swidden agriculture, very low population density, and large tracts of unused climax forest. Intergroup warfare was endemic, the prize being the possession of secondary brush in various stages of regrowth from previous agricultural use. Given the apparent labor differential in clearing primary vs. secondary forest, warfare over previously cultivated areas was a more economical course of action than was opening up new areas for cultivation.

Cooperation and competition are frequently seen as polar processes but, as is argued in detail later in this book, competition may be the major stimulus to cooperation—and in fact almost demand cooperation as a solution to particularly acute problems of competition.

A number of positive responses to population pressure may be postulated. As can be readily seen, some of these responses are classifiable as competitive responses; others, cooperative:

1. A change in the technology of food production resulting in an increase of food extracted per unit of land or an increase in the percentage of land in cultivation.
2. Changes in social and economic structure that result in a more efficient exploitation of land or distribution of food within the same technological pattern of food procurement.
3. Specialization of individuals and communities, either in crops best adapted to specific microgeographical niches or in non-

food-producing activities. For the latter to relieve population stress it must relate, however, to supra-local market patterns and agricultural surpluses in nearby areas.

4. Political control of surplus food produced in areas exterior to the local areas.
5. Local migration or segmentation of physical communities, or emigration to other areas.
6. Warfare which reduces or stabilizes the population.
7. Other positive checks on population growth such as infanticide or birth control.

Negative checks to population would be famine and/or a combination of nutritional imbalances accompanied by diseases.

Earlier in this book the flexibility of cultural adaptation to environmental stress was emphasized. The major stress undoubtedly revolves around food supply. Theoretically, a population faced by an adaptive stress may respond positively or negatively and, if positively, in a variety of ways, some of which may be more adaptive than others. It is our contention, moreover, that certain types of environments place a premium on those responses that lead ultimately to the evolution of civilization.

In summary, population growth, competition, and cooperation are cited as critical and coordinate processes in the evolution of civilization. In the following section the operations of these processes in the specific evolution of Mesoamerican civilization will be examined.

Part TWO

The Evolution of Mesoamerican Civilization

V / BASIC GEOGRAPHY

The Mesoamerican area is highly complex geographically; over distances of 60 to 80 kilometers one may encounter nearly all of the world's environments. This remarkable variation is a function of latitude and topography. Elevations vary from sea level to nearly 5,500 m. above sea level; temperatures from tropical to arctic; rainfall from near-desert conditions to areas with nearly 6,000 mm. of annual precipitation; soils from laterites to siernozems; topography from steep canyon valleys to flat riverine flood plains; and vegetation from xerophytic, through steppe, mixed forest, boreal forest, tundra, tropical grassland, jungle, and tropical rainforest. Mesoamerican civilization was found wherever maize could be grown; it is perhaps the adaptability of the Mesoamerican maize farmer to this fantastically diverse landscape that is the most impressive achievement of this civilization.

Each small area of Mesoamerica presents in reality a unique micro-geographical setting; any gross classification of these environments is accordingly somewhat misleading. Nine broad ecological types might be defined, however, on the basis of variations in altitude and precipitation.

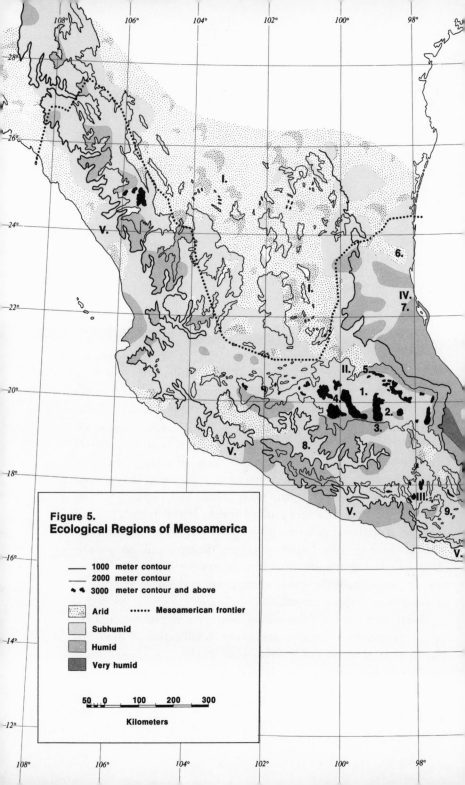

Figure 5.
Ecological Regions of Mesoamerica

——— 1000 meter contour
——— 2000 meter contour
◆ ◢ 3000 meter contour and above

⠠⠄ Arid   •••••• Mesoamerican frontier

░ Subhumid

▒ Humid

▓ Very humid

50 0   100   200   300
Kilometers

Regions:

I.   Northern Plateau
II. Central Plateau
III. Oaxaca—Guerrero Highlands—Sierra Madre del Sur
IV. Gulf Coast Plain
V.   Mexican Pacific Coastal Plain
VI. Guatemalan Pacific Coastal Plain
VII. Yucatan Peninsula
VIII. Guatemalan Highlands

Subregions:

1. Basin of Mexico
2. Puebla Basin
3. Morelos—Puebla Escarpment (Amacusac Basin)
4. Valley of Toluca
5. Valley of Tulancingo
6. Sierra de Tamaulipas
7. Panuco Basin
8. Balsas Basin
9. Valley of Oaxaca
10. Isthmus of Tehuantepec
11. Central Valley of Chiapas
12. Peten

Ecological Types	Typical Areas
1. Tierra Caliente (0 to 1000 m.)	
a. Arid (below 800 mm. annual precipitation)	Northwestern Yucatán, Isthmus of Tehuantepec
b. Subhumid (800 to 1200 mm.)	Central Veracruz, lowland Huasteca, Oaxaca coast, Central Valley of Chiapas
c. Humid (over 1200 mm.)	Petén, South Gulf Coast, Pacific Coast of Chiapas and Guatemala
2. Tierra Templada (1000 to 2000 m.)	
a. Arid (below 500 mm. annual precipitation)	Tehuacán Valley, Meztitlán Valley
b. Subhumid (500 to 1000 mm.)	Southern Puebla-Morelos Valley of Oaxaca, Mixteca Alta
c. Humid (over 1000 mm.)	Escarpments of Pacific and Gulf Coast Plains, Highland Guatemala
3. Tierra Fría (2000 to 2800 m.)	
a. Arid (below 500 mm.)	Portions of Hidalgo, Eastern Puebla
b. Subhumid (500 to 1000 mm.)	Most of Central Plateau
c. Humid (over 1000 mm.)	Higher slopes of most highland and escarpment areas

The delineation of ecological types by altitude zones is based on temperature tolerances of crops. For example, cacao does not do well above 1,000 m.; the pulque-producing variety of maguey is found primarily above 2,000 m.; and the growing season for maize is reduced to 6 to 7 months above 2,000 m.

The distinction between subtypes (arid, subhumid, humid) is based on the distribution of agricultural crops as a whole and on variations in agricultural techniques necessary for maize cultivation. For example, the designation "arid" means that maize and most other pre-Hispanic cultivates, except under very exceptional conditions (unusually humid soils), would require irrigation for dependable production; "subhumid" refers to a rainfall pattern in which irrigation is not necessary but its application results in a substantial increase in production and has a striking effect on crop stability. Some crops, such as cacao, would require irrigation if planted in areas classified as subhumid. Other crops, as maguey and cotton, will not grow well under humid conditions.

Differences in temperature and rainfall not only affect the distribution of crops but require different methods of cultivation of the staple crop: maize. At the time of the Conquest (as in contemporary Mesoamerica) there were probably as many systems of maize cultivation as microenvironments. These may be grouped for convenience, however, into the following of Wolf's (1966) paleotechnic types: Long-term Fallowing Systems, Sectorial Fallowing Systems, Permanent Cultivation, and Infield-Outfield.

We will now attempt to apply the ecological principles stated previously to the overall picture of Mesoamerican culture history. The archaeological data are not entirely satisfactory for many areas of Mesoamerica, nor for some potentially critical time periods. In the discussion, therefore, attention will be focused on those areas that played unusually significant roles in the evolution of Mesoamerican culture as a whole and for which data are good.

The discussion is organized by stages based on Service's levels of social organization. Since it is by developmental stage rather than chronological period, the date of inception and termination of each stage will vary considerably from one area of Mesoamerica to another, variations in precocity and retardation which in themselves are of particular interest. Where the terms Formative, Classic, and Postclassic are used they refer to chronological periods as currently employed by Mesoamerican specialists (see Figure 2).

VI / BANDS AND TRIBES IN MESOAMERICA

Bands

The band level of social structure is generally associated with a hunting-and-gathering subsistence base. Since the emphasis here is upon the evolution of more complex socio-economic systems, we will discuss only incipiently agricultural bands.

HISTORY AND DISTRIBUTION

Agriculture is a precondition of civilized society. Evidence of the origins of agriculture in Mesoamerica is substantial only in two areas, the Sierra de Tamaulipas on the northeastern frontier and the Tehuacán Valley in the Central Plateau (cf. MacNeish 1958, 1964). The Sierra de Tamaulipas is a low mountain area with a climate varying from arid to subhumid. Because of its northern latitude it has a temperature regime similar to that of the Tierra Templada even though the elevation is below 1,000 m. The environment, therefore, fits into types 2b and 2a (see table on p. 104). The Tehuacán Valley environment is on the borderline between 2b and 2a. In both areas frosts are absent, and summer rainfall is sufficient to permit agriculture, particularly on alluvial fans and terraces where soil humidity is greater. Large, dense populations, however, cannot be maintained here without irrigation.

The band stage characterizes these two areas possibly as early as 8000 B.C. and ends around 2500 B.C., and perhaps even prior to 2500 B.C. in Tehuacán, with tribal society. In the Tehuacán Valley the beginning of plant domestication may have occurred as early as the El Riego phase (7200 to 5200 B.C.), but by the Abejas phase (3400 to 2300 B.C.) the evidence of agriculture is incontrovertible. At that time squash, chile peppers, avocados, maguey, amaranth, gourds, beans, zapotes, maize, and cotton all had achieved the status of agricultural plants. The basis for a varied, rich, well-balanced, artificially produced nutritional complex was therefore well established. The history of occupation of the Valley between 8000 and 1500 B.C. may be summarized as follows:

Over this long period of time a gradual improvement of the productivity of agricultural plants made village life possible by 2500 B.C. Correlatively, there was a decline in the significance of hunting and gathering.

At the time of inception of agriculture, the social structure involved a seasonal shift from what MacNeish calls micro- to macro-band residence. Micro-bands, consisting of single nuclear or possibly extended families migrating independently through the dry season in search of food, gathered into small multifamily macro-bands during the rainy season when food, particularly wild grasses, was more abundant.

Subsequent history involved a gradual increase in the period of macro-band residence as agriculture played an increasingly more significant role in the diet. The latter process was closely related to the botanical improvement of the plants themselves. By the Abejas phase there may have been all-year macro-band residence, with a small hamlet consisting of 5 to 10 families. There is no evidence of larger social aggregations, however, and the hamlet was no larger in size than the earlier macro-bands.

There was, however, a definite overall increase of population of the valley.

It is difficult to generalize from the Tehuacán data above; much more work is obviously required in other Mesoamerican areas. Theoretically, the data indicate that the drier, middle temperature zones of Mesoamerica were the primary centers of agricultural development, particularly of the two key crops—maize and beans. In theory, wild maize may have been as tolerant of variations of temperature (but probably not of such variation in rainfall, since forested areas would not be natural settings for wild grasses), as domestic maize. Wild maize pollen has been reported from the Basin of Mexico at an elevation of at least 2,240 m. above sea level.

The evidence from the Tehuacán Valley for the introduction of more productive foreign varieties (Early Tripsacoid) during the Abejas phase, suggests multiple contemporary centers for maize domestication. Mangelsdorf *et al.* (1964) offer the possibility that the Balsas Basin may have been the source of this exotic maize, since tripsacum has been reported from that area. Note that the environment of that area generally ranges between types 2b and 2c. Tehuacán, therefore, may have been marginal to the primary areas of maize evolution. In summary, the entire area embraced by those portions of the Central Plateau and Sierra Madre del Sur (which has a dry Tierra Templada environment) was probably the scene of multiple experimentation in plant domestication.[4]

ECOLOGICAL PROCESSES

One could argue from the Tehuacán evidence that plant domestication is in one sense as much a botanical process as an ecological one. It is the association with particular climatic characteristics that indicates that selective factors other than purely

[4] Recent evidence has tended to substantiate this statement. Kent Flannery reports indications of an incipient stage of plant domestication in the Valley of Oaxaca comparable in age and content to that reported by MacNeish from Tehuacán.

genetic ones were at work. The drier mountain areas are natural demographic pressure areas, with wild plants, particularly edible seed plants, being the only really substantial source of food. At the same time, precisely in a habitat where overall aridity tends to reduce their quantity and restrict their distribution to a few relatively small areas, a population would depend to an unusual extent upon such foods. Sooner or later a hunting-and-gathering people who depended upon and presumably preferred this type of food, would be faced with the problem of an increasing population depending on a static food supply in a relatively unproductive environment. The beginnings of plant domestication may have been as simple as the artificial flooding of wild grass plots or extending them by a combination of flooding and broadcast sowing using very simple brush dams as was done by the historic Owens Valley Paiute (cf. Steward 1938). We have here quite an excellent illustration of Romer's Rule. In the case of an area like the Tehuacán Valley, the presence of high mountain walls and tropical jungles at the exit of the valley into the coastal plain would tend to restrict emigration as a solution to the demographic problem and to stimulate simple artificial methods of increasing the local food supply.

In the humid lowland areas scattered evidence seems to indicate an early focus on shellfish gathering and fishing. Data from Mesoamerica particularly are rather scanty, but research along the Caribbean shore and Pacific littoral of South and Central America indicates a widespread pattern of selective adaptation to sea foods prior to the development of productive agriculture. The presence of dense natural vegetation, lack of wild grasses, and abundance of marine and riverine food resources would have tended to retard the evolution of artificial food production. However, the possibility does exist in these humid lowlands for a very early root crop agriculture involving sweet manioc or sweet potatoes, though no evidence of this has been found archaeologically in Mesoamerica. Most researchers, moreover, seem to feel that cultivation of the tropical root crops originated in the

Orinoco-Caribbean lowlands of Venezuela or Colombia. Further-more, if Reichel-Dolmatoff (1965) is correct, manioc may not have been cultivated in Colombia much before 1000 B.C. so that it would probably have reached the Mesoamerican area only at a time well after maize had already been adapted to the tropical lowlands. The fact that the root crops in the Meso-american lowlands are always secondary crops would support this reconstruction.

Data from Colombia tend to justify the preceding arguments rather well. Reichel-Dolmatoff postulates a long period (3000 to 1000 B.C.) of shellfish gathering along the Caribbean coast. The introduction of manioc around 1000 B.C. did not drastically alter the ecological system. Although it resulted in some shift of residence from littoral to riparian locations, agricultural com-munities were limited to the Caribbean plain; wild food re-sources from the rivers remained the principal staples, largely perhaps because of their high protein content. It was only with the introduction of a productive type of maize from Mesoamerica around 500 B.C. that this encysted ecological system was finally dissolved. The result was a spread of agriculture up the Andean valleys, rapid growth of population, and by B.C./A.D., the establishment of a pattern of chiefdom socioeconomic structure.

Tribal Society

DEFINITION

Archaeological definition of tribal social systems in Meso-america has never been attempted. In the absence of good settlement pattern studies all that can be done here is to assume that cultural complexes characterized by sedentary agricultural settlements but lacking community stratification had a tribal social structure. It is possible but not very probable that such villages were socially autonomous. "Autonomy" is always rather relative at best.

We have noted the close correlation between agriculture and the tribe as the minimal level of social structure. It is possible that the population in Early Formative times in Mesoamerica was so small that band social structure was characteristic. We have noted, however, that some North American tribes had unusually low densities, undoubtedly much below that of the Basin of Mexico in the Early Formative phase. On the other hand, it was also demonstrated that even in rich environments tribes tend to be weakly developed with only a hunting-and-gathering economy. On the basis of data from the Teotihuacán Valley (Sanders 1965) one could tentatively define a number of tribelets, as indicated by hamlet clustering, for much of the Formative period (1000 to 300 B.C.). When the Tehuacán Project is terminated it may be possible to do the same there. In the Teotihuacán Valley such societies could not have numbered more than a few hundred each.

HISTORY AND DISTRIBUTION

Using the archaeological definition given above, a tribal societal stage for Mesoamerica could be defined for a great number of areas. The following archaeological complexes may be classified in this stage: Early Zacatenco in the Basin of Mexico (Piña Chan 1958; Vaillant 1930); El Trapiche on the Central Gulf Coast (García Payón 1950); Pavon-Ponce-Aguilár-Chila on the North Gulf Coast (MacNeish 1954); La Venta Pre-Complex A on the South Gulf Coast (Drucker, Heizer, and Squier 1959); Cotorra in the Central Depression of Chiapas (Dixon 1959; Lowe 1959); Mamom and early Chicanel in the Petén (Smith 1955); Arévalo in the Guatemala Highlands (Borhegyi 1965); Ajalpan in the Tehuacán Valley (MacNeish 1964); and Ocós on the Pacific Coast of Guatemala (Coe 1961b). Chronologically, the inception and duration of this stage varied from area to area. In the Teotihuacán Valley it probably began around 1000 B.C. and lasted until the appearance of the first tiny chiefdoms (circa 300 B.C.). In the southern part of the Basin of Mexico it may have started as early as 1500 B.C. and ended around 800 B.C. with the Middle Formative chiefdoms of Tlatilco, Tlapacoyan, and possibly Cuicuilco. In the Petén the stage apparently started around 1000 B.C. and lasted until the final phase of Chicanel at Tikal. Generally speaking, it is archaeologically a poorly defined stage in the evolution of Mesoamerican society—perhaps because the development of chiefdoms entailed a rapid growth, and the tribal stage would therefore have been of brief duration in many areas.

ECOLOGICAL PROCESSES

Coe and Flannery (1964) have argued that agriculture probably began in the Central Highlands but that sedentary village life was initiated in the tropical lowlands, possibly on the coastal plain of Guatemala. Their suggestion, based primarily on Coe's La Victoria excavation, is that shellfish resources permitted sedentary residence prior to the introduction of agriculture, which was later added to the ecosystem; an existing pattern of sedentary life would have given the population time to develop more productive varieties of maize that would in turn permit an agriculturally based sedentarism.

In a more recent paper (Coe and Flannery 1967) they reiterate the primacy of settled village life in the tropical lowlands on the basis of additional excavations and settlement pattern surveys in the Ocós area. First they define two primary ecological zones, coastal and piedmont, with subtypes within the former category. They further subdivide the Formative into six phases: Ocós (1300 to 1025 B.C.), Cuadros (1025 to 850 B.C.), Jocotal (850 to 775 B.C.), Conchas I (775 to 500 B.C.), Conchas II (500 to 300 B.C.), and Crucero (300 B.C. to B.C./A.D.).

During the Ocós–Cuadros–Jocotal phases population was light and distributed in a number of small sedentary villages or hamlets located on estuary or river banks. At least during the Cuadros–Jocotal phases subsistence was based on a combination of maize agriculture (a primitive, non-tripsacoid maize) and wild resources—fish, molluscs, crabs. No direct evidence of cultivation is present for the preceding Ocós phase. During the subsequent Conchas I and II population increased without, however, alteration of the basic settlement pattern. A near abandonment of the riverine-estuary location occurred during the Crucero phase, when heavy occupation shifted to the piedmont, a more favorable location for agriculture. The Classic and Postclassic population remained heavy in the piedmont.

Far from demonstrating a causal relationship between the sedentarism of a marine-riparian subsistence base and that of agricultural villages, the history of occupation of this area parallels that noted above for Colombia. The initial restriction of population to the coastal strip suggests instead heavy reliance on wild food resources and a relatively unproductive agriculture. If it was the introduction of more productive varieties of maize that stimulated the population explosion on the piedmont, it is difficult to see the causal or functional relationship between the earlier Ocós–Cuadros–Jocotal–Conchas ecosystem and the Crucero and post-Crucero developments. We note also that while these processes were taking place along the coast of Guatemala, sedentary village life was already well established in Central Mexico, based upon agricultural subsistence.

A recent report by Coe, Diehl, and Stuiver (1967) of excavations at San Lorenzo Tenochtitlán indicate the high probability of established chiefdoms on the Gulf Coast plain at least sixty kilometers inland from the beach by 1000 B.C. This would argue for considerable time depth of sedentary village life in the same area. The location of the site, furthermore, near the foothills of the Central Highlands, would seem instead to point to a higher valley like Tehuacán as the setting of the primary achievement of sedentary village life. The Tehuacán data in fact point to sedentary agricultural communities as early as 2500 to 2300 B.C., and data from the Valley of Oaxaca would tend to support such a conclusion.

We see, in summary, no reason to assume estuary-riverine

shellfish gathering and fishing as a necessary precondition for an agriculturally based sedentarism. Sedentary life can be permitted by economic bases other than agriculture under certain circumstances; but in our view this fact is irrelevant to arguments of continuity.

VII / THE CHIEFDOM STAGE IN MESOAMERICA

Definition

    For the chiefdom level, the archaeological data
are much more abundant and of greater pertinence to this work.
Archaeologically, societies of this type are identified on the basis
of site stratification. If, in a local area, there are numerous contemporary sites, some without civic architecture, and/or others
with very small civic centers, and still others with markedly
larger ones, then one can safely infer the presence of relatively
large, stratified social systems involving a number of communities. When this evidence is combined with striking variations
in the richness of tomb furniture, the archaeologist can assume
the existence of a society in which social stratification—or at
least ranking—is a major factor in integrating the social system.

    We have earlier examined the distinction between ranking
and true stratification as drawn by Fried (1960). The former
is associated with chiefdoms, the latter with political states or,
as we are calling them, civilizations. Although ranking differs
in principle from stratification, the distinction is often difficult to
infer reliably from archaeological evidence. Empirically, the
appearance is, in fact, quantitative rather than qualitative with

relatively complex chiefdoms located along a continuum in close proximity to the position of relatively simple states. Despite the difference in principle of organization, the distinction here would appear to matter comparatively little to the archaeologist, at least for present purposes.

Chiefdom social structure could exist with a variety of specific physical settlement patterns. Models of at least three types are presented below:

1. Ceremonial centers with a civic precinct and very small residential groups made up of the chiefly lineage, plus perhaps a small group of service personnel. The other lineages would be scattered over the countryside in nuclear family, extended family or lineage settlements. These settlements would support the chiefly lineage by food tribute and themselves consist of full-time farmers or farmers-part-time-craftsmen with specializations based upon local resources. This is the typical Polynesian pattern.
2. The entire chiefdom could have resided in a single, large, compact nucleated center.
3. A relatively large population could reside at the center with the balance of the population residing in smaller settlements as in 1.

Type 1 settlement patterns are much more characteristic of chiefdoms; Types 2 and 3 would occur only under such unusual circumstances as intensive warfare, intensive agriculture, or very uneven distribution of some critical resource like water or land. Types 2 and 3 are much more likely to occur on the state or civilized level of societal development since they are linked with the evolution of urbanism. Structurally, chiefdoms may be characterized as secular or theocratic (cf. Steward and Faron 1959) depending upon the primary function of the higher statuses.

History and Distribution

The chiefdom level of social structure was achieved in at least one area of Mesoamerica prior to 1000 B.C. (South Gulf Coast), was definitely established in a number of areas during the chronological Middle Formative (1500 to 600 B.C.), and was distributed all over Mesoamerica excepting the northwest frontier (the area between Michoacán and Sinaloa) by Late Formative–Protoclassic times (600 B.C.–300 A.D.). In much of Mesoamerica chiefdoms probably persisted until well into the Classic period, and in a few areas, for example, in the northwest, up to the Spanish Conquest.

One interpretation of Mesoamerican chronology, vigorously defended by Coe (1965b, c), postulates the inception of what we are calling chiefdoms in the humid Tierra Caliente of southeastern Veracruz and adjacent western Tabasco. The specific culture complex is called Olmec. Coe argues that all other complex societies of Mesoamerica were the product of stimulus diffusion or migration from this area. His argument is in reality a restatement in modified form of the earlier ideas of Covarrubias (1957). Covarrubias, however, was reluctant to accept a lowland origin of this complex, preferring to regard it as a highland development which subsequently became established on the Gulf Coast. The substance of the argument, however, is based on the spread of a sophisticated, specialized art style with its accompanying religious concepts (particularly the anthropomorphic-feline rain god) from the South Gulf Coast to a huge area extending from Central Mexico to Salvador, and on the apparent correlation of the rise of stratified society in those areas with the arrival of this style. The spread of the Olmec style is visualized as a catalyst in the transformation of simple societies into complex ones, possibly indirectly by trading contacts. Coe (1965a) has recently suggested that, as far as Central Mexico was concerned, the stimulus was a Jade Route—a parallel to the Bronze Age Amber Route from the Near East to northern Europe—protected by military colonies, from the Gulf Coast across the southern escarpment of the Central Plateau to Guerrero.[5] We shall subsequently question his view of the organization and the cultural patterning of this trading network. Others (cf. Coe 1962; Piña Chan 1960) have suggested migrations of missionaries who settled in foreign areas, establishing themselves as a dominant group and introducing complex religious institutions.

The objects found in the status burials in sites in the Basin of Mexico in the Central Plateau such as Tlatilco and Tlapacoyan do comprise a distinctive style that appears intrusive when compared to materials found in contemporary and earlier village sites in the same area. These objects have generally been considered Olmec, and researchers have suggested an introduction, perhaps even a migration, from the South Gulf Coast. Numerically however, if one limits the term Olmec to refer to the specific La Venta–Tres Zapotes–San Lorenzo style, a great number of the objects are decidedly non-Olmec. Furthermore, in sites located immediately over the mountains in southern Puebla (Las Bocas) or Morelos (Atlihuayan, Gualupita, Chalcatzingo) (cf. Coe 1965a; Vaillant 1934; Piña Chan 1955), the style is clearly local, indigenous, and again predominantly non-Olmec while including a few borrowings from the Olmec, most notably motifs relating to the anthropomorphic-feline symbolism. In other words, we seem to have a sophisticated Middle Formative regional and religious tradition on the southern es-

[5] This is a dissected, gradually sloping escarpment with a subhumid Tierra Templada environment. Today the area is included within the state of Morelos, the southern half of Puebla, and the northern part of Guerrero. Grove (1967) notes that the association of the major Central Mexican Middle Formative sites in this area is with mountain passes or strategic valley mouths, ideal locations for the control of trade routes. This would tend to support Coe's hypothesis of the importance of trade networks at this time.

carpment of the Central Mexican Plateau that was contemporary with the South Gulf Coast Olmec development and with which it was in close contact. We suggest calling this non-Olmec Central Mexican Middle Formative style Amacusac, after the drainage basin that dominates the area. It is interesting and undoubtedly significant that this early style occurs in the same general area where MacNeish found evidence of an early development of agriculture (Tehuacán Valley). The evidences found at Tlatilco and Tlapacoyan in the Basin of Mexico may well have been the product of small scale migrations, but from the Amacusac area rather than from the South Gulf Coast. We feel, Coe to the contrary, that the specific Olmec style played only a minimal role in the overall evolution of Central Mexican civilization. This is clearly demonstrated by the lack of significant Olmec influences in the Late Formative and post-Formative cultures of the area. A number of writers have pointed out that the general Formative tradition of Central Mexico is distinctive, so much so that the correlation of phases here with those of areas to the south and east can be done only with considerable difficulty. (Wauchope 1950; Coe 1962; Piña Chan 1960; Sorenson 1955; Willey 1966.)

The same generalizations apply to the so-called Olmec influences in other areas of Mesoamerica. The supposed Olmec influence in the Danzante style of Monte Albán I is vague, ambiguous, and obviously generic rather than specific. The relationship does not seem to support a hypothesis of Olmec migrations or missionizing; nor does the assumption of Olmec stimuli, direct or indirect, carry one far toward understanding the growth processes of Monte Albán. The recent work of Flannery, *et al.* in this area suggests very strongly that this evolution was essentially a local process having an indigenous base.

Much of the supposed "Olmec influence" that has been asserted for various Mesoamerican areas has consisted of little more than resemblances of art styles. As we observed in Chapter III, however, the structural inferences that can be reliably drawn from this type of evidence are severely limited. We are concerned with the kinds of processes and traits which, no matter what their ultimate origins, function as parts of locally integrated evolutionary systems. Such processes and traits derive their significance and can be examined meaningfully solely with reference to their position within the local system. Even decisive, reliable, and incontrovertible evidence of foreign influence upon a local art style would not clarify to any great extent the organizational patterning of the diffusion situation. To recapitulate our earlier statement on this topic, diffusion cannot be viewed as a purely mechanical process, but rather as taking place under certain kinds of cultural conditions.

We see the Middle Formative situation, rather, in the following light. All over central and southern Mesoamerica shortly after 1500 B.C. population growth had reached a level that permitted and encouraged the development of a chiefdom level of social structure. The geographical diversity of the area was a major stimulus toward trade, on one hand, and cultural diversity on the other. The result was the emergence of a variety of regional cultures in constant mutual contact. It is this interactive system, called by Bennett (1948) a "regional co-tradition," that provided a ready mechanism for the spread of religious concepts.

Since it seems improbable to us that a truly proselytizing religious system ever evolved in Mesoamerica, we find it difficult to accept the idea of an Olmec missionary group. In the Old World proselytizing religions do not appear until well into the Iron Age—post-600 B.C. Prior to this date, religious systems were highly parochial, involving primarily the idea of patron gods of ethnic groups, states, or communities. The case of the Hebrews as the Chosen People is pertinent. In the sixteenth century each city state in Central Mexico had its own patron deity, as did each of the Mesopotamian city states in the third millenium B.C. Foreign gods were frequently incorporated into the religious pantheon, particularly as a result of the military success of their adherents or as a means of reinforcing the allegiance of conquered territories; but a truly proselytizing religious concept was lacking.

In all of these suggestions, as we have observed, there is a certain confusion between the diffusion of religious symbols represented in art styles and the evolution of social structures. In the first place, there are enough specific differences between even the apparent religious concepts of Middle Formative chiefdoms in Central Mexico and those on the South Gulf Coast to argue against population movements. A number of religious symbols found at Tlatilco have yet to be identified at La Venta, particularly the beings with dual, deformed, masked, or death characteristics. Baby face figurines, long considered as an integral part of the Olmec style, are much more common in the Central Plateau than in the Olmec heartland, and the larger hollow ceramic variety is distinctively a Morelos–Puebla development. Coe himself in his recent publication on the Central Mexican Middle Formative illustrates a bewildering variety of art motifs in ceramics from Tlatilco, Tlapacoyan, Gualupita, Chalcatzingo, Atlihuayan and Las Bocas, with the observation that much of the stylistic complex is non-Olmec and probably indigenous (Coe 1965a).

Second, the archaeology indicates profound differences in social and economic structure. In Central Mexico there was a settlement pattern consisting of nucleated villages or towns as centers with dependent hamlets (the Type 3 pattern) in contrast to the ceremonial center-hamlet pattern of the Gulf Coast. Evidence from Tlatilco would suggest that females occupied the higher statuses (as attested by status burials involving women as central figures accompanied by sacrificed men and children); whereas La Venta art suggests that males occupied the higher statuses there. In summary, striking differences are apparent in both religious symbolism and societal structure between the South Gulf Coast and Central Mexico during the Middle Formative period.

Coe may well be correct as to the significance of the Jade

Route. The diffusion of the jaguar god could have been the product of these trading contacts, but much of the culture of the Middle Formative Central Mexican chiefdoms must have derived from local roots and processes. One outstanding problem in Coe's theory is his suggestion that "Olmec pochteca" were responsible for the maintenance, first of all, of the Jade Route, and second, for the diffusion of Olmec ideology. This seems to us to involve a misinterpretation of the structure of the pochteca as documented for Aztec times (Sahagun Book IX 1959), along with an exaggerated idea of the nature of the Olmec society. It would seem that the most striking structural characteristic of the Aztec pochteca was not merely their status as a hereditary guild of specialists in long-distance trade in luxuries, but rather, precisely, the fact that their activities were directed by, and carried out within the context of, a well-developed state organization. We prefer to view the structure, accordingly, as intimately bound up with economic policy and other needs of an expansionist political hierarchy, for which the pochteca served as one arm. In the absence of such a structural matrix, among the Olmec, there may well have been specialized, hereditary groups of merchants—but not, we feel, pochteca on the Aztec model. As we shall see in a subsequent section of this book, we do not believe that these conditions in fact obtained in Middle Formative times. Such a mechanism would probably not have been necessary for the maintenance of the Jade Route. What the archaeological evidence suggests is that the South Gulf Coast chiefdoms were larger in population and constructed more imposing civic centers than elsewhere in Mesoamerica during Middle Formative times. Even this generalization is subject to argument, however; and there may have been equally imposing centers on the Chiapas-Guatemala Coast, or at Monte Albán and Kaminaljuyú during the Middle Formative phase, centers whose development may have been quite independent of happenings in the "tropical heartland."

Agricultural Systems

The archaeological evidence indicates that coeval with the evolution of chiefdoms in the Middle and Late Formative phases, a variety of distinctive agricultural systems and a more effective level of ecological adaptation were achieved. It seems probable that during the final phases of the band and throughout the tribal stages, various subtypes of swidden cultivation were practiced in Mesoamerica.

In the more humid areas of Mesoamerica today (Highland Guatemala, Tierra Templada of Veracruz and Hidalgo, Balsas Basin) a variant of swidden cultivation called tlacolol (Wolf's sectorial fallowing system) is practiced, usually on slopes.

In flat areas, however, more intensive methods of cultivation are preferred, as the soils are more fertile and less susceptible to erosion. The cultivation procedures followed both in the Tierra Templada and in tropical lowland swidden are, in most essentials, identical. The important differences between tlacolol and tropical swidden are found in the use of the hoe to prepare land for sowing and for weeding and in the shorter fallow cycle characteristic of the former. In the humid Tierra Templada areas where tlacolol cultivation is practiced, the ratio of land lying fallow to that being cultivated may be as low as 1:1 in unusually fertile soils, but is more commonly 1:2 or 1:3. The ratio required by swidden cultivation in lowland tropics, by contrast, ranges from 1:3 up to 1:12, with a mode in the middle ranges. In tlacolol cultivation the major factor that determines the ratio is soil fertility, since weed regrowth is slower and the use of the hoe enables the cultivators to control the natural vegetation more effectively. It is true that tlacolol fields in some areas, where slopes are unusually steep or soils unusually thin, may suffer so severely from erosion as to be permanently abandoned; or alternatively these fields may have to be fallowed as long as tropical swiddens; but this is unusual. In lowland swiddens, by contrast, the length of the cycle is determined more by weed regrowth, particularly that of grasses.

Although theoretically the shorter cycle of tlacolol should result in a higher demographic capacity, the reverse is generally true. Actual yields per unit of land planted or per hours of work are considerably higher in tropical swiddens, thus compensating for the lower percentage of land in use. Furthermore, in most Gulf–Caribbean lowland areas there is a winter rainy season which permits the raising of two crops per year in a single field. The yield, however, of the winter crops is usually much less than that of the summer crops since the precipitation is significantly lower; the term "double cropping" frequently encountered in the literature is, therefore, somewhat misleading. Other advantages of tropical systems are the slower rate of erosion and the possibilities of raising specialized crops with a high market value.

The conclusions found in the literature on swidden cultivation are extremely conflicting. Some writers characterize it as wasteful, unproductive, and deleterious to the biotic balance; others claim for it an extraordinary productivity. The truth, as usual, lies somewhere between the extreme statements. In terms of man-hours of work per kilogram of food produced it is one of the most productive systems of farming in the world; as long as the population density remains moderate—Pelzer (1945) suggests twenty persons per km² but this would vary according to a variety of factors—the biotic balance is not permanently altered. The major demographic limitation of the system is that a large percentage of an area, in some cases as much as 80 to 90 percent, is out of production in any given year. Actually, there is a certain advantage to this, since a variety of wild natural products for food, fuel, medicines, and housebuilding are conveniently available to the cultivators; in the Yucatán Peninsula even deer and small game are relatively abundant. The important point here is that swidden cultivation with a balanced, artificially produced nutritional complex will support densities high enough to maintain both chiefdoms and nonurban states.

Swidden cultivation and its highland variant, tlacolol, are widespread systems of cultivation in Mesoamerica today; the former was the only system of any consequence throughout the pre-Hispanic history of the Gulf Coast and Yucatán Peninsula. Tlacolol was probably the only system practiced over huge areas of the Highlands throughout the Formative period and has persisted as a major system in the humid Tierra Templada of contemporary Mesoamerica.

A major archaeological problem is that of the possibility of either hydraulic or infield-outfield systems of cultivation in the drier highland areas during the Middle and Late Formative phases. Both of these systems will support considerably greater populations than either swidden or tlacolol. MacNeish suggests a possible Middle Formative, certain Late Formative date for the inception of irrigation in the Tehuacán Valley. Palerm and Wolf (1961) postulate irrigation at Cuicuilco in the Basin of Mexico in Late Formative times. It could date from the Terminal Formative or Protoclassic, however, since sherds of that period are reported by Bennyhoff and Heizer (1965) under the lava flow. The evidence from the Teotihuacán Valley Project suggests a Protoclassic date in that area with possible inception during the Late Formative. At both Cuicuilco and Teotihuacán the development of hydraulic agriculture correlates very well with the development of large nucleated settlements. Possibly hydraulic agriculture was the food-producing base for the small nucleated Middle Formative chiefdoms of Morelos and Puebla, but no evidence has been reported to date.[6]

---

[6] Fowler, in a paper delivered at the International Congress of Americanists at Mar del Plata in 1966, cites evidence of Late Middle–Late Formative irrigation at Amelucan, a site comparable in date and size to Cuicuilco and located near Puebla. Kent Flannery (1967) reports Formative irrigation systems in the Valley of Oaxaca, a view confirmed by Neely, in a paper given at the thirty-second annual meeting of the Society for American Archaeology, Ann Arbor, Michigan, 1967. In

Social and Economic Structure

The specific social and economic structure of the Formative Mesoamerican chiefdoms remains to be defined. We see no justification, however, for Coe's statement quoted below:

> A more mundane explanation of the Classic and pre-Classic states of Mesoamerica shows structural unity between the earliest—the Olmec, and the latest—the Aztec. I do not believe the Aztecs were very different from all the peoples who preceded them in Central Mexico (Coe 1965a: 122).

Coe seems to feel that political, economic, and religious institutions remained static for over 2,000 years. Although we believe that there has probably been more continuity between Classic and Postclassic cultures than has formerly been stressed, this is a somewhat different problem. Particularly in the Central Plateau, the Teotihuacán–Toltec–Aztec sequence is a dramatic illustration of Steward's cyclical-conquest phenomenon (1955b). In the developmental sequence terminology of Willey and Phillips (1958), Teotihuacán could be classified typologically as either Postclassic or Classic. Teotihuacán may well have been a true empire, and the political system, therefore, more closely resembled the Aztec than previous syntheses of Mesoamerican history have suggested. In view of Coe's argument of structural continuity, however, the existence of a pan-Mesoamerican empire centered, as he claims Olmec in fact was, on the Gulf Coast would be in every sense an anomaly rather than an example of continuity, since no large states were present in that area in Classic or Postclassic times. As we indicate below, there are significant differences in settlement patterns between the Middle Formative and later periods that reflect in fact striking differences in social,

---

summary, positive evidence is rapidly accumulating to support the antiquity of irrigation and its functional relationship to the evolution of large social systems in Highland Mesoamerica.

religious, and economic institutions. We believe that Service's chiefdom type of socioeconomic structure, rather than the state, can be fitted more plausibly with the Middle–Late Formative archaeological data.

During these times urbanism was only nascently developed in the Highlands (Monte Albán and Cuicuilco may have been the first transitional urban communities to evolve, possibly also Kaminaljuyú and Cholula). No definite proof of markets in any Formative period site has been presented, and sites of truly monumental scale, indicating definite units of supra-chiefdom size, are absent. La Venta, Tres Zapotes, and San Lorenzo Tenochtitlán would all be third- and fourth-rate sites under Morley's classification of Maya centers. Recent studies of Maya settlement patterns by Bullard (1962) suggest that Maya sites of that size were centers of small local states of perhaps 5,000 to 10,000 people. The Central Mexican Middle Formative chiefdoms were probably much smaller than that, and the Gulf Coast chiefdoms may in fact have been somewhat larger, although these are tentative conclusions. In comparison to Early Classic Central Mexico all architectural activities at La Venta together represent less labor than the construction of the Moon Pyramid at Teotihuacán (see Figures 6, 7, 8, 9).

Even the massive stone sculpture at La Venta would not have required a labor force beyond the size of a chiefdom. Stirling (1955) has suggested that the massive stone heads represent chieftains, possibly of a dynastic line, which means that only one would have been carved per generation of chiefs. All that was needed, therefore, was the manpower necessary to move a block of stone 20 to 30 tons in weight from the quarry to the site once a generation, plus a small corps of full-time craftsmen to work the stone into its final form. A chiefdom would easily be capable both of integrating populations of that size and of maintaining the Jade Route postulated by Coe.

The focus on the funerary cult with elaborate status burials suggested by a number of writers as characteristic of the later phases of the Formative also suggests a chiefdom social structure. Gulf Coast Formative settlement patterns, as far as they are known, offer rather striking parallels to Polynesian patterns, with ceremonial centers (the larger Polynesian ones, like marae Mahaiatea in Tahiti and tohua Vahangeku'a in the Marquesas, are of comparable size and complexity) and dependent population dispersed in hamlets (cf. Suggs 1960). Much of Service's characterization of the general structure of the chiefdoms was based on the more elaborately organized Polynesian examples. Polynesian chiefs had both secular and religious functions and had courts made up of secondary secular and religious officials and royal craftsmen, a pattern that could have closely resembled the structure of the Olmec chiefdoms. Within Polynesia there was considerable variation in the size of chiefdoms, the secular power of chiefs, the elaborateness of the court, and the degree to which leaders and craftsmen were full-time (Sahlins 1958). This same picture would fit the total Mesoamerican Middle and Late Formative scene rather well.

Ecological Processes

We will now explore the ecology of the Formative chiefdoms in Mesoamerica and attempt to explain why and how they evolved and the reasons underlying their spatial distribution. The three basic ecological processes outlined previously—population growth, competition, and cooperation in a setting of microgeographical complexity—were critical.

Although the archaeological data are not entirely satisfactory, the evidence suggests that Mesoamerica was well populated by 1500 B.C. and that the nutritional complex was sufficiently developed to provide the basis of sedentary village life and tribal society. As we have stated, a tribal stage of social structure at this time probably existed, and in some areas the first small chiefdoms emerged.

Even as early as the Middle Formative phase, agriculture,

because of the intense microgeographical variation, must have varied in its specific characteristics from area to area. There was undoubtedly a great variety of types of maize and of swidden cultivation techniques. Furthermore, even within a single mountain valley or coastal strip there tends to be a very uneven distribution of resources. In the lowland areas significant variables would be location with respect to coast and rivers; such topographical variations as foothills, hillsides, flood plains, and interfluvial ridges; and variations in rainfall and soils. These factors would affect crop distribution and productivity, nonagricultural food resources and other raw materials (clay, shell, and stone, for example). In the Highlands such contrasts in resources were considerably greater. Archaeological evidence from the Early Formative sites demonstrates that trade was extensive even in the prechiefdom stage.

This microgeographical zoning has several significant effects. First of all it stimulates competition within a local area over resources. Second, since broken topography acts as a barrier and since the microgeographical zoning is often sufficiently extreme to make difficult the spread of specific subsistence techniques over wide areas, migration as a response to population pressure is greatly inhibited. Response to population pressures, therefore, takes the form of more intensive or specialized adaptations to the local environment resulting in even greater cultural differentiation and interdependence from ecological zone to ecological zone. The net result is a very rapid population growth in each zone; hence the critical density level for chiefdoms and states is achieved at a much faster rate than in large, relatively uniform geographical regions. Carneiro (1961), in a very provocative paper, stresses the difference between what he calls "circumscribed" and "open" environments. The Amazon Basin, for example, is a huge, relatively uniform area with almost limitless space for population expansion. The normal economic response to population pressure in such a setting would be segmentation and emigration. An enormously long period of time would thus be required to achieve the critical density level for the evolution of complex societies in such an ecological setting. The same generalization may apply to the Eastern Woodland area. The fact that the hunting-and-gathering Californians achieved a population density higher than the agricultural Woodland groups at the time of discovery may have been primarily the product of these two distinctive demographic responses to population pressure. The need for riverine protein resources in the case of the Amazon Basin settlements would tend to limit population movement and distribution; there is in fact a possibility that chiefdoms did occur in some riverine strips. Meggers and Evans (1957) in several papers have recorded the migration of a group with a chiefdom level of social structure from the Caribbean coastal plain to Marajó Island in the mouth of the Amazon. The archaeological sequence of the island starts with a culture complex that includes large burial mounds with richly stocked status tombs. In the succeeding phases, mound building disappears, and the art generally deteriorates. Meggers and Evans argue that the tropical environment was not sufficiently productive to sustain a complex society. A more convincing argument would be that as the population increased, the almost limitless agricultural land on the mainland acted as an incentive to emigration. The result was a steady reduction of population density until chiefdom social structure could no longer be maintained. The combination of a small isolated area of relatively high population density, abundance of land around it, lack of competition with similar societies, and the generally centrifugal tendency of swidden agriculture would, we believe, cancel out the integrative efficiency of a chiefdom. In the highland valleys of Mesoamerica and in the relatively narrow coastal plains—areas containing hundreds of small circumscribed ecological zones—this demographic filling-in process would be much faster, and the critical level for complex social systems achieved relatively early.

In Service's discussion of chiefdoms he observes that the

historic distributions of chiefdoms coincided with regions composed of small circumscribed microgeographical zones (the
larger Pacific islands, Intermediate Area, West Indies); he sees
the chiefdom type of social structure as a response to the need
for an effective distribution of highly localized natural resources.
Theoretically, periodic raids could solve the problem of the
supply of raw materials for each local group, but a regular
supply of goods could hardly be sustained in this manner. For
relatively small populations tribal social structure would provide
a social setting within which informal trade, perhaps conducted
by means of fictive kin groups, could solve the problem. Another
solution might be found in ceremonial exchanges between normally hostile local groups, as in the case of the Trobriand Kula.
One could argue, however, that as the population became larger
and denser, and as trade orbits widened, there was a stimulus
toward the evolution of more effective systems of distribution.
Chiefdoms were the product of this need.

One of the basic characteristics of chiefdom social structure
is the presence of a core lineage that enjoys privileged status and
control of the distribution system. Local variations in productivity in a geographically complex area would stimulate the
growth of such a system, since some local groups would enjoy
demographic superiority over others. In the Mesoamerican South
Gulf Coast there are striking differences in productivity of
riverine flood plains in contrast to nonalluviated interfluves.
Flood plains may be cultivated with much shorter cycles, the
winter crop is more dependable, and commercially profitable
crops such as cacao may be grown. Foothill settings offer equally
desirable advantages. It was no accident that the two largest
Classic Maya centers in the area, Comalcalco and Palenque, and
the three Olmec centers were located in similar niches. In the
arid highlands the alluvial plains, when irrigated, were more
productive than were piedmonts or hillsides; all of the major
Classic and Postclassic centers were therefore situated in localities with ready access to such sectors.

In summary, variations in productivity within small zones and between adjacent zones would place some groups in an advantageous competitive position. In such a setting egalitarian tribal society could be transformed quite readily into a ranked or stratified one. We believe that the evidence of an apparent short duration of the tribal phase in the evolution of Mesoamerican society, at least in certain nuclear areas, is not because there has been insufficient research, but because the evolution of non-egalitarian society, once the critical demographic level had been achieved, was indeed a rapid process, and the major controlling factors were ecological. The chiefdom is a large, productive economic system in which a great number of specialized units are organized by a privileged group to facilitate the distribution of products. The economic functions of tribes are more limited, comprising primarily those related to occasional emergencies. Chiefdoms, with their tighter structure, offer obvious military advantages over tribes, so that chiefdoms evolving among tribal groups, stimulate the development of other chiefdoms. The rise of Gulf Coast Olmec chiefdoms may, therefore, have been a factor stimulating such developments in the nearby areas. In this sense Coe's (1965a) argument that the Olmec influence acted as a stimulus to cultural development beyond the Gulf Coast areas is defensible. This too may be considered a kind of "foreign influence," although in a sense an indirect one and not the customary meaning of this term. It is for this reason, among others, that we feel the attribution of culture change to foreign influence, without postulating a plausible mechanism for its operation, tends to be meaningless or misleading, itself requiring explanation.

The history and distribution of Formative chiefdoms within Mesoamerica presents an extremely complex picture; anthropologists today are still far from understanding the processes that govern this chronological and spatial patterning. The evidence previously assembled suggests an initial development of labor-intensive methods of agriculture, including irrigation, during the Formative period in the arid portions of the Highlands. This development was functionally related to the emergence of the first complex chiefdoms in those areas, apparently in Middle Formative and Late Formative times. Over most of Meso-america, however, including the arid highlands, various forms of swidden cultivation seem to have been characteristic. Lowland swidden agriculture is generally more productive than highland tlacolol (in terms of yield per work hour and per geographical zone), so that the larger and earlier Gulf Coast chiefdoms, if in fact they were larger and earlier, would be understandable and expected. A relatively large class of non-food-producers, consisting of the chiefly lineage and craftsmen, could be easily supported; the larger size of particular chiefdoms would enable them to control, maintain, and organize supra-local patterns of trade. The spread of the Olmec feline rain god cult is thus readily understood in terms of this social and economic setting.

The overall impression of the Mesoamerican Formative period is of relatively light population and geographical selectivity. This is probably the result of two processes, one historical (the distance of areas from centers of plant domestication—the location of which, of course, is ultimately itself an ecological phenomenon), the other ecological (the economic implications of various types of agricultural system). If the center of plant domestication was in the intermediate altitude, subhumid region of Oaxaca and the Balsas Basin, then some areas would have been marginal simply because of distance from these centers (for example, the northwest and northeast frontiers). Within those areas easily accessible to this postulated hearth of plant domestication, assuming initially a swidden system of cultivation, the tropical lowlands would be the most favorable environment, the humid highlands intermediate, and the arid lands (primarily but not entirely highland) the least favorable because of the dual problems of erosion and drought. Areas above 2,000 meters elevation would have the additional disadvantage of a frost season.

It is increasingly evident, however, that the first experimentations with labor-intensive patterns of agriculture were taking place in this highland zone during the Middle Formative period. We feel that these developments were functionally related to the emergence of chiefdoms in these zones, possibly prior to, at least contemporary with, the Gulf Coast lowland florescence. It would seem likely, however, that the initial developments in hydraulic agriculture would have been small in size and their effects on productivity limited at first. The Gulf Coast florescence can be explained on the basis of the high productivity of swidden agriculture in this region and the early stabilization of exploitation on this basis. Its demographic potential would probably have been higher than that of the incipiently hydraulic chiefdoms of the Highlands.

With further development of both infield-outfield cultivation and hydraulic agriculture in the Highlands, however, the initial advantage of the tropical lowlands would dissipate and the demographic balance ultimately shift. As we shall demonstrate, this is precisely what happened in the succeeding Classic and Postclassic periods. This dissipation of advantage actually began in the Late and Terminal Formative, as the emergence of a great number of large regional centers and the decline of Olmec artistic influence demonstrates.

The Lowlands, because of their initially greater productivity, would have filled in demographically comparatively quickly. From this point on, little fundamental change occurred in principle. In the Highlands, however, the shift from swidden-tlacolol to hydraulic cultivation, even given a relatively minor initial impact, would ultimately provide a basis for increased population, increased social complexity, and dominance of areas having such systems over areas which lacked them—a striking illustration of what Sahlins and Service (1960) have called the Law of Evolutionary Potential.

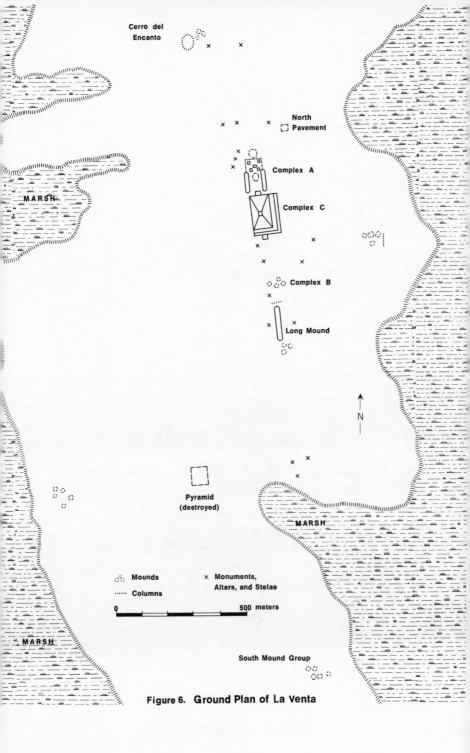

Figure 6. Ground Plan of La Venta

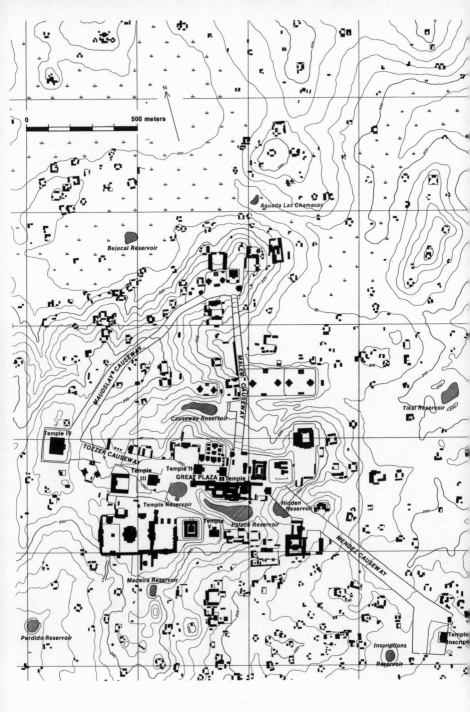

Figure 7. Ground Plan of Tikal

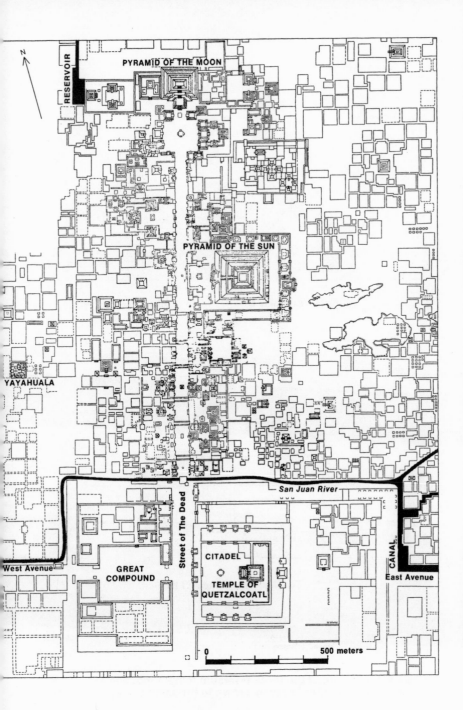

Figure 8. Ground Plan of Teotihuacan

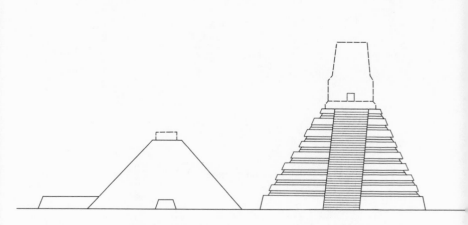

La Venta (Complex C)   **Tikal (Temple IV.)**

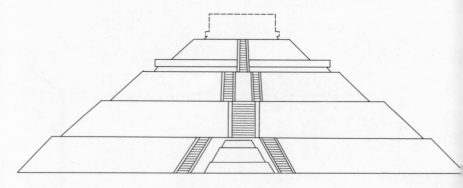

Teotihuacan (Temple of the Sun)

50   0   50   100 meters

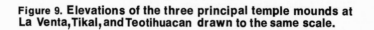

Figure 9. Elevations of the three principal temple mounds at
La Venta, Tikal, and Teotihuacan drawn to the same scale.

VIII / CIVILIZATIONS IN MESOAMERICA

Definition

A definition of civilization was presented in Chapter II. A major problem, as in the case of the lower levels of social complexity, is that of archaeological identification. The chiefdom level of socioeconomic structure in Mesoamerica was defined archaeologically on the basis of small-scale site stratification. Chiefdoms in Nuclear America, whether the prehistoric Middle Formative Mesoamerican or the historic highland Colombian Chibcha, varied considerably in the quality of their material remains. Some archaeologists would probably classify the Olmec culture as a civilization. We freely admit that much of the taxonomy used, as applied to prehistoric cultures, is subjective and that there is room for argument. As sophisticated and skilled as Olmec art was, however, there is a substantial qualitative and quantitative difference in richness of content between the material remains of Classic and Postclassic periods in Mesoamerica on one hand, and those of even the most elaborate Formative cultures on the other. This increase in quality and quantity must relate to a corresponding increase in the amount and degree of occupational specialization and consequent changes in the character of economic institutions. In architecture the contrast is even more striking; no Formative site is comparable in size, quality, or complexity to the great Classic and Postclassic centers. Monumental architecture is perhaps the best index of the degree of complexity of social systems. The post-Formative periods contrast with the Formative primarily in the presence of centers of truly monumental size, thus adding another level or two to the pyramid of site stratification. (See Figures 6, 7, 8, 9.)

Archaeological data as well as sixteenth-century documents indicate clearly that there were two types of civilization in post-Formative times: urban and nonurban. Earlier syntheses of Mesoamerican culture history postulated that these two types were temporal, that during the Classic period there were nonurban civilizations, succeeded by urban civilizations in the Postclassic. Recent research has demonstrated, however, that the differences are spatial and probably ecological rather than temporal. In regions of swidden or tlacolol cultivation urbanism is absent or poorly developed whatever the time period. It is present in both the Classic and Postclassic periods in connection with hydraulic agriculture. The significance of infield-outfield agriculture without hydraulic characteristics is not clear. In fact, the only Mesoamerican areas where urbanism is definitely present are the core area of the Central Plateau and the Valley of Oaxaca.

History and Distribution

Recent research suggests that the earliest development of civilization occurred at either Teotihuacán or Monte Albán and that it preceded such development elsewhere by at least three and possibly by as much as six centuries. Both of these earliest civilizations in Mesoamerica were urban, probably developing from earlier nucleated chiefdoms (our Type 3) in the same areas.

A fairly detailed picture of the evolution of Teotihuacán will soon be available as a result of the Teotihuacán Valley Project, directed by Sanders, and particularly from the Teotihuacán Mapping Project of René Millon. The Teotihuacán Valley was occupied for approximately 1,000 years by a sedentary agricultural society prior to the rise of the city. The settlement pattern data suggest a simple tribal society, occupying primarily the elevated portions of the Valley and practicing tlacolol cultivation during much of this long period. The Valley at this time was marginal demographically and socially to the west-central and southwestern parts of the Basin of Mexico.

Between approximately 1000 and 300 B.C. population growth was relatively slow; subjective estimates suggest a doubling every two or three centuries. By 300 B.C. a series of tiny chiefdoms emerged. Between 300 B.C. and B.C./A.D. several striking changes in the ecosystem occurred: The population probably doubled every generation, settlements shifted to the alluvial plain, and toward the end of this period, at least half of the population was concentrated into a single, huge, sprawling, nucleated center at the site of the Classic city. Millon (1964) feels that at this time Teotihuacán was already a city and that there was extensive architectural activity. By the time of Christ, there was at least valley-wide political integration, comprising an area of approximately 500 km². The subsequent history of Teotihuacán is one of expansion of the size of this nucleated center, increase in density and socioeconomic differentiation of the population of the center, and expansion of the orbit of its political influence. By the Miccaotli phase Teotihuacán had certainly reached the status of a city and the Teotihuacán culture the status of a civilization. The subsequent history of Central Mexico was one of cyclical rise and decline of urban civilizations with changing centers of political and economic power.

A comparable sequence of events following a similar time table apparently occurred at Monte Albán. In startling contrast to its Formative period precocity, the South Gulf Coast was relatively static during the Classic and Postclassic. For the old Olmec heartland there were changing styles of figurines, pottery, and architecture with cyclic occurrences of highland Mexican influences (Early Classic from Teotihuacán, Late Classic and Postclassic from Cholula, Tula, and Tenochtitlán) possibly because of conquest. No centers comparable in size to Monte Albán or Teotihuacán appeared throughout the Classic and Postclassic periods. For the Central Gulf Coast Tajín represented the first major center comparable to Teotihuacán or Monte Albán to emerge; its florescence, significantly, seems to have occurred in Late Classic times following the collapse of Teotihuacán and the consequent power vacuum on the Central Plateau. In the lowland Huasteca or North Gulf Coast there are no major centers reported before the Postclassic (Tantoc, Cacahuatenco).

In the Maya Lowlands a number of centers such as Copán, Comalcalco, Tikal, Calakmul, Piedras Negras, Yaxchilán, Palenque, Uxmal, and Cobá attained monumental size during the Late Classic period. This was also the period of maximum skill in all of the arts and crafts—architecture, sculpture, painting, and ceramics—and final development of writing and calendrics. Some of the Late Classic Lowland Maya craftsmanship remains unexcelled in the history of Mesoamerica.

There is the strong possibility that the chiefdoms of lowland Mesoamerica did not undergo the transformation of social structure we are calling civilization until Late Classic times and then only in certain areas. Recent attempts to analyze Classic Maya socioeconomic structure seem to favor a relatively small, only slightly differentiated society at least through the Early Classic (Willey 1964; Vogt 1964). It has been postulated that second-class centers like Uaxactún may have been serviced by organized populations of 5,000 to 10,000 persons (cf. Bullard 1962). Vogt has suggested that the religious statuses (clearly represented in Maya art), although arranged in a graded hierarchy, were part-time positions filled by the residents in outlying hamlets. He suggests a rotation system similar to the santo-cargo system found among contemporary Maya speakers at Zinacantan in the Chiapas Highlands (Vogt 1961).

Harris (1964) has pointed out the advantage of the fiesta-cargo system to an exploiting upper class dominating a subordinate peasantry, in effect, a means of preventing capital accumulation and therefore power on the part of the dominated group, while at the same time giving that group some semblance of a stake in the perpetuation of the system. Although his data are post-Hispanic, the pre-Hispanic situation of social stratification was remarkably similar structurally. It is, therefore, highly likely that an institution similar to the fiesta-cargo system existed, with similar functions, in pre-Conquest times. Such an institution seems to us to be ideally suited to the inferred sociological picture of the Lowland Classic Maya. In contrast to the social strata in the urbanized highlands, where social integration of various classes was achieved by close economic interdependence of these classes in the production and exchange of goods and services, the Lowland economic system appears far simpler and, accordingly, lacking in the multiple mutual reinforcement of many kinds of interconnecting links. In effect, the Lowland upper classes had a good deal less to do, and were in a sense more "parasitic" than was the case for their Highland counterparts. Vertical social integration would therefore have been a more serious problem in the Lowlands in the absence of economic symbiosis, and such an institution as the fiesta-cargo system could have been a solution. Interestingly, Harris' modern data suggest strongly that the worst "excesses" of the system tend to occur in areas where craft specialization and its correlate, an intensive system of markets, are less well-developed. In a community such as Tzintzuntzan, where the fiesta coincides with a large market and acts as a stimulus to commerce, the exploitative character of the fiesta is lacking, and the carguero has a good chance of making a profit.

Willey and his coworkers found very little evidence of social

stratification in their excavations and survey of rural sites in the
Belize Valley; the burial furniture of rural tombs was comparable to that found in the ceremonial centers (Willey *et al.*
1965). Based on this fact and on the occurrence of ceremonial
architecture in outlying hamlets and small ceremonial centers,
they argue that Maya society was well integrated and that the
suggested gulf between peasant and priest was nonexistent. Vogt
has postulated a plausible mechanism for this integration. Furthermore, Willey and Bullard suggest (1965) that craftsmen,
presumably part-time, lived scattered throughout the rural settlements (a pattern perhaps comparable to contemporary Hindu
India where groups of specialized craftsmen reside in rural
settlements, though in the case of the Maya, the caste features
were undoubtedly lacking).

The extraordinary florescence of Late Classic Maya art and
calendrics and the size of the mentioned macroceremonial centers
would, however, indicate the gradual development of a professional priesthood, residing permanently at the ceremonial center
and accompanied by cadres of professional craftsmen who were
directly attached to the priesthood and the gods. Even the largest
Maya center, Tikal, however, lacked truly urban population
concentrations. The settlement density around the site is comparable to Bullard's rural "zones" and the arrangement of houses
is identical. In the vicinity of the ceremonial civic precincts,
however, there have been found numerous multiroomed vaulted
structures that were probably residences of a sacerdotal-temple-
craftsmen class. Tikal and other macroceremonial centers probably possessed priestly colleges and trained the professional
priests for service in secondary centers like Uaxactún.

In part much of the recent argument concerning the urban
status of Tikal in particular (W. Coe 1965; Andrews 1965;
Willey and Bullard 1965) arises from a confusion of the terms
"civilization"—a status which Tikal in Late Classic times had
indisputably attained—and "urban," which, according to the
definitions presented here we feel they did not. There may have

been a very slight tendency toward nucleation of population in the vicinity of the ceremonial focus, but this is insufficiently great to warrant a designation of "urban." Foreign influence may be cited as a factor, considering that there is considerable evidence of trade with Teotihuacán during Early Classic times, including one structure of somewhat problematical date (5D-43) in Teotihuacán style (W. Coe 1965) indicating the possibility of a resident foreign colony. Accordingly, Tikal as a whole may have functioned as a sort of regional capital, at least on the level of *primus inter pares*, through which foreign relations, so to speak, were channeled. The "foreign colony" at Tikal, whether ambassadors, merchants, spies, ecclesiastics, or whatever, would inevitably have been full-time specialists, and, as such, would have required goods and services from the local population. They provided, in effect, an urban component for the settlement in which they resided; a modern analogy would be that of the governmental-diplomatic colony of Washington, D.C. Some slight stimulus toward urbanism may, therefore, have been present; however, from the evidence of the response as reflected in settlement patterns, the stimulus was indeed slight.

Agricultural Systems

In 1519 two basic systems of cultivation were practiced in Mesoamerica: swidden and various forms of infield-outfield. The former, as we have noted, can be divided into lowland and highland varieties. The essential characteristics of both have been previously defined. Swidden was the primary system of agriculture throughout areas of environmental types 1b, 1c, and 2c (see p. 104). In areas with 1a, 2a, 2b, and 3abc environments varying forms of infield-outfield cultivation were characteristic.

In tlacolol cultivation, unlike swidden cultivation, weed growth is not a serious problem, and the major factor that makes fallowing of fields imperative is instead declining soil fertility.

Erosion on hillsides, particularly in the drier sectors, also compounds the problem. In Mesoamerica, with the near absence of domestic animals, soil restoration must have been a major problem. As long as the population density remained low and land was abundant, tlacolol cultivation was a satisfactory adaptation. As population increased, the problem of supporting a growing population residing in ecologically circumscribed zones became acute. The archaeological data indicate that this problem emerged in some areas of Mesoamerica as early as the Late Formative and final centuries of the Middle Formative phases. Various types of infield-outfield agriculture evolved as a response, in turn resulting in a higher level of population density. This new level of density in time must have generated new pressures.

The success of infield-outfield agriculture depends in part upon variations in soil fertility, in part upon techniques of soil restoration. In some areas of highland Mesoamerica, natural processes such as alluviation in mountain valleys permitted continuous use of bottom land. A system of cultivation resulted in which social groups like villages, families, or kin groups possessed land in both valley bottom and hillside locations and cultivated the former continuously, the latter with a short rotational cycle. In other areas the calmil system was in use, characterized by a relatively dispersed settlement pattern with each house surrounded by a relatively large house lot. (Palerm [1955] based on contemporary data suggests .5 hectare as the maximal size for a nuclear family residence.) In this system refuse from humans and animals (dogs, turkeys) and use of the lot for garbage disposal or excretory functions produced enough organic refuse to permit continuous cultivation and relatively high production. From one-third to one-half of the family's subsistence needs can be provided from this permanently cultivated field. The balance of food is provided from large fields located outside the village cultivated on a rotation system. In some highland areas a combination of permanently cultivated bottom lands, plus calmil on terrace systems situated on the lower slopes, plus extensive cultivation of the higher lands permitted a population density in excess of the potential of either swidden or tlacolol cultivation.

This demographic advantage would be enormously increased with irrigation. Irrigation, even in areas where annual rainfall permits relatively dependable cropping, results in a sizable increase of yields since it permits humidity regulation; the water used in irrigation frequently also carries soil in suspension and plant nutrients in solution. Floodwater irrigation in particular, since it is based on torrential accumulations, is extremely rich in suspended materials; but even spring water contains dissolved minerals.

The densest pre-Hispanic population in Mesoamerica was achieved in a core area of the Central Plateau and adjacent escarpment (Basins of Mexico, Puebla, and upper Balsas). The total population of this demographic heartland in 1519 was at least 1.5 million in an area of 20,000 km² or a density of approximately 75 persons per km². A more reasonable estimate would be 2.25 million or a density of 112.5 per km².[7] In no other area of comparable size in the New World was a more effective adaptation to an environment achieved by a pre-Hispanic population. Within the area population was not evenly distributed; there were areas of unusually high population densities (Cholula plain, alluvial plains and adjacent piedmonts of Texcoco and Tenochtitlán, Chinampan). All of the major political and population centers were located within these areas of unusually dense population. The history of this population growth correlates directly with an increase of the percentage of infield and permanent cultivation over outfield and tlacolol. The soils generally are of high natural fertility and can be kept under continuous cultivation by calmil fertilization and floodwater and

[7] If the Cook and Simpson and Cook and Borah calculations of Conquest period population are used, these figures would be two to four times as high.

perennial irrigation. Added to these techniques of widespread applicability was the extraordinarily intensive system of cultivation called chinampa. True chinampas are artificial islands constructed of alternate layers of vegetation and mud in shallow fresh water lakes. Special features include the use of seed beds to shorten the growing season (thus permitting a continuous succession of crops in a single year), frequent fertilization using mud from the lake bottom and lake vegetation, and perennial irrigation. Chinampas were constructed in the form of narrow rectangles to facilitate bucket irrigation and natural seepage. When planted in maize, the highest yields in pre-Hispanic agriculture were achieved—up to 3,000 to 4,000 kg. per hectare (cf. West and Armillas 1950; Sanders 1957). In recent times, much of the land has been used for truck gardening and a similar situation probably obtained, if to a lesser degree, in Aztec times. Spatially this system in the highly specialized form described above is limited to the lakes in the Basin of Mexico. Lorenzo (1960), however, describes a system practiced in the Valley of Oaxaca that is strikingly similar. In the valley floor the water table is apparently relatively high, only a few meters below the surface. Farmers excavate a series of pits to water level at intervals along the long edges of their fields, which are in the form of narrow rectangles. As in the case of chinampas the plots are irrigated by buckets and scoops. Flannery (1967) notes the association of Early Formative sites in the Oaxaca Valley with a three-meter water table—an association which may suggest the antiquity of the system which he calls "pot irrigation." Excavations by Orlandini (1967) confirm at least a Middle Formative date for this method. A very similar system is found in the Teotihuacán Valley in the area of the springs, where the water table is less than a meter below the surface. Farmers dig trenches completely around their fields; seepage into the ditches produces a continuous water supply; and fields are irrigated by scoop from the water-filled ditches. They even plant huejote trees along the field edges as in true chinampas to protect and consolidate the field edge. The total distribution of this type of irrigation is not known.

Up to this point we have been concerned primarily with agricultural systems in the sixteenth century. Archaeological research on the pre-Aztec history of agriculture in Central Mexico is still in its infancy.

One of the most critical areas of recent research has been the determination of the history and significance of irrigation in the culture history of Mesoamerica. Research has established that irrigation was widespread in Mesoamerica at the time of the Spanish Conquest, dates back at least to the Late and Terminal Formative phases and was of considerable demographic and, derivatively, of political and economic importance. True hydraulic agriculture (see p. 88), as Wittfogel calls it, however, was not characteristic of Highland Mesoamerica with the exception of Central Mexico.

Indirect evidence from the Teotihuacán Valley Project indicates that perennial irrigation of the alluvial plain of the Lower Valley based on springs and floodwater irrigation of the Middle Valley formed the subsistence base of the Early Classic city. The slopes were probably terraced and irrigated using floodwater irrigation, as was the case in the Aztec period. The growth of the city, particularly in its early phases, was apparently related to the development of these techniques of intensive land use. How widespread intensive versus extensive cultivation was in the Basin of Mexico generally, is not known. Superficial surveys suggest that the population of the Basin as a whole during the Early Classic period was probably no more than one-third of the population in 1519, perhaps 300,000 to 500,-000 people.

On the other hand, the population of the Teotihuacán Valley was approximately 100,000 or equal to that achieved in Aztec times. This suggests that in Early Classic times there were local foci of intensive cultivation near cities and towns but that much of the area was still cultivated using extensive techniques.

Cuicuilco in Late Formative times was apparently situated in a similar compact area of hydraulic agriculture with most of the Basin under tlacolol cultivation.

In the Texcoco section of the Basin there is even a suggestion that Early Classic settlement tended to be concentrated in the piedmont and that the alluvial plain was in only partial use. This would indicate only a moderate population for that area, since the plain was the locus of nearly all the population centers and was intensively cultivated, along with the piedmont, in the sixteenth century. The picture in Early Classic times then is one of a moderately dense overall population for the heartland, with a number of local, densely populated zones (Teotihuacán Valley, Cholula Plain, probably a number of others) with a variety of agricultural systems being practiced, ranging from tlacolol to hydraulic, and in which centers of political power were closely related to areas of hydraulic agriculture. The model here is very much that of infield-outfield cultivation writ large.

The ecosystem of contemporary northern Nigeria strikingly parallels our model of the Late Formative–Early Classic in the Central Plateau. Modern Kano, Sokoto, Katsina, and Zaria are large, tightly nucleated population centers with a partly urban, partly rural subsistence base. Each is located within a small area of very intensively cultivated land, with some irrigation. In the immediate hinterland of Kano, for example, some 90 percent of the land is under cultivation; population densities exceed 175 persons per square kilometer at the core, tapering off to a range of 100 to 175 on the fringes. Between such nuclei lie areas with much lower population densities, associated with more extensive patterns of land use, and dominated economically and politically by the population centers (Buchanan and Pugh 1966).

The Late Classic (or Terminal Classic) and Early Post-classic period (Toltec period) witnessed a heavy population loss in the Teotihuacán Valley, almost certainly a local phenomenon related to the collapse of Teotihuacán itself as a focus of power.

For the Basin as a whole evidence suggests continuous population growth, probably correlated with an expansion of intensive agriculture, that reached a peak by 1519. Recent evidence from Armillas' Chinampan Project (personal communication) seems to point to a Postclassic date for the inception of chinampa cultivation reaching a peak in Aztec times—the final phase in a history of increasingly intensive use of resources.

Society and Economy

The level of social evolution defined as civilization was certainly present in Central Mexico at the time of the Spanish Conquest; it was, furthermore, clearly an urban civilization. Space does not permit a full analysis of Aztec social and economic structure, but we shall briefly summarize its salient characteristics.

Physical communities were differentiated into rural types, including hamlets and villages, and urban types, including towns and cities. The rural settlements varied in form from linear to radial and in density from rather dispersed to tightly nucleated, according to their location, with linear-dispersed settlements occurring primarily in terraced piedmonts and nucleated radial settlements within alluvial plains. Populations of rural settlements ranged from a few score up to several thousand. Towns varied considerably in population but tended to sort into two size ranges—3,000 to 4,000, and 5,000 to 6,000 inhabitants. Cities had populations in the tens of thousands. The largest city was Tenochtitlán with a minimum of 60,000 and possibly as many as 120,000 inhabitants.[8] Approximately 25 percent of the population of the Basin of Mexico resided in towns or cities in 1519.

Sociopolitically, the Basin of Mexico was divided into some

[8] Calnek (personal communication) suggests estimates double our upper figure, and Willey (1966:157) gives a population estimate of 300,000 persons.

sixty semiautonomous divisions, each with a population range of between 12,000 and 50,000 and an average territory of approximately 130 km². All of them paid tribute to and were politically dependent on one of the three centers: Tenochtitlán, Texcoco, or Tlacopán.

Each of the sixty divisions included a town or small city as an administrative center and dependent rural communities. Each state was ruled by a hereditary ruler generally called a tlatoani or tlatoque, who had despotic powers and was surrounded by an elaborate court characterized by the expected protocol. He resided in a large multiroomed masonry palace complex, built and maintained by corvée labor.

Society was stratified into two levels: the pipiltin or nobles who were descendants of the reigning and former tlatoanis and the macehualtin or commoners. Since there is some indication that these divisions were endogamous, they might virtually be termed castes. The macehualtin were divided into social classes with residence in either town or rural settlements, based primarily on occupation. In the town were the professional warriors or tectecuhtin, the pochteca or merchants, and such full-time professional craftsmen as the goldsmiths, lapidaries, and featherworkers. The merchants and craftsmen were organized into hereditary guilds occupying residential wards within the town. The status of such groups, particularly that of the warriors, was superior to other macehualtin. Although great numbers of other craftsmen also resided in the town, it is not clear whether they were full- or part-time specialists, or whether they were organized into guilds. The bulk of the macehualtin were farmers residing in the rural settlements. Part-time specialization based on local resources, however, was characteristic of such rural settlements and a distinctive feature of Central Mexican economic life, persisting into the present. Each town had a market to facilitate the exchange of these various specialized products. Along with the "free" craftsmen and farmers were three depressed classes, the mayeques who were equivalent to European serfs, a temporary-slave class that included individuals who had sold themselves to pay off debts or had committed crimes, and finally a true slave class derived from prisoners of war. The mayeques were attached to estates either held by the state for assignment to office holders or privately owned by the nobility (cf. Caso 1959).

Tribute commitments to the tlatoani were based on class-caste affiliations as well as on economic specialization. While all classes and castes were required to perform military services, the pipiltin and tectecuhtin were exempt from all other taxation. While merchants and craftsmen were required to pay tribute in the goods they produced, they were exempt from corvée labor. Farmers were required to pay tribute in agricultural produce as well as in corvée labor.

In addition to the position of the tlatoani, the administration of even small states was characterized by an elaborate bureaucracy of officials (cf. Calnek 1966) including ward division heads in the towns, tax collectors, treasurers, judges, priests, ambassadors, and even a police force. Occupants of such positions were appointed by the ruler from either the nobility (pipiltin) or warrior (tectecuhtin) classes and were supported by the state, usually by granting hacienda-like estates with mayeques to the office holder during the term of office. Each of these statuses had well-defined privileges, duties, and powers. Economic, political, and religious statuses were all distinguished by differences in dress, food habits, housing, and respect accorded them.

The social organization of rural settlements included a pyramid of kinship-based residential groups of varying size. The largest unit was the calpulli, often called a barrio by the Spaniards. Its structure has never been fully understood but its functions are well described by them.

The functions of the calpulli were multiple. In the economic sphere it was a unit of land tenure, corvée labor, and tax payment. Politically each had a council of extended-family heads and a hereditary chief as an arbiter of disputes within the unit, custodian of the land maps, and representative of the calpulli to the tlatoani. Each calpulli apparently fought in warfare as a military company, and maintained its own military school (the telpochcalli). Finally, the calpulli possessed social functions, probably including, to a greater or lesser extent, some kinship aspects; these latter are discussed below in greater detail.

The calpulli was divided into small units referred to by the Spaniards as "barrios pequeños" (when a Náhuatl term is given, the term calpulli is also used for the subdivisions) whose functions are not clear, although they apparently were administrative and tax units of some kind and had a local administrative official—the tequitlato or tequitano. Archaeological survey suggests that they were residential units, either physically isolated hamlets or ward-like divisions of larger settlements. Below this level were extended patrilocal families residing in multifamily houses and nuclear families occupying apartments in such structures.

Depending upon the characteristics one chooses to emphasize, it is possible to interpret the calpulli in many ways, so diverse as often to be actually in conflict with each other. Debate concerning the nature of this unit has been prevalent since the sixteenth-century chroniclers first described it; modern interpretations are, if anything, still more divergent. The reasons for this are several, ranging from the difference of descriptions offered by the conquistadores themselves to changes in general anthropological theory over the past eighty years. We shall proceed to analyze and attempt to interpret the structure of this group, taking as our starting point the general agreement of nearly all writers that it comprises the fundamental unit of Aztec social structure and that it was a territorial unit.

In addition to the characteristics mentioned above, there is strong evidence that the calpulli was a kinship as well as a residential unit in spite of Moreno's (1931) arguments to the contrary. On the basis of analysis of sixteenth-century marriage and baptismal records, Carrasco (1961) feels that it was an endogamous unit, a conclusion strongly implied also by Zorita (1942). Considering the function of the calpulli as a landholding unit, endogamy may well be related to an ecological situation of intensive agriculture and population pressure; endogamy would serve as an admirable device of minimizing disputes over rights of land tenure that would otherwise be likely to result.

If, as seems probable, the calpulli was both localized and endogamous, the problem of lineality wanes in importance, for the present analysis at least. In the case of the calpulli there seems to have been a patri-bias; in effect, however, the unit would probably best be treated as essentially bilaterial in respect to descent. Contrary to the early views of Morgan (1877) and Bandelier (1880), this is evidently not a clan, in Morgan's sense, although Vaillant (1941) adopted this hypothesis in modified form and not without difficulty. Given the nearly general agreement that it was at least in part a corporate kinship group, we may well ask what kind of group. The absence of a functionally significant principle of lineality removes it from the "clan" category. One exceptionally significant additional characteristic also differentiates the calpulli from the clan: It was clearly nonegalitarian in terms of the statuses of its members, and, according to some accounts (Zorita 1942:31; Monzon 1946:38), not only ranking but stratification was the principle involved. Members held different amounts of land; calpullis differed among themselves in the extent of land held with some being "greater" than others. The chief was clearly selected from a core lineage of higher status than the others.

The possibility of considering this as a deme in Murdock's (1949) terminology has been raised (cf. Sanders 1957, 1965), but this is in certain respects not completely satisfactory. Murdock defines the deme (1949:62) as essentially a consanguineally related, endogamous local group structured into families. Beyond this, however, he pays scant attention to the special properties of this kind of group, and, furthermore, has failed to note what we consider to be one of the most important attributes of the calpulli—its strongly nonegalitarian character. Apart from distinguishing this type from unilineal groupings defined with far more specificity, his treatment of the deme is based more on negative characteristics, on what it is not, and is generally extremely superficial, primarily because of Murdock's failure to employ technoeconomic functions as classificatory criteria.

Analysis of the calpulli rather in the framework of the conical clan as defined by Kirchhoff (1959) seems to us to be more productive. Whether, indeed, a unit by definition ambilateral, internally stratified, and with a tendency at least toward endogamy ought to be called a clan of any type is debatable; the usage does violate the customarily accepted concept of the clan as defined either by Morgan or by Murdock. Clearly, however, this type of unit seems consonant with the nature of the calpulli insofar as this is inferable from ethnohistoric and archaeological evidence. If the calpulli is considered a conical clan, furthermore, a number of ethnographic parallels are suggested that cast further light on the nature, distribution, and evolutionary potential of this type of unit. Much of the controversy concerning such groups seems to lie in a concentration upon structural minutiae and idiosyncrasies to the neglect of the regularities, the fundamental similarities that we feel exist among the various examples. We feel that along with the calpulli, the ramage (Sahlins 1958) of Polynesia, and the Peruvian ayllu may also be considered as instances of this general structural type. There is, in other words, a striking association of this phenomenon with a level of cultural development at or above the chiefdom—an association which we feel is far from accidental. Such units are in their organization the whole in microcosm.

Given the characteristics of states as presented by Service and followed generally in this work, the conical clan appears to be an institution well suited to the ecological and sociological processes occurring at these levels. Another characteristic of the conical clan in general and of the calpulli in particular that seems to us salient is the extreme variability and flexibility of this group—in size, rank, stratification, and relative emphasis on one or another of the principles on the basis of which we distinguish it as a type. It may be this variability, which to our knowledge has not been emphasized by any of the writers on the subject, that is in part responsible for the welter of controversy. Most of the chroniclers who have described the calpulli do not necessarily state the exact area from which the information was drawn. The Aztec Empire was far from uniform in ecology, in demography, in ethnic and linguistic affiliations of component groups, in closeness of integration with the center at Tenochtitlán. To expect uniformity in all details of a unit like the calpulli in the face of these extreme diversities would seem to be utopian. The implicit assumption, furthermore, that Aztec social organization was in any real sense static is similarly unwarranted. Even within relatively short periods of time variation in details of social structure should be expected, particularly when one considers the remarkably rapid expansion of the Empire, which does not seem even to have reached a period of stabilization prior to its decapitation by the Conquest. Under such circumstances, the flexibility of the conical clan would clearly be a feature of no small adaptive significance. Its power to expand, to incorporate new groups at various levels, and to organize for the efficient exploitation of additional lands within the framework of higher levels of sociopolitical structure would have been tremendous.

The position of a corporate group within such a larger framework, in other words, would act as a determinant of its structure and functions. In addition to the geographic, demographic, and ethnic diversity of the Aztec Empire, we are dealing also with wide variation in factors such as social class, and urban as opposed to rural setting. It is primarily the fact that the calpulli existed very much as a structural part of a stratified and state-organized society that led Moreno to deny that it had, at the time of the Conquest, virtually any kinship functions whatever, maintaining rather that it was purely a residential unit within the state. What we have mentioned, however, as the most significant aspects of its kin-based nature do not seem incompatible with these higher levels of organization—in fact, they replicate it in miniature in the way that an egalitarian clan would obviously not.

With the present interpretation of the calpulli as a whole, we are in a position to examine what seems to be one of its components, the almost equally puzzling barrio pequeño of the Spanish chroniclers. Whether these were the individual patri-lineages comprising the calpulli, or were smaller conical sub-clans above the lineage level remains unclear. It seems that both hypotheses are equally tenable, and more likely still that the term barrio pequeño was very probably applied to both alternatives interchangeably without distinguishing the two situations. Like the calpulli, the barrio pequeño varied in size and in function. If one visualizes a rural community as com-posed of, normally, a single calpulli, towns and cities were probably complex in this respect. In the setting of the town, the barrio pequeño very likely served as the unit of craft specializa-tion.

Cities were much larger units characterized by daily markets and considerable full-time occupational specialization in non-food-producing activities. They served as centers of large states, composed of scores, and in the case of Tenochtitlán hundreds, of semiautonomous tributary states of the type we have de-scribed. The social organization of cities was accordingly com-plex. According to the Codex Osuna, a Spanish tax document dating from the mid-sixteenth century, Tenochtitlán was com-posed of some 60 to 70 barrios, each approximately comparable in size to the rural calpulli. Most recent studies mention but twenty of these units, and, to complicate the picture further, there is ample precedent for using the term "calpulli" to refer to each of the four principal geographical subdivisions of Tenochtitlán. It might, however, be more fruitful to regard these Four Quarters as "hue-calpulli" (great calpulli) a division more complex in nature and on a higher structural and demographic level than that of its components. A concept of a basic conical-clan structure makes this interpretation feasible. Doubtless the residential principle was probably more operative than the kinship or other features at this higher level. Again, in Tenochtitlán it is likely that both the calpulli and the barrio pequeño also served as craft guilds, some of whose production was disposed of in the market, while other such cadres of professionals worked only for the state. The overall political structure of Tenochtitlán seems to have been similar to that of smaller city-states, differing in size of court, internal complexity and more elevated hierarchical position, rather than in any way in principle.

The most significant aspect of Central Mexican economics, aside from the intensiveness of the agricultural base, was the intense symbiosis among social subdivisions focused on the market system. This symbiosis integrated units within the urban communities, rural and urban units, and rural with rural into a complex web of interdependence; its integrative functions were both horizontal and vertical.

The ethnographic data from other areas of Mesoamerica are not as well documented. The fundamental characteristics of Aztec society and economics seem to occur in varying levels of intensity and complexity in Central Mexico and the Oaxaca Highlands; much of it may perhaps apply to Highland Guatemala as well.

In contrast there was a striking difference from this general pattern in the tropical lowlands, although, as in the case of highland areas, it would be a gross and misleading oversimplification to assume that considerable variation of social structure was absent in the lowlands. For example, large unilineal descent groups comparable to sibs have been suggested for the Lowland Maya, whereas none have been reported for the Huastec or Totonac (Roys 1943, 1957; Palerm 1952–3). All tropical lowland areas, however, shared certain features of social and economic organization regardless of the details of social structure, and the overall Lowland pattern stood in striking contrast to that of Central Mexico.

Lowland society was stratified into two social levels, an upper level in control of the political or religious institutions and a lower level whose tribute in labor and goods supported this hierarchy. The upper class resided in civic centers composed of masonry palaces or monasteries—probably with a small class of commoners who were servants, retainers, or professional craftsmen and who worked directly for either the temple or state. Urbanism of the highland type was rare, particularly in areas of swidden agriculture. There is some evidence of towns and small cities in the more arid portions of the lowlands, as at Cempoalla where urbanism was associated with hydraulic agriculture and at Mayapán where foreign mercenaries established a political system of Central Mexican type. There is both documentary and archaeological evidence, however, that Mayapán was really a massive ceremonial center in which the local rulers and their immediate retainers were required to reside part of the year as a technique of social control. Andrews (1965) has asserted that Dzibilchaltún was a true city, the largest in the New World, and that it covered 50 km^2. The prepublication map really does not justify this claim at all; one has the impression that he has considered as a single site what in reality is a segment of regional settlement that includes ceremonial precincts, elite residential complexes, and rural settlements. By his definition the entire Lower Valley of Teotihuacán would be a single giant Aztec city!

A significant indicator of the difference in intensity of economic specialization between Lowlands and Highlands is the frequency of market encounters. The sixteenth-century sources in speaking of the Gulf Coast, when markets are mentioned at all, refer to twenty-day markets. In the Basin of Mexico there were five-day markets in towns and daily markets in the major centers. In support of this conclusion, we cite evidence adduced by Chapman (1957) to the effect that the specialized long-distance commerce carried out in ports-of-trade in the Maya area was the prerogative of the Maya nobility. Such activity for the Aztecs was not a function of the nobility, but of a specialized class of long-distance traders, the pochteca, a class which while almost surely controlled politically by the state, was, strictly speaking, neither noble nor quite commoner. This group, although tribute-paying (and hence non-noble), paid only in the goods in which they dealt, most frequently luxury goods, and were exempt from corvée labor. The pochteca, and possibly other such specialized groups, occupied an intermediate status in the Aztec hierarchy. The entire Aztec social system was, therefore, more complex than the Maya in that it comprised a greater number of levels. Still more significant is the strong implication that trade of all types—market as well as port-of-trade—was of greater volume and importance in the highlands, as compared to the Lowland pattern, where volume was relatively small and a class of full-time specialists to handle the activity was neither necessary nor economical.

The documentary evidence indicates that civilization, as we have defined the term, was characteristic of the areas of swidden agriculture, but that urbanism was generally lacking. The state and some full-time craft specialization (restricted primarily to the direct needs of state and temple) were present; part-time specialization by rural communities was characteristic but lacked the intensity of that in highland areas; society was highly stratified and was characterized by a more sacred, less secular ethos.

Archaeological evidence demonstrates that this arid highland-humid lowland contrast in society and economics has great time depth; we noted the inception of this divergence in societal type as early as the Middle Formative. By Early Classic times the contrast is marked. Perhaps the most convincing way of demonstrating the dichotomy between the two types of civilization is by a comparison of the two largest sites that represent them, Tikal and Teotihuacán. Recent studies by Millon, from which only brief preliminary reports have been published (1964, 1967), plus earlier research by Armillas (1950), Millon (1960), and Sanders (1965), have established the urban character of Early Classic Teotihuacán. Millon has confirmed the presence of markets and craft specialization by ward, a wide range of social status, large population (85,000 at the peak), formal planning of residential as well as civic precincts, population density of a clearly urban level, and some formally organized political system, possibly with the priesthood as the power elite. Recent excavations by the Instituto Nacional de Antropología e Historia and the Teotihuacán Valley Project (Sanders 1965) point towards a considerably more militaristic orientation of Teotihuacán society than had been supposed.

The city apparently reached its maximum population in the Xolalpan phase. At this time it covered approximately 19 km^2 (Millon 1966), with an overall density of 4,500 persons per km^2. With respect to plan the Xolalpan city was divided into two zones—a central, planned, more densely settled area measuring 6.75 km^2 and an amorphous, less densely settled peripheral zone of 12 km^2. Within the core houses consisted of large multifamily complexes, each arranged around a central patio and enclosed by a compound. The sizes of the compounds varied but were apparently based on a grid of fifty-seven meters or divisions of fifty-seven, and were separated only by narrow alley-like streets. Millon estimates the population of the core at 40,000 persons living in an area of 5 km^2 (the remaining 1.75 km^2 of the core being occupied by avenues and civic buildings). The density of population in the core was therefore 5,200 persons per square kilometer; excluding the area of civic buildings and avenues, 8,000. Data on the population of the periphery are not yet well controlled, but he assumes a pattern of decreasing density. The overall density of this area is estimated at approximately 3,750 per km^2.

The demographic and settlement patterns at Teotihuacán are in striking contrast to those at Tikal (Carr and Hazard 1961). (Cf. Figures 7, 8.)

At Tikal a surface survey was conducted over a total area of 16 km², an area slightly smaller than Xolalpan phase Teotihuacán. Within this area 2,745 structures were mapped. Approximately 2,200 consisted of small stone platforms that functioned apparently as substructures for nuclear family houses built of pole-and-thatch. The platforms rarely occur singly but usually in groups of two, three, or four around the sides of small patios, probably the archaeological equivalent of extended families. The average number of platforms per square kilometer is calculated at 137. The house groups are not evenly distributed over the grid; rather they occur in hamlet-like aggregations separated by empty or lightly utilized spaces, these spaces being occupied primarily by swampy bajos or steep slopes. The hamlets tend to occur on relatively level ridge tops or natural terraces. The pattern is similar in density and distribution to rural settlement elsewhere in the Petén (Bullard 1960) and offers a striking contrast to Teotihuacán with its overall planning, avenues and streets, and high degree of congestion.

It is difficult to estimate the actual population residing within the 16 km². There is the problem of contemporaneity of occupation. Preliminary testing seems to indicate a gradual increase in number of houses from Middle Formative to Late Classic, and nearly all houses tested have a Late Classic occupation. Even if these preliminary data were interpreted as indicating contemporaneity of all houses during the final phase of the Classic, there are still the problems of the size of families, and of the use of specific structures within a house group. If we assume that each platform houses a nuclear family and that each nuclear family had an average membership of four persons, then the total population residing in the small houses would be calculated at 8,800 with a density of 548 persons per square kilometer. On the other hand, if each house group is considered as the residence of an extended family with portions of the structure used for storage, ritual, or communal cooking, then the figures could be significantly lower. Based on an early sixteenth-century census of Tepoztlán in Central Mexico, Carrasco (1964) estimates the average household size (nuclear and extended families combined) at 5.6 members. This could reduce the estimate of the population of Tikal to approximately 5,000 or a density of but 312 persons per square kilometer.

The density calculations of between 312 and 548 persons per square kilometer of lower class residents are far below those of any known urban community and yet exceed by a wide margin the potential of a rural population using swidden agriculture. How then to explain the settlement pattern at Tikal? Two possible models are suggested here:

1. Tikal was a macroceremonial center that drew its food supply from a much larger region based on tribute collecting. This plus the labor requirement for its mammoth building projects resulted in a relatively dense population that was supported in part by tax collection from outside and in part by local swidden agriculture. The population then would consist of part time farmers-laborers.

2. The probability exists that only a fraction of the residential structures were occupied simultaneously. As a general principle we would argue that the more dispersed is the settlement pattern of an archaeological site the less likely were the structures in contemporaneous use. Even in tightly nucleated settlements in Central Mexico today (Sanders 1965) up to 20 percent of the houses may be abandoned or unoccupied in any single year due to migration or extinction of family lines. With houses built of perishable materials the tendency towards abandonment would be greater. In areas of northern Yucatán today (Sanders 1962–3), where swidden agriculture provides the subsistence base, a high percentage of the population resides in settlements of hamlet size (below one hundred inhabitants), and entire settlements may be occupied for periods of only ten to twenty years. We

mention the possibility that at Tikal, therefore, component hamlet clusters may have been occupied for short periods of time, abandoned, and reused. The tendency for reuse of specific house sites would be intensified during the Classic period because of the use of masonry substructures. Maya ceramic chronology in current use would be unable to detect such shifts in residence since it deals in blocks of time of at least one century.

The balance of the structures at Tikal consist of public buildings (pyramid temples, large platforms, altar platforms, and ball courts) and apparently larger vaulted multiroomed masonry structures that were probably elite residences. These structures are grouped into complexes, arranged around masonry plazas, and connected by masonry causeways. The civic complexes occur on the tops of hills and high ridges and are concentrated into a central zone that covers 150 hectares. Almost certainly the elite residences were continuously occupied and could have housed a population of 2,000 or 3,000.

In summary, Tikal, the largest of the lowland Mesoamerican centers, probably had a population of 2,000 or 3,000 political, religious, and economic specialists plus an additional maximum of 8,800 or minimum of 2,000 or 3,000 part-time farmers-laborers-craftsmen, or full-time subsistence farmers, the latter residing in settlements of a distinctly rural type. This population cluster represents the maximum expression of nucleation during the Classic period in the swidden areas of Mesoamerica and was of course far below the levels of population size, density, and internal complexity Millon has demonstrated for Teotihuacán.

Other striking differences between Tikal and Teotihuacán are apparent in the scale and character of the civic architecture, and these differences surely reflect the differences between the agricultural potential of hydraulic as opposed to swidden agriculture on one hand, and the intensity of the political-imperialistic focus on the other. The huge compound defined by Millon that includes the Ciudadela and market measures nearly 1,000 by 500 meters. It covers as much ground as the total of all civic buildings at Tikal! There is no other building complex in Meso-america that so dramatically illustrates economic and political centralization as this enormous complex. When one adds to it the enormous pyramids of the Sun and the Moon with their associated building complexes the monumental scale of Teo-tihuacán staggers the imagination.

Since the excavations at Tres Zapotes, Kaminaljuyú, Uaxac-tún, and Monte Albán, researchers have noted the wide and pervasive influence of Teotihuacán on the contemporary regional civilizations of Mesoamerica. More recent research in the Gulf Coast and Highland and Lowland Maya areas has amplified this picture. In a previous section of this volume and in another context we mentioned briefly some of the implications of this contact.

The influence varies in nature and intensity from area to area and involves portable objects of clay and stone of which some were probably manufactured at Teotihuacán itself and others locally manufactured that either duplicate Teotihuacán objects or combine Teotihuacán and local styles. Also present are close copies or stylistic syncretism in nonportable stone sculpture and painting in the Teotihuacán art style. Of particu-lar significance is the presence of architecture that closely ap-proximates the stylistic characteristics of that of Teotihuacán itself. The reasons for stressing the diffusion of architecture as evidence of expansion of states are obvious: a local group may well purchase portable foreign objects as exotic household furni-ture or even bury them with their dead but (particularly where the local society has a highly evolved religious system) such a group does not voluntarily supply the manpower required for the construction of monumental civic buildings to serve foreign gods. The introduction of large-scale ceremonial architecture of a foreign style in a local sequence, therefore, is evidence that the foreign power in some manner has secured control over the surplus labor of a local population. Bennett (1946:143) in speaking of the diffusion of Inca architectural style in the Andes has stated:

> Archaeological evidence confirms the historical accounts of the center and spread of the *Inca* Empire. That the Cuzco region was the major center is indicated by the numerous important cities found there, and by the quantity of excellent *Inca* stone masonry. . . . As mentioned above, the distribution of *Inca* style can be traced by archaeological evidence and *Inca* mixture with local styles is easily demonstrated. In other words, even without historical documentation, the archaeological materials would reflect the powerful influence of the *Inca* throughout the whole area and the wide spread of the typical Cuzco style would suggest conquest.

In each case the stylistic syncretism replaces a rich, vigorous, highly developed, local stylistic tradition and strongly implies the acceptance of Teotihuacán religious concepts. Tlaloc, apparently the patron of Teotihuacán, is found represented in painting and sculpture in places as distant as Tikal and Kaminaljuyú. Typically, objects of Teotihuacán manufacture or local copies (the cylindrical tripod vase occurs repetitively in this respect and is considered, in fact, diagnostic of the Tzakol and Esperanza ceramic complexes) occur as part of the burial furniture of high status individuals. Most researchers have assumed that in great part this influence resulted either from mercantile contacts, possibly involving resident Teotihuacán merchants in foreign centers, or from religious pilgrimages.

The data from the Teotihuacán Valley Project (trophies of human bones, ritual cannibalism, and abundance of projectile points [Sanders 1965]) plus accumulating evidence of militarism from Teotihuacán art suggest otherwise. There is archaeological evidence of an organized program of enforced nucleation of scattered rural population into planned nucleated villages and towns in the Central Plateau during the final phase of the history of the city, somewhat parallel to the sixteenth-century *congregación* policy of the Spaniards. All of this points to a more imperialistic emphasis in Teotihuacán culture than has been previously suspected. The parallel in both the history of research and characteristics of the social system between Tiahuanaco in the Central Andes and Teotihuacán in Mesoamerica is truly extraordinary. In both cases early research revealed widespread pan-culture-areal diffusion involving ritual symbols and practices, the mechanics of which were assumed to be a combination of trade and pilgrimage networks; in both cases fuller documentation revealed a more secular, militaristic process.

The nature of the archaeological evidence of Teotihuacán influence in the Maya area reveals two distinct types of sociopolitical patterning, which would merit separate analytical models. In Highland Guatemala, at the site of Kaminaljuyú, it appears highly likely that we are dealing with a situation of actual colonization from the Central Plateau. Esperanza phase Kaminaljuyú represents at least a partial rebuilding of an earlier settlement as a replica of Teotihuacán, and Central Mexican influence in portable objects is similarly far-reaching. Given the distance and the difficulties of terrain separating these two sites, it would first of all seem exceptionally improbable that so great a degree of control could have been exerted in the absence of military force. Second, a political development of this nature itself requires explanation. A plausible one may lie in the unusually strategic location of Kaminaljuyú, which was in the Guatemala Highlands and in an excellent position from which to control access to the lowlands of the Pacific Coast Plain. This latter area, in Aztec times, comprised the province of Xoconusco, a principal cacao-growing region which was also an objective of the Aztec state. Political control of Kaminaljuyú by Teotihuacán would have given the latter a virtual monopoly of the highly lucrative cacao trade; what we are suggesting here is a Cacao Route, analogous to the Amber Route of Bronze Age Europe and the Jade Route of Middle Formative Mexico. Certainly such commerce would have acted as a powerful motivation to a Central Mexico-based state to maintain so distant a colony at no inconsiderable expense and difficulty, given the level of development of transportation and communication. In support of the postulated antiquity of this, a pattern well-documented for Tenochtitlán, Chapman (1957) observes that Xoconusco, of all the cacao-producing areas, was tributary to the Aztec state. The others had what she considers a port-of-trade status. According to her own hypothesis, trade preceded tribute, a pattern which, if true, would tend to support our conclusion of pre-Aztec Central Mexican political control of this area.

At Tikal, on the other hand, the archaeological evidence of actual political control is more equivocal. We have in a preceding section described the nature of the impact of Teotihuacán upon Tikal and feel that a model of mercantile and/or diplomatic contacts with the strong likelihood of a resident foreign enclave may explain the situation in the Maya Lowlands rather than the colonization model applicable to Kaminaljuyú. One obvious difficulty with the mercantile model lies in the paucity of exportable resources of the Lowland Maya. Importation of staples to the Meseta Central from so great a distance would have been uneconomical with primitive transportation and with the presence of many nearer and more exploitable sources. None of the principal luxury goods documented for later times originates in the Petén rain forest; cacao does not grow well, nor is jade found there. One may well ask what the inhabitants of Tikal were using to pay for their imported goods; there must have been a balance-of-payments problem of no mean proportion. Copal incense could be one possible answer, and another might be personnel. If, however, we regard the Petén as comprising part of a larger Guatemalan Symbiotic Region (Sanders 1956), Teotihuacán influence here might become more explicable in political terms as arising from the protection of the strategic colony of Kaminaljuyú, from which the Teotihuacán influence may have in fact emanated directly. The situation is not by any means clear, but the Lowland Maya situation does appear to be structured very differently from the Highland Maya one. At this level we are obviously dealing with problems in foreign policy of empire, and inference and reconstruction leave considerable room for debate.

Teotihuacán, because of the size of the religious architecture and apparent absence of a royal palace or palaces, does still seem more religious and less secular in orientation than, say, Tenochtitlán, and the power elite at Teotihuacán may well have been priests. Stating it another way, there was a single hierarchy of power at Teotihuacán in which secular and religious functions were combined, in contrast to the two separate bureaucracies of Tenochtitlán. Even at Tenochtitlán, however, the tlatoani was the ultimate religious authority and played a supervisory role in public ritual. The spread of Aztec political influence was accompanied by a spread of gods and ritualistic practices as well, so that the separation of state and temple was never complete.

Data from the Classic period in the areas of swidden cultivation demonstrate that the ceremonial center-hamlet settlement pattern has considerable time depth. Initiated in Middle Formative times and with the addition of macroceremonial centers in the Late Classic phase, the pattern persisted until the Spanish Conquest and, in some areas, into the present.

Ecological Processes

The differences between chiefdoms and civilizations, as we have previously observed, are both qualitative and quantitative. In the evolution of civilization two social processes were involved: (1) increasing size of society accompanied by those changes in social structure necessitated by such growth to provide continued, effective social integration and (2) increasing differentiation based on occupation, wealth, and power. There seems to be a continuum of development of these processes from band to tribe to chiefdom to nonurban civilization to urban civilization.

The three primary ecological processes involved in such societal development have been population growth, cooperation, and conflict in a microgeographically complex environment. Although other processes were undoubtedly at work, we believe that these ecological processes were of critical significance. Since the stage of societal development we have here defined as civilization is essentially an outgrowth and intensification of patterns found in the earlier chiefdom level, it will be useful at this point to briefly summarize our arguments concerning the ecological patterns and processes diagnostic of chiefdoms.

1. A variety of productive systems were developed, adapted to the various microecological niches.
2. Because of these locally specialized ecological systems, the response to population growth took the form of an increasingly intensive use of resources and specialization rather than emigration. The result was an increase in population density.
3. Competition between local groups in a varied environment over the primary resource (agricultural land) was intense. Because of variations in productivity, there was a corresponding variation in population density and consequently in the size of these groups within an area.
4. Prior to the formation of chiefdoms, the local groups were probably unilineal kin groups varying in size from lineages to clans with sodalities linking such groups horizontally as in tribal social systems.
5. Because of these variations in ecological adaptation, variations which are found not only in the productivity of the staple crop but also in specific food and other resources, there was a strong stimulus toward the development of institutions to facilitate exchange.
6. The response to these stimuli was the socioeconomic system that Service calls chiefdoms, in which particular local groups enjoying demographic superiority, were able to establish a

hierarchical social structure focused on a core lineage that monopolized power positions and acted as a distributive agency for locally specialized units.

7. The earlier phases of agricultural use of an area would tend to be characterized by extensive systems of cultivation. These are more productive, as measured by the critical ratio of food produced per hour of labor, and do not require initial and continued investment of labor in the construction of canals, dams, or terraces.

Since certain types of environments were more favorable than others, the chiefdoms in those areas tended to be larger in size and better able to control regional trade routes. Particularly vigorous chiefdoms were distributed in the South Gulf Coast, Chiapas–Guatemala Coast, Pacific Coast, and Guatemala Highlands. For both swidden and tlacolol cultivation these are prize areas. There seems to have been a particularly strong religious focus in these larger Formative chiefdoms, possibly as a technique of integrating dispersed settlements. This emphasis continued in the Classic and Postclassic periods as one of the distinctive characteristics of Mesoamerican civilization. It was particularly highly developed in the tropical lowland civilization as we have noted and correlated closely with Service's observation of the ritualized definition of the hierarchy in the social structure of chiefdoms.

The ecological processes outlined above and the geographical characteristics we have emphasized would apply to the entire region between northwestern Mexico and northwestern Argentina—the previously defined Nuclear America, throughout which at least a chiefdom level of social evolution was achieved. As has been pointed out, civilizations were limited to Mesoamerica and the Central Andes. We believe the reasons were ecological. Central America (that is, the area between Guatemala and Colombia) is a geographically diverse area, but it lacks entirely the Tierra Fría or Tierra Templada arid or subhumid components. Colombia and northern Ecuador, with respect to thermal zones, are as diverse as Mesoamerica, but both lack the arid highland components; in the case of Colombia, the high Andean area was intensively occupied only in the final pre-Hispanic period.

A major geographical difference between the Mesoamerican-Central Andean areas on one hand and the Intermediate Area on the other, therefore, was the presence in the former areas of extensive regions of arid highland or coastal environments conducive to the development of hydraulic agriculture.

Mesoamerica differs from the Central Andes in that one particular highland area tended to dominate the political and economic development of Mesoamerica during the Classic and Postclassic periods. Prior to this point, we have simply referred to this area as "Central Mexico," the "Central Plateau and neighboring southern escarpment" or the "heartland of Central Mexico." Sanders has referred to it as either the Central Mexican Symbiotic Region (1956) or Nuclear Mesoamerica (1962). It was, as we have noted, the main scene of development of hydraulic agriculture in Mesoamerica. (See Figure 10, p. 192.)

The Central Mexican Symbiotic Region includes the Central Plateau and adjacent southern escarpment. In a broad sense it includes the modern states of Michoacán, Mexico, Puebla, Tlaxcala, Morelos, and northern Guerrero but within it is a smaller core where the majority of the population was concentrated in 1519. This core was the center of the two Postclassic pan-Mesoamerican empires, Toltec and Aztec, and in Early Classic times was the location of Teotihuacán, the most vigorous of all of the great Classic civilizations of Mesoamerica. It may have been one of the places of origin of Mesoamerican agriculture and of sedentary village life, and played a significant role in the evolution of chiefdoms. In short there is no area of comparable size in Mesoamerica that played such a vital role in the overall history of the region.

With respect to our classification of Mesoamerican environments the core consists of two parallel east-west strips. One, to the north, includes two plateau basins (Mexico and Puebla) located above 2,000 m. (our Tierra Fría zone) and with annual rainfall falling generally in the subhumid category; the other, to the south, is a strip of escarpment drained by the Amacusac river system that falls into our Tierra Templada subhumid category. The significant characteristics of the area for the evolution of civilizations were the great range of elevation, generally dry climate, relatively large but internally complex and circumscribed zones of good agricultural land, water for irrigation and the chain of the lakes in the Basin of Mexico that provided a setting for chinampa agriculture, a rich source of animal protein foods, and a medium for efficient transportation of bulky goods to the urban markets. Particularly important was the contrast between the Tierra Templada with its longer growing season for tropical crops and its potential all-year cropping and the Tierra Fría with its more restricted crop complex and shorter growing season but much more extensive plains and lake products. In the Colonial and Republican periods of Mexican history there is abundant documentation of the intense trade between these two strips.

In contrast, in the Central Andes there was no single area that played a comparable historical role; instead, centers of political and economic power tended to shift from one small valley to another. The only other comparable Mesoamerican area of arid to subhumid highland environment is found in the Sierra Madre del Sur of Oaxaca and Guerrero, but the valleys are small, comparable in size to those of the Central Andes; and, like the latter, tend to be more cut off from each other by vast tracts of marginal to unusable, dissected terrain which makes intercommunication difficult. The largest such topographical unit in Oaxaca is the Valley of Oaxaca, with a surface area of only 700 km².

In Central Mexico the core area is divided by mountains into three large, mutually accessible basins. The Basin of Mexico plus the adjacent upper Pánuco (Tula River) Valley has a surface area of 8,000 km². The adjacent West Tlaxcala—Cholula–Atlixco Plain and Amacusac Basin have surface areas of 4,000 km² each. Around this core were plateau surfaces and mountain basins of comparable size (East Puebla–Tlaxcala, Valley of Toluca, Valley of Tulancingo), easily accessible to the core and of lesser, but still considerable, population density. This huge stretch of arid to semiarid highlands covered a surface area of nearly 35,000 km² and had a population of between 2 million to 3 million in 1519. This is equivalent to the entire population of the Intermediate Area and over half the population of the Central Andes in the sixteenth century. The core measured 20,000 km² and had a population of 1.5 million to 2.25 million inhabitants in 1519.

In our discussion of the history of civilizations in Mesoamerica the extraordinary historical role of Teotihuacán during the Early Classic period has been emphasized. This critical role included one of political dominance comparable in nature to that exercised by the Late Classic-Postclassic centers located in the same region. If anything (in spite of what may have been a considerably smaller demographic base), the centralization of power seems, on the basis of the archaeological evidence, to have been even greater than that of Tenochtitlán. Since we feel that this dominance is based on ecological factors, we attempt to clarify these factors and relate them to the evolution of Mesoamerican civilization.

The two characteristics of the ecological system of the Central Mexican area that were the primary stimuli toward evolution of urban civilization were hydraulic agriculture and economic symbiosis. We shall examine first the hydraulic agriculture hypothesis.

Characteristic of a civilized population are the presence of large numbers of non-food-producing specialists—economic, political, and religious—and sociopolitical organization on a large scale, both vertical and horizontal. Since these specialists must be supported by the surplus production of others, a productive agricultural economy is essential. The fact that the agricultural and transportation technologies of Mesoamerica were primitive placed a premium on intensive patterns of land use, the ideal being a very dense population concentrated into a relatively small area. The less dense the population, the larger the territory needed and the greater the consequent strain on socioeconomic integration. Irrigation, terracing, and chinampa agriculture provided precisely that type of subsistence base.

In irrigation agriculture primary and secondary canals must be excavated and cleaned annually by cooperative labor; the larger the system, the greater the size of the organized labor force required. This cooperative labor must be planned and organized. Although in theory this can be done by decentralized and relatively informal arrangements among groups of politically autonomous or at least nonhierarchical units, it is much more effective when there is a state-like social structure. The larger the system, the greater the necessity that formal patterns of authority be established.

Some irrigation cooperatives are based on local water sources so small that they are of subcommunity or community size. Since they are small, the same informal patterns of control and group organizations that are effective in small non-hydraulic societies work well. When a large number of socially and physically discrete settlements are involved, however, especially when the pattern is one of intensive agriculture in areas of severely limited land and water resources, conflicts arise which require or stimulate more formal patterns of delegation of authority. There is, therefore, considerable variation in the social aspects of irrigation agriculture. The crucial variables seem to be the amount of the land dependent upon a single integrated system and the proportion and economic significance of irrigated to nonirrigated land used by the cooperative.

Aside from the organizational requirements of cooperative labor and maintenance, cooperation is also necessary to regulate water distribution so that each farmer and each community receives water. While this task may or may not be accomplished by centralization of authority, such centralization is undoubtedly the most efficient solution. One of the most common sources of conflict among modern communities in the Valley of Teotihuacán today is over the water allotment because in the Valley the supply of water is less than that of land. When a system of centralized authority for water allocation is established, hydraulic agriculture provides that authority with an extraordinarily effective weapon against recalcitrant peasants or communities—the withholding of water. The result can be a very despotic political system.

Agricultural systems may, therefore, play an economic role (essentially a permissive role, that is, that of productivity) or a social role (in that cooperation on a supracommunity scale is required) in the evolution of civilization. Chinampa and terrace cultivation involve only the economic role; neither normally requires large cooperative undertakings for success. Terrace agriculture, however, does stimulate at least suprafamily cooperation in that the maintenance of the entire terrace system is vital to the continued productivity of each and all of the individual components. Although one disintegrating terrace jeopardizes the entire system, it would be rare for such mutual needs to involve stable units above that of the local community. They may involve such cooperation (examples are state-organized terrace construction in Peru and state-constructed dikes in Lakes Xochimilco–Chalco to control chinampa flooding), but such high levels of cooperation are usually undertaken when the development of both the agricultural techniques and the state has already achieved a high level of maturity. Irrigation is the only agricultural technique of the three that has, even in its formative development, both economic and social effects in the development of civilizations.

The most elaborate presentation of the preceding theoretical construct is undoubtedly that of Wittfogel in his book *Oriental*

Despotism (1957). His ideas are summarized more compactly in his 1955 paper, a brief resumé of which follows:

1. Wittfogel uses the term "hydraulic agriculture" for a system of agriculture that is based on large-scale government-directed water control and construction of water works. He uses the term "hydraulic societies" for societies that possess such works, whose social evolution is functionally correlated with their construction, and who have "inordinately strong governments." Such societies are centered around the state; there are no other institutions capable of competing with it.

2. The basic institutional features of hydraulic societies included control of private property, monopolistic bureaucracy, incorporation of church with state, and the unchallenged role of the state as a principal entrepreneur of public works, especially hydraulic.

3. Not all hydraulic societies were equally evolved in the characteristics listed above. As Wittfogel states, they vary in "hydraulic and managerial density." He correlates these variations with the degree of significance of irrigated versus nonirrigated land in the economy of the particular group. The term "Compact Hydraulic Society" refers to those situations where the majority of cultivated land is irrigated and a high percentage of land holders are therefore under the direct control of the state. "Loose Hydraulic Societies" are those where there is a sizable amount of nonirrigated land. He also uses the term "Marginal Hydraulic Society" for cases in which irrigation is lacking, but where the societal characteristics are present as the product of introduction of such techniques from a hydraulic society.

With respect to the evolution of hydraulic society he postulates several basic stages. The first stage involves a large number of separate community irrigation systems. The pueblos of the American Southwest are cited as an example of this developmental stage.

The second stage involves the evolution of a "hydraulic region," a relatively large area with a single, integrated system controlled by a dominant community. If such a stage occurs in a desert area, then a compact hydraulic society evolves; if there is rainfall and a considerable amount of nonirrigated land, a loose hydraulic society is the result. He also suggests that in areas such as the Near East, loose hydraulic societies may have preceded compact hydraulic societies in the nearby mountain areas, and that irrigation was introduced into Mesopotamia by a loose hydraulic society. Its managerial density, he suggests, increased as it adapted to the desert conditons. He postulates a final stage when the compact hydraulic state established hegemony over nonhydraulic or loose hydraulic societies in supraregional empires. In this stage there is a decline in the density of the hydraulic bureaucracy, and the overall society becomes a loose hydraulic society. This type is the product of two processes. First, the incorporation of land not served by the hydraulic system and therefore not subject to the same controls; concomitantly there is increased complexity of the property tenure system, with private land holdings as well as those of community and state. Second, as the limits of the potential wealth based directly on irrigation agriculture are reached, there is increasing emphasis upon the importance of commercial specialization. Further development results in a type of society he calls "semi-complex" rather than "complex" hydraulic society because the state is still the supreme economic power and is involved in the new sources of wealth.

Few attempts were made to discuss the role of irrigation in the evolution of Mesoamerican civilization until Armillas published his 1949 paper, "Notas Sobre los Sistémas de Cultívo en Mesoamerica." Prior to this, Spinden (1928) suggested briefly and without elaboration the probably crucial role of irrigation in the beginnings of Mesoamerican civilization.

As a result of stimulus from Armillas, a theoretical school has developed in recent years and several people have written extensively on the subject. Following Armillas, Steward (1949), West and Armillas (1950), Palerm and Wolf (1961), Millon (1954, 1957), Wolf (1959), and Sanders (1965) have all stressed the importance of hydraulic agriculture in the evolution of the civilization of the Central Mexican area. Most of this research has involved analyses of documentary references to Aztec period irrigation and archaeological identification of Aztec systems. These studies have demonstrated conclusively the economic and integrative role of irrigation in the Central Plateau for that period and have focused attention on the role of the Aztec states as entrepreneurs of hydraulic works. Based on the relative amounts of irrigated versus nonirrigated land, a loose hydraulic society certainly existed in the area in 1519.

The major problem has been archaeological, that of establishing the antiquity of irrigation and of hydraulic society and of evaluating their roles in the genesis and growth of Mesoamerican civilization as a whole. It is theoretically possible that hydraulic agriculture began in Aztec times and that the civilizations of Teotihuacán, Tula, Xochicalco, and the pre-Aztec Cholula were not based on hydraulic agriculture. We feel, however, that this is highly improbable. Of course, even if it could be demonstrated that irrigation agriculture developed contemporaneously with the earliest civilization in the area, there still remains the difficult problem of evaluating in an archaeological setting the cause-effect relationship between hydraulic agriculture and civilization.

Millon (1962) and Millon *et al.* (1962) have published two papers in an attempt to qualify the absoluteness of theoretical assumptions of the interaction between irrigation and centralized political systems. Using an essentially comparative and synchronic method in his paper "Variations in Response to the Practice of Irrigation Agriculture," he evaluates the correlation between small irrigation systems and centralized authority. Seven small contemporary irrigation systems from East Africa, Ceylon, Japan, Bali, Iraq, Arabia, and Mexico (the Teotihuacán system) are compared. We summarize his conclusions as follows:

The use of irrigation by a community or group of communities clearly introduces a special factor that is potentially both integrative and disruptive in social interaction. The operation of the system requires cooperation but may produce conflicts, especially in those situations where the supply of one critical component, water or land, acts as a limiting factor. In the management of small irrigation systems a variety of arrangements is possible. No absolute relationship exists between the size of a small irrigation system and the degree of centralization of authority in its utilization.

The emphasis was upon small systems because Millon has been concerned in his research with the role of irrigation in Central Mexican culture history, and all of the systems in that area may be classified—in his terms—as "small." His conclusions are undoubtedly valid as far as they go, but there are a number of methodological problems and implicit assumptions in his study that are open to serious argument and question.

Although undoubtedly Millon did not intentionally convey this impression, nevertheless there is the implicit assumption in his discussion that ecological adaptation is static. Obviously, if one conducts a purely synchronic study such as this one, there is always the problem of time and the level of success of adaptation of a people to an area. For example, the El Shabana of Iraq, one of his sample groups, were apparently recent immigrants into the area and were formerly pastoralists! The evolution of any ecological system requires time, and as we have stated, a particular group may not necessarily select initially the most effective solution to an ecological problem. Our argument is that over a long period of time the practice of irrigation presents certain problems and stimuli, and that there is a strong selective force analogous to biological natural selection in favor of centralized control. The overall history of Iraq certainly justifies this assumption.

A second assumption is that a local group with an irrigation system organized along essentially traditional lines is free to resolve the problems of conflict and cooperation. In all cases cited by Millon the irrigation cooperative was a unit within a larger national political and social system. He cites cases in both Japan and the Teotihuacán Valley where federal troops intervened in conflict situations to prevent physical combat between communities. As we shall argue later, conflict is probably one of the major stimuli to the evolution of centralized control in history of irrigation systems.

Several of the examples employed, the Sonjo of East Africa, Pul Eliya in Ceylon and the Nahid in Arabia, involve social groups so small (single communities in the case of the first two) that traditional kin ties would be sufficient to integrate the society regardless of the absence or presence of irrigation. The same really applies to Bali, where although the individual cooperatives do crosscut village lines, they involve a population of only 5,500 to 7,500 people each. In Millon's study the only two samples that are really comparable in that they are both relatively large supra-community systems with a respectable antiquity are the cases of a group of twelve villages in Japan and the Teotihuacán Valley system involving sixteen villages. The latter is centralized, the former is not. It is interesting to note that in both cases the national government has had to intervene to prevent warfare over water rights. In summary, all of his examples are of groups within highly altered, evolved, secondary or tertiary states.

In the second paper "Conflict in the Modern Teotihuacán Irrigation System" Millon *et al.* elaborate on the disruptive effects of an irrigation system with insufficient water to supply the available irrigable land. He stresses conflict between upstream and downstream cultivators over the theft of water by upstream communities, conflict over the right of Atlatongo to a permanent supply of water from the San José Canal, conflicts between ejidatarios and "proprietarios pequeños," and between users of the San José and San Antonio Canals which both derive water from a single source.

The theoretical position defended here is that it is precisely this conflict that stimulates the selective process in favor of centralization of authority—the more severe the conflict, the greater the need for and probable evolution of centralized control. One of the significant facts that emerges from his discussions in the 1962 papers is that such systems do not work effectively unless there is a highly centralized authority.

Other arrangements may be possible or workable, but this does not negate the principle that a functional relationship exists between centralized power and relatively large irrigation systems, or that the former is an effective solution to the problem of the operation of the latter. If population growth is one of the major achievements of the evolution of ecological systems, then the development of centralized control of irrigation systems can be readily understood. It controls conflict within the cooperative, permits a more efficient use of water and land, and provides the cooperative with an economic and organizational advantage over groups external to the system.

Adams in three papers—"The Origin of Cities" (1960a), "Early Civilizations, Subsistence and Environment" (1960b), "A Synopsis of the Historical Demography and Ecology of the Diyala River Basin, Central Iraq" (1962a)—and a book—*The Evolution of Urban Society* (1966)—has also challenged the functional relationships between irrigation and warfare on one hand, and the rise of cities and states in Mesopotamia on the other. His major criticism is based on the sequence of events as reflected by archaeological data from Mesopotamia. Most writers on Mesopotamian history (cf. Childe 1957; Frankfort 1951) have been convinced of the economic and social-integrative role of irrigation in the evolution of Mesopotamian states. They have also argued that the history of Mesopotamia is one of coalescence of small centers into large ones as the result of wars fought over land and water resources. The growth of large centers and that of states in Mesopotamia were apparently correlative processes, so that the term city-state is frequently and cogently applied. Adams' major criticism is based on the following considerations.

In Late Predynastic and Early Dynastic times the population of Mesopotamia resided in a series of compact, tightly nucleated towns and cities each with its own isolated zone of irrigated land. This agricultural zone was irrigated by a series of short-length canals that breached the natural levees bordering the streams and even on a local level were not integrated into a master system. Each town or city was surrounded by a zone of artificially irrigated land; the zones were separated from others by marshes, unimproved desert, pasture, and areas of either floodwater or rainfall agriculture. The ethnic and ecological components of the area were therefore complex, with hydraulic farmers, fishermen, extensive cultivators, and herdsmen.

Large multistate integrated irrigation systems did not appear until the Iron Age. He argues therefore that states long predated the kinds of large irrigation systems that might engender power structures of the type that Wittfogel defines as hydraulic and that furthermore both land and water were sufficiently abundant so that competition over such resources could not have been a major factor in their growth.

We comment on his arguments as follows: His picture of the Sumerian town or city state is strikingly similar to the ecological characteristics we have outlined for the sixteenth-century Aztec. The interdigiting of hydraulic and nonhydraulic zones plus the additional components of fishermen and herdsmen with the consequent unevenness of demographic potentials of each economic pattern would stimulate competition and power systems of the Central Mexican type.

Frankfort analyzes Predynastic society as being composed of a number of nucleated, autonomous, spatially isolated temple communities dedicated to the worship of a single god. The god owned the land and canal system, the temple was his residence, and the attached population his tenants. Within this "household" were the priests, his "administrators," professional craftsmen, and farmers. Presumably such a household included the outlying population components noted by Adams as well as the residents of the nucleated towns. Each temple household involved a centralized control of resources, production, and distribution: The land was owned by the god; seed and draft animals were provided by his administrators; and the temple was a public granary, craft workshop, and redistribution agent. This structure resembled in many ways the chiefdoms described by Service with the difference that the system focused on the position of the god rather than a chief. These chiefdoms were small in size, numbering perhaps only a few thousand members each.

In Early Dynastic times, Frankfort argues, such town-temple estates coalesced into cities. In the Sumerian city the temple estate continued to function and the population was divided up into a number of these temple estates each with its own patron god, priestly order, craftsmen, and tenant farmers. Although many of the elements of chiefdom structure persisted, the larger community required a more formal political system and a new position—the "lugal" or secular dynast—was created. Although markets remained incipiently developed in Early Dynastic Sumeria there was an increasing tendency for the craftsmen to produce goods for sale and a market economy was emerging. By the end of the fourth millenium B.C. all of the characteristics we have defined as civilization were fully evolved.

In answer to Adams' arguments we would respond therefore as follows. In all probability the small canal systems in Predynastic and Early Dynastic times were administered by the temple estates and therefore we can postulate a correlation between their control and the emergence of first a chiefdom, then a state-like political system. The local Early Dynastic Sumerian canal systems were individually as large as the Central Mexican systems. Such local systems were therefore individually large enough to have played an integrative role in the growth of the state. In his 1962 study Adams shows in detail a history of gradual nucleation of villages into towns and towns into cities, all linked with the development of the aforementioned local systems. In other words, the city-state itself was the significant irrigation cooperative, not all of Mesopotamia. The evolution of supersystems involving large areas of the Mesopotamian plain is simply the end product of a process that began on a local level. The sequence of events in Mesopotamia of growth of society from village to town to city to regional state in reality is a striking demonstration of the interaction between hydraulic agriculture and large societies.

With respect to the warfare hypothesis, Adams admits the importance of the role of warfare in the social evolution of Mesopotamia. If they were not fighting over land and water, what were they fighting over? Mesopotamian tax records seem to point clearly to an economic motivation in war. We feel that Adams' error here is in assuming that war over land and water means war over unimproved desert and uncontrolled rivers. In reality an irrigation system represents an enormous investment in capital and labor. In the setting of ancient Sumeria when the population of a city state outgrew its irrigated zone, that state was faced with two alternatives: expansion of the system, or the conquest of neighboring states and regularized exploitation of their established irrigation systems by means of tribute. The latter is actually a more economic response. The conflict was therefore over canal systems and improved land.

The small size of the individual hydraulic areas in Central Mexico (none of them supported a population in excess of 100,000 persons in 1519) would seem to weaken our argument concerning the significance of irrigation in the evolution of states. If one considers, however, the interplay of the two processes of competition and cooperation within the geographical setting of Central Mexico, the role of hydraulic agriculture seems clear. The complex interdigiting of hydraulic and non-hydraulic zones with their consequent variations in population density, the short distances between hydraulic zones, and the dramatic contrast in productivity between hydraulic and non-hydraulic agriculture in a sharply circumscribed environment would provide an extremely competitive social environment. The combination of a system of agriculture that requires coopera-tion, the consequent uneven distribution of population, and a competitive social environment would all act to stimulate the development of highly organized, centralized political systems. Once the communities of a hydraulic zone were organized in this fashion the resultant state would enjoy an obvious competitive advantage over neighboring nonhydraulic zones and more dis-tant hydraulic zones of smaller size or less efficient organization.

By a process of imperialistic expansion into these other areas, larger political systems would result which in turn would be in an advantageous position with regard to wider regional con-figurations. The Basin of Mexico was consistently a center of power because of the unusual number and close spacing of hydraulic zones. By this process a very small hydraulic zone (in the case of the Teotihuacán Valley a maximal size of 50 km² of permanently irrigated land served by a single permanent source of water and perhaps an additional 50 km² of floodwater-irrigated plain) could play an exceptionally critical role in the evolution of even the largest Mesoamerican states.

We believe that it is in this way especially that the Central Mexican ecological pattern differs from that in the Lowlands. Previously discussed was the role of variations in the produc-tivity of the natural environment of the Gulf Coast in the evolu-tion of Formative chiefdoms. The differences, however, are neither quantitatively nor qualitatively comparable to those between hydraulic and nonhydraulic zones within Central Mex-ico. Furthermore, hydraulic agriculture, in contrast to swidden agriculture, permits, because of its greater productivity, larger social aggregations with the same level of transportation and communication, and these larger aggregations stimulate in turn more effective levels of social integration. The result was the transformation of the chiefdom level of social structure into states.

We are calling the second ecological process in the evolution of Central Mexican civilization symbiosis (cf. Sanders 1956). If from the broad evolutionary viewpoint the primary function of the hydraulic process is the improvement of subsistence, the primary function of the symbiotic process is the efficient procurement of raw materials and finished technology although subsistence may be directly or indirectly involved. By symbiosis is meant the economic interdependence of social and physical population units in a given region to the advantage of all. In a broad sense symbiosis is characteristic of all human social interaction; even the family as a social group is essentially an economic partnership with divisions of labor on the bases of age and sex. No human community has probably ever been completely self-sufficient. What particularly characterizes civilization is the intensity of such specialization and exchange and the size and complexity of the component units involved.

In this brief survey of Mesoamerican biophysical environments we have noted that the one striking, salient characteristic of the area as a whole is its extraordinary diversity. The tight microgeographical zoning results in a corresponding diversity and highly localized distribution of raw materials. In the discussion of chiefdoms this question was posed: How can a small community situated in a given area obtain the raw materials or finished products necessary for the maintenance of a stable economy? Several possible methods were suggested: Periodic raids on the territory of the haves by the have-nots; informal and formal trade between mutually hostile groups via some ceremonial safe-conduct institution like the Kula; a chiefdom type of social structure in which the chief acts as a focus of redistribution of surpluses. The last approach clearly is a more efficient one, but chiefdom social and economic institutions work effectively only under conditions of relatively small areas and populations. Another response, and one capable of resolving the problem on a much greater scale, is organized trade based on markets and part- or full-time community specialization.

McBryde's superb analysis of patterns of trade and specialization in the Southwest Highlands of Guatemala (1947) is a good example of this level of development; such systems, however, are difficult to maintain except when the communities are part of some larger sociopolitical structure such as a regional state. Wholly aside from the need of a peaceful and stable political climate for the successful establishment of such economic patterns, the traditional, repetitive market encounters of people from different communities would tend to produce a feeling of community of interests and social identification that should act as a subtle integrative factor. Whether market systems precede states or are made possible by states is not really pertinent here. The important consideration here is that they are functionally related.

On the basis of diversity of needs and mutual interdependence of zones, Mesoamerica may be divided into a series of regions for which the term "Symbiotic Region" is useful. Each consists of zones of contrasting environments, and each has a highland and a lowland component. Highland Chiapas and Lowland Tabasco, for example, would comprise a Symbiotic Region, as do the Central Plateau and Central Veracruz, and Highland and Pacific Coast Guatemala. In the case of none of these Symbiotic Regions is the association of component zones with each other inevitable. A Symbiotic Region is therefore not rigidly bounded or circumscribed; Highland Guatemala, for example, could just as easily form a unit with the Petén (and in Classic and Late Formative times probably did) or with Pacific Coastal Guatemala; and Highland Chiapas with either Pacific Coastal Chiapas or the Tabascan plain. The interrelationships of the components of these regions are complex and overlapping.

We have little patience with attempts to derive complex manifestations from single sources via simple cultural processes, and are not implying that all of the regional cultures of Mesoamerica derive their specific characteristics from Central Mexico. As has been made abundantly clear, the theoretical emphases of this book are evolutionistic and ecological, with each regional variant of Mesoamerican civilization seen as the product of essentially local processes. However, the implication of the concept of economic symbiosis is that when areas were in constant historic contact, such contacts were a primary force in the enrichment of local cultural traditions. It is also evident that a number of areas acted more frequently as donors than as recipients, or, in other words, that events there had greater repercussions on the area as a whole. This is where the Central Mexican Symbiotic Region is outstanding. Its uniqueness was, we believe, the product of its peculiar geographical characteristics. In no other Symbiotic Region of Mesoamerica do we find both highland and lowland components in which intensive agriculture and dense population were so characteristic.

There seems to be a general correlation between population density and the degree of symbiosis. Darwin in 1859 noted that even in plants and infrahuman animals there is a marked increase of specialization as the density of living creatures increases in a given area. Later Durkheim (1933) applied this principle to humans and discussed the relationship between symbiosis and population density. The denser the population the greater the competition over the prime resource, agricultural land, and the greater the stimulus toward agricultural or non-agricultural specialization. Intensive agriculture in small, artificially productive areas such as the core lands of hydraulic societies is perhaps one of the most powerful stimuli to such specialization.

This process works in several ways. On the level first of food production some crops are basic foodstuffs (for example, maize) that vary however in their maturation by ecological zone; others are highly prized but consumed in small quantities (for example, chile peppers); some are demanding in soil and water requirements (maize), others of temperature (tomatoes), while still others are tolerant of a greater range of conditions. The solution is a regional system of agricultural specialization in which particular farmers in particular localities may grow only particular crops. Intensive agriculture, in contrast to extensive cultivation, produces shortages even in basic raw materials for peasant technology. For example, villagers in the lower parts of the Basin of Mexico must purchase all of their wood products, in some cases even firewood, since the natural vegetation has been completely destroyed by agricultural activities. On the Gulf Coast, on the other hand, where slash-and-burn cultivation with its succession of cultivated fields and forest in various stages of regrowth is practiced, each farmer has such raw materials in his holding.

In the case of the Central Mexican Symbiotic Region the stimulus is further increased by the mountainous terrain. The combination of tropical latitude and great altitudinal range has provided an extraordinary variety of environments, each with specific resources and each presenting somewhat different problems to primitive cultivation. This variability is based on the behavior of frosts, temperature, rainfall, vegetation, absence or presence of lakes, and topography. The intense microgeographical zoning, with many diverse ecological niches in close proximity to each other, must have acted as a powerful stimulus to local specialization of production. Combined with the demographic growth and the increasingly intensive methods of land use attested to by the archaeological data, the selective pressure would have been heavily in favor of the development of trade and the establishment of stable symbiotic patterns. The importance of trade, and the volume of such trade correlative with the density of population, would lead to additional local specialization, in nonagricultural as well as agricultural production.

In summary, the evolution of Central Mexican civilization can be conceptualized as the product of the three ecological processes mentioned: population growth, competition, and cooperation in a unique environmental setting. Extensive agriculture

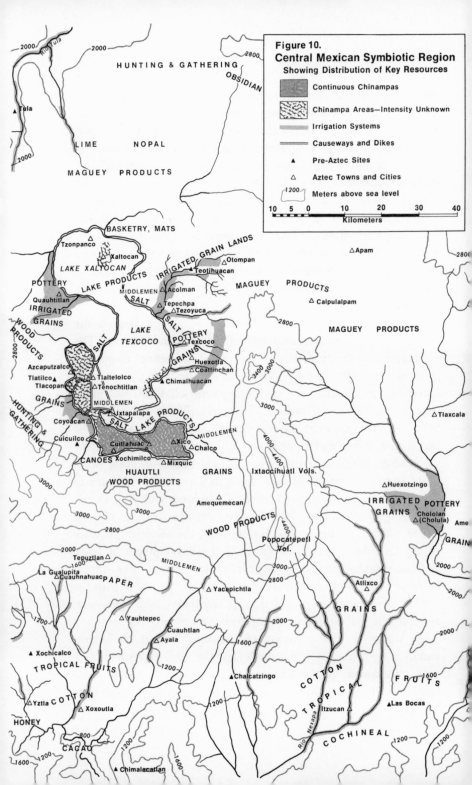

Figure 10.
Central Mexican Symbiotic Region
Showing Distribution of Key Resources

	Continuous Chinampas
	Chinampa Areas—Intensity Unknown
	Irrigation Systems
	Causeways and Dikes
▲ | Pre-Aztec Sites
△ | Aztec Towns and Cities
1200 | Meters above sea level

10 5 0   10   20   30   40
Kilometers

with a balanced nutritional complex resulted in population growth in an unusually variable environment with exceptionally sharply circumscribed ecological niches. As these niches became completely occupied, new methods of cultivation developed in response to population pressure that permitted in turn still denser populations. One of these methods, hydraulic agriculture, involves a subtle interaction of competition and cooperation, both within the hydraulic zone and in the relationship of a hydraulic to other zones, that favored the evolution of the state from an earlier chiefdom level. The complex environment combined with the special characteristics of intensive agriculture to stimulate first the development of the chiefdom type of economic specialization and distribution and, ultimately, of market systems that provided another dimension to large group integration.

Up to this point the discussion has been concerned only with the evolution of civilization generally in Central Mexico. The ecological factors that led to urbanism have not been discussed. The presence of large urban centers in Central Mexico has been one of the most intriguing problems of New World archaeology. The development of urbanism in Central Mexico, as in Mesopotamia, was, we believe, correlated with the development of the state and can be viewed as an outgrowth of the same basic processes.

In order to clarify the following discussion, it would be worthwhile to repeat the definition of urbanism presented in Chapter I. Urbanism was defined as a complex of three interrelated processes: population growth, socioeconomic differentiation, and, particularly, *nucleation*. The first two are major processes in the evolution of civilization generally. The particularly distinctive characteristic of urbanism is the concentration of a *large socioeconomically differentiated population into a single physical community*.

In the case of Central Mexico, urbanization seems to have been a local process. We have previously traced the evolution of Central Mexican society through the levels of band, tribe, chiefdom, and civilization. In this reconstruction true cities appeared with Teotihuacán and the achievement of civilization. Urbanism might possibly have evolved from a tribal pattern in the same area that included large, nucleated, nonurban settlements. Nucleation of population into large physical units has certain advantages and disadvantages even with a tribal level of social structure. Social integration may be more easily achieved in the case of a population residing in large nucleated settlements. If, furthermore, the social setting is one of competition, there would be obvious military advantages in this settlement pattern even at this lower level of integration. There are, of course, disadvantages; if the economic livelihood of the community is agriculture, a nucleated settlement is obviously less convenient than one with houses dispersed among the land holdings in smaller territorial units.

Nonurban (both tribal and rural) settlement patterns may be viewed as the product of three sets of factors: direct environmental (water supply, topography, and so forth), social, and economic. With respect to social structure, nuclear families, extended families, lineages, clans, or demes have a strong tendency to be expressed as physically differentiated entities. A nonurban population above the band level dispersed in nuclear family homesteads, however, is extremely rare and tends to be found in areas of commercial agriculture in modern industrial states. Apparently the need for protection, for some level of economic cooperation and desire for social contacts in preindustrial societies leads to communities larger than the nuclear family. The level at which communities stabilize seems to be the product of primarily economic factors, particularly the type of agriculture practiced.

We are not arguing here for an absolute causal relationship between economic factors and settlement type. Settlement patterns in any given historical situation are the product of a complex balance of a great number of factors. What we are saying is that economic factors, particularly the subsistence system, are critical variables in the expression of nonurban settlement pattern. We would also argue that since there is greater stability in the subsistence system than in most of the other factors involved, it will tend to be the dominant factor over long periods of time.

Theoretically, it is always more convenient for a farmer to reside near his agricultural land. If the agricultural system is extensive as in the case of swidden, and a considerable amount of land is required to maintain the population, then there would be strong pressures against residence in large nucleated settlements. It would be inconvenient to get to and from fields and particularly so to transport the harvest on human backs from field to home. On the other hand, as we have noted, completely dispersed settlement is very rare. The result is usually a compromise with the population distributed in a great number of small nucleated settlements that Sanders (1957) has referred to as hamlets. These are frequently no larger in size than the band and are frequently occupied by a single lineage. This seems to have been the most common settlement type for the Maya area. The more intensive the agriculture, on the other hand, the greater the variability of settlement patterns. Hydraulic farmers particularly may reside in a great variety of settlement types.

External factors such as conquest states may in specific historical situations impose alien and basically unstable patterns. In the sixteenth century, to facilitate conversion and taxation the Spanish imposed a vast, ambitious program of resettlement of the native population into larger nucleated communities—the *congregación*. This was applied all over Mesoamerica regardless of the enormous variations in ecology. In Central Mexico where agriculture was intensive and a native pattern of larger nucleated settlements was already in existence, the program involved only minor readjustments. In Yucatán it met with considerable resistance, and the sixteenth-century population decline (unlike the situation in most of Mesoamerica, where it is attributed to foreign diseases), is blamed on the *congregación* policy. The *Relaciones Geográficas* are replete with references to the hardships produced by the policy: Communities established by the Spaniards lost from one-half to two-thirds of their populations in the forty years between 1540 and 1580.

Generally, however, the program was successful in Yucatán, where the majority of the Maya today reside in large nucleated settlements. Factors promoting stability were the vigilance of the Colonial administration, a native tradition for organization of large societies, relative population stability during the period between 1600 and 1900, introduction of beasts of burden in the sixteenth century and in the twentieth century, highways and bus transport (modern Maya travel in buses to milpas 30 to 40 kilometers from their villages), commercial agriculture and part-time craft specialization within the context of modern transportation and national economy. Although the nucleated settlements established by the Spaniards have survived, all over Yucatán there is a strong tendency for proliferation of satellite hamlets whose populations are extremely unstable. Farmers may shift residence from permanent village to hamlet, move on in ten years to another hamlet, or return to the village. In some districts over half the population in a single year resides in such temporary settlements (cf. Sanders 1962–3).

In the Philippines in a setting of swidden agriculture and dispersed settlement the *congregación* policy was a complete failure. In this case the factors were probably a combination of the weakness of the Spanish administrative control and lack of native institutions to organize large societies effectively.

It is possible that at various times in the pre-Hispanic period the native states attempted such programs of resettlement to facilitate administration of dispersed swidden-based farmers. Archaeological evidence of these experiments however, is absent. We noted the attempt of Teotihuacán to carry out a *congregación* policy. It is significant that this was apparently applied only in Central Mexico, possibly at Kaminaljuyú—in other words, in highland areas.

Under certain kinds of situations, because of the multiplicity of determinants of settlement pattern, the expected correlations of particular settlement patterns with agricultural systems do not in fact obtain. Such factors as the limited and localized distribution of a critical resource like water, or a very hostile social environment with the resultant defense requirements, could lead to a pattern of nucleated settlements with an economic base of swidden agriculture. Bearing in mind such exceptions, however, a survey of contemporary and sixteenth-century settlement patterns in Mesoamerica suggests that the size and density of settlements is closely related to the productivity of agriculture. In areas of hydraulic agriculture rural populations tend to be distributed in large nucleated settlements; in areas of swidden cultivation the population tends to be dispersed in hamlets of extended family or lineage size. The correlation is so ubiquitous that one is tempted to shift the argument around and say that corporate localized kin groups above the lineage level originate as the product of a process of nucleation of lineages stimulated perhaps by competition and permitted by increasingly intensive agriculture. If one argues that nucleation is an advantageous pattern, from the point of view of social integration intensive agriculture permits, whereas extensive agriculture militates against, the process. With a system of unusually productive agriculture, as in the case of chinampa cultivation, a surprisingly large, entirely rural, community can be maintained with a completely agricultural subsistence base. San Gregorio Atlapulco, a contemporary community in the chinampa area, for example, had a population of 5,500 persons in 1950. Nearly all of the fields held by the village lie within a radius of three kilometers from the village.

Furthermore, we would apply Darwin's principle of the relationship between the density of living creatures in an area and degree of specialization to the individual human community as well as to the population of a district. As the nucleated, initially rural settlement increased in size there would be an increasing tendency for the population to expand their economic activities into trade and craft specializations and correspondingly reduce their dependence on agriculture. Possibly there is a gross arithmetical relationship between community population size and the degree to which urban characteristics evolve; one of the chinampa communities, Xochimilco, had a population of 15,000 persons in 1920. At this time, although agriculture was still the primary source of subsistence for the majority of the population, the community had a permanent market and great numbers of part- and full-time specialists in nonagricultural activities.

The functional relationship between intensive agriculture and the growth of cities seems obvious. It is most probable that urbanism developed in response to continued population growth of large nucleated rural settlements in a setting of intensive agriculture. We might use the term "primary urbanism" for this type of socioeconomic evolution. As such communities became urban they acted as catalysts in the development of secondary urban communities either by transforming older rural settlements by expansion of trade or direct colonization at the termini of trade routes. The foregoing argument is really no more than a restatement of V. Gordon Childe's primary hypothesis with the population-specialization interaction added.

The specific factors within a growing nucleated settlement that would operate to produce specialization are numerous and multifaceted:

1. When the population reached sufficient numbers it would provide a local clientele large enough to support non-agricultural specialists.
2. The increasing distance to agricultural lands as the community increased in size during the early phase of growth would tend to make it increasingly inconvenient to subsist by agriculture alone.

3. During the later phases of growth the unequal distribution of the community's permanently cultivated and improved lands would force individuals into nonagricultural specialties.
4. The relationships between the community and other communities, both dependent and independent, would act as a further stimulus to urban growth.

Such growing settlements would also increase in density as well as in total population as proximity to the market became important to an increasingly specialized population.

Wholly aside from the permissive aspect of intensive agriculture generally, hydraulic agriculture would require cooperation in production and further stimulate nucleation. While there is no absolute need for the cooperating population to reside in a single settlement, such an arrangement simplifies organization of work and distribution of water and (given the Central Mexican pattern of intense local specialization of production, with concomitant dependence of virtually all communities on a market network) the provision of basic subsistence needs, as well as the distribution of other commodities.

Urbanism in Central Mexico probably had its roots, therefore, in a preurban settlement pattern of large nucleated settlements located in areas of hydraulic agriculture. This pattern probably had its inception in the Tierra Templada sector during Middle Formative times and was extended into the Tierra Fría sector in the Late and Terminal Formative phases. The development and spread of this pattern of nucleated settlement was apparently coeval with the evolution of tribal social structures to the chiefdom level.

A variety of factors operating as functionally integrated parts of an overall evolutionary system gradually transformed a nucleated, essentially nonurban community into an urban one. First, growing social and economic differentiation occurred between the center, located in a hydraulic zone, and its dependent settlements in less favorable localities within hydraulic zones (for example, downstream locations) or in nearby nonhydraulic areas. As hydraulic and other intensive methods of cultivation were improved or extended, the centers and political divisions increased in size, and a large administrative class emerged, which required the services of a great number of non-food-producing specialists. The highly productive agricultural economy permitted the accumulation of a considerably greater food surplus and therefore enabled the society to support increased numbers of non-food-producing specialists. The pattern of local part-time specialization provided a constant source of semiskilled labor that could be readily converted to full-time occupational specialization.

Since settlement studies have not been conducted to date in the rest of the Central Mexican area, the process of nucleation described above can be verified only for the Teotihuacán Valley. The data we have seem to support the situation outlined above. An incipient development of hydraulic agriculture may have occurred as early as Late Ticomán times (500 B.C.), associated with two nucleated villages in the alluvial plain. Contemporary with these communities was a large number of hillside hamlets with a subsistence probably based on tlacolol cultivation. In the Patlachique phase (200 B.C.) there were two large nucleated villages or towns, probably centers of chiefdoms, one in the lower end of the valley, the other located at the springs. Their location suggests a pattern of competition that may be related to Millon's upstream-downstream type of conflict characteristic of village interaction in the Valley today. By Tzacualli times (B.C./A.D.) the lower valley settlement was abandoned and a large town covering 12 km^2 evolved on the site of the Classic city (Millon 1964). The data from the Teotihuacán Valley Project indicate that at that time at least 50 percent of the population of the entire valley, and almost 100 percent of the population that cultivated land served by the irrigation system, resided in a single nucleated settlement. This process of nucleation continued throughout the history of Teotihuacán until at least 80 to 90 percent of the total population (and this correlated with an enormous overall demographic increase) of the Valley resided in a single, densely nucleated settlement. The post-Formative growth of this gigantic nucleated settlement was accompanied by increasing socioeconomic differentiation and expansion of political control over a huge hinterland as has been previously outlined.

We have discussed the advantages of nucleation for tribal and chiefdom levels of social structure. The advantages are even greater for the civilized level since the vital functions of the state, particularly tax collection, organization of corvée labor, mobilization of military resources, market exchanges, and religious ceremony can all be much more effectively activated within a pattern of nucleated settlement. As both the Spanish conquerors and apparently also the Teotihuacán elite who preceded them discovered, a nucleated population is considerably easier to control than a dispersed one; both acted accordingly. Given the size and density of population requisite to the state level of organization in the first place, and with relatively undeveloped communications systems, a dispersed population would probably have led to an intolerable sociopolitical chaos. Nucleation in a civilized society can therefore be considered as a social invention with the primary function of socioeconomic integration and control. The history of Teotihuacán is an extraordinary example of the operation of the factors and processes outlined above. We believe that the settlement pattern data show that the hydraulic process was in operation in a setting of local military competition in the initial development of the city. As the city grew in size and political influence, however, the population became considerably larger, ultimately surpassing the productivity of the local hydraulic zone; an increasing percentage of the population became non-food-producers—the situation was in a sense permissive, in a sense almost forcing. The history of Teotihuacán is an example of an unusually vigorous, really spectacular response to the ecological stimuli outlined in previous chapters.

In our reconstruction of the history of Mesoamerican society we have repeatedly invoked the concept of a Nuclear Area. In the Formative period, particularly as the chiefdom level of social structure developed, certain small areas were the scenes of unusually vigorous regional cultures that had striking influence on neighboring areas. Some of these areas, such as the highlands of Guatemala, Pacific Coast of Guatemala, and South Gulf Coast, in striking contrast to their Formative precocity, were provincial areas during the subsequent Classic or Postclassic periods, the periods in which civilization emerged. We have noted, furthermore, the possibility that chiefdom social structure had persisted in some areas well into the Classic period. Also noted were the absence of civilization in the Intermediate Area, its presence in the Central Andes, and its apparent initial appearance within Mesoamerica at Teotihuacán. We believe the culture history of this huge area between Central Mexico and Bolivia clearly indicates that the developments of a state level of political organization, civilization generally, and urbanism in particular in the New World, were in fact closely interrelated historical processes, and that their origin and development were functionally related to hydraulic agriculture in arid environments.

We have referred to the spread of Teotihuacán influence and/ or control to the various regions comprising the culture area of Mesoamerica as a whole. In so doing we have attempted the reconstruction of the sociocultural patterning of that influence, particularly in the two key examples of Kaminaljuyú and Tikal. Such influence can be viewed in terms of the effects of a critical Nuclear Area upon those non-nuclear zones that came, for various reasons, within its orbit. We have distinguished two interrelated categories of conditions determining the nature of that influence: first, the nature of autochthonous cultural development in the recipient culture which would make it more or less likely to accept the diffused patterns and which would govern the ways and extent of acceptance; second, the kinds of local repercussions in the recipient culture resulting directly from the nature and extent of foreign domination. These repercussions would depend in part upon the nature of the recipient culture and in part upon such factors as its resources or strategic location, which would affect the degree to which it could be integrated into a wider political system as well as the overall terms of that incorporation. In addition, we may now distinguish a third class of factors which would also govern the nature of foreign influence: the institutions of the Nuclear (dominating) Area itself, the extent to which they are exportable to other types of ecological and political settings, and the kinds of repercussions they would be likely to induce when imported into such settings of various types.

Specifically, we feel that Teotihuacán did impose, on a virtually pan-Mesoamerican basis, the particular techniques of government that it developed and nurtured in a setting of hydraulic agriculture. These techniques included the concept of a professional ruling class divorced from kinship, a centrally administered judicial system, efficient corvée labor organization combined with systematic tribute and taxation, and a professional military class for effective execution of sanctions. The incentives for the Nuclear Area to export these techniques of control and the effectiveness of their functioning in other areas was seen to vary enormously from a situation of actual colonization at Kaminaljuyú to one of more diffuse, less intensive domination at Tikal. In the former case, the resources controlled by Kaminaljuyú rendered profitable what might otherwise be viewed as a dangerously expensive overextension of Teotihuacán power. Conversely, the closeness of integration of Kaminaljuyú with the economy and politics of the mother city acted to alter, in effect, its economic base, which became inevitably and inextricably linked with the fortunes of the center. Supporting this interpretation are the strong indications of the contemporaneity of the fall of Teotihuacán and that of Kaminaljuyú, which in effect collapsed as a local center of power when the Nuclear Area on which it depended withdrew its control.

The situation was otherwise at Tikal. If Teotihuacán did, as seems highly probable, attempt to impose a hydraulic political system, certainly this attempt lacked the spectacular success it achieved at Kaminaljuyú. The productive system of the Petén was certainly capable of supporting so expensive a system, as has been amply demonstrated. On the other hand, there would seem to have been considerably less incentive for Teotihuacán to have attempted the completeness of control evidenced at Kaminaljuyú. We have noted the paucity of economically exportable resources in the Lowland Maya area, and there is little if any archaeological evidence of such exports. On the other hand, however, we have postulated a possible reason for the considerable Teotihuacán influence noted at Tikal. If we assume a linkage of the Petén with Highland Guatemala into a Symbiotic Region, the Teotihuacán presence at Tikal may be seen as part of a strategy of safeguarding and pacifying the region upon which the Kaminaljuyú colony was dependent.

Even when an area can in theory support a hydraulic-like upper class of specialists, it must also have a need for such a class. If this elite is not to be entirely parasitic, it must have a function in terms of the local socioeconomic system. In hydraulic areas this function is clear and has been discussed in detail elsewhere. We turn now to consideration of this factor in the dynamics of the Maya states, the economic base of which was swidden agriculture.

Considering only the condition present in an ostensibly isolated Petén, it would be difficult to determine what this class did, so to speak, to earn its keep. Swidden agriculture involves little, if any, necessity for the cooperative labor of large numbers of people to maintain and insure efficient production. Similarly, there would have been little inducement for centralized control of local trading and markets in a region having no marked internal geographical variability, a precondition for wide diversity in production, in harvesting periods, and in the distribution of essential resources. In theory the little community could continue to function quite well without either marked social stratification or its consequent political controls. But if swidden agriculture is not demanding of elaborate social control, its productivity would assure an expanding population in the course of time. Larger numbers of people require social institutions that smaller numbers of people can neither require nor support. Also it is conceivable that an elite, given a sufficiently large and dense population relative to the carrying capacity of land cultivated necessarily by extensive techniques, may have served to regulate the agricultural cycle and the reallocation of lands to maintain the balance of the total system.

However, the fact that the Petén was in many ways not isolated but instead tied in, if tangentially, with other, more highly developed societies, with which it entered into regular and patterned relationships, alters the picture considerably. In our prior discussion of the urban versus nonurban character of Tikal we mentioned the point that political functions localized in a settlement, functions dependent upon the position within a more expanded network, alter the structure, function, and status of that settlement on even the local level. This sort of phenomenon, while not turning Tikal into what we would call an urban community, could conceivably raise the level of development from that of chiefdom to that of state; it would definitely intensify the tendency to stratification already present. Furthermore, the position of the elite would be immeasurably strengthened. Not only would this group have some function (in effect, the conduct of foreign relations), but in turn this new position would make them considerably more receptive to the diffusion of the techniques of government from a hydraulic civilization.

A new cycle of local competition for control would therefore result, and the consequent higher level of group integration would be reflected archaeologically in increased site stratification. It is interesting to note that following the collapse of Teotihuacán in the Central Plateau, the Maya "capital" at Tikal bears witness to a 50- to 60-year hiatus in building activity between the Early and Late Classic phases. Contemporary with this, in the Nuclear Area, there seems to have been a power vacuum. Not an absence of the hydraulic state, but rather a lower level of integration still on the principle of the hydraulic macro-state. The Late or Terminal Classic in Central Mexico was a period of struggle for hegemony among several competing centers, the growth of which would have been stimulated by the fall of the central power. Of the three competing states—Xochicalco, Cholula, Tula—the last-named succeeded ultimately to the mantle of Teotihuacán as a pan-Mesoamerican power. Even in this period of essentially local retrenchment, however, these would still have been what we are calling large political systems in the Highlands; their continuing presence would stimulate the continuation of the state level of organization in other areas of Mesoamerica.

We emphasize this point because slash-and-burn agriculture with its low population density and necessarily dispersed settlement pattern would militate against the effective functioning of the state. The absence of an urban center with its integrative economic mechanisms would further reduce the effectiveness of integration of a socially stratified society. A swidden-based state would be predictably less stable and more weakly organized than a hydraulic state. Even the largest of the swidden-based lowland states probably involved territories of only thousands of square kilometers and populations of only tens of thousands. Our argument is, in effect, that the swidden-based state represents a response to the stimulus of the hydraulic. It seems to us increasingly likely that the "civilizations without cities" are what Fried (1960) would term secondary states, formed as a response to pressures set up by the nearby presence of a preexisting state, itself either pristine or secondary but with a hydraulic and urbanized base. We have proposed a plausible model for the analysis of the conditions under which such developments occur.

In the prior discussion of minimal size for states on pages 74–75 we noted the presence of states in sixteenth-century Central Mexico with populations as low as 12,000 persons and suggested a minimum size of 10,000 for this type of social structure. Actually there were several states with populations of 5,000 to 6,000—a size that could be effectively organized at a chiefdom level. In view of our arguments about societal size and social structure the small size of these states needs explanation. It seems to us highly improbable that states that small would have existed without the presence of larger states in the same general region. The presence of large states stimulates societies of relatively small size to organize themselves on the same basis—this stimulation may occur as the product of internal development, as a technique of self-defense, or because the smaller society was at some previous period assimilated by a larger one that introduced the state level of administration. The first process could be termed primary stimulus; the second two secondary. Following this argument, the extraordinary historical role of centers like Teotihuacán and Monte Albán in the evolution of Mesoamerican civilization as a whole takes on increasing significance. The impact of these centers is similar to that of large chiefdoms on smaller societies (as outlined on page 132), except that the secondary stimulus would be more significant at the level of civilization since the incorporative capacities of chiefdoms were so limited. Viewed in this framework the historical differences between Olmec and Teotihuacán "influence" are clarified.

The competitive interaction between large and small societies within a geographical region therefore is one of the most vital stimuli to social evolution. This process would operate on all societal levels in the history of a culture area, from bands to states. The Aztec Empire, probably the largest macro-state in

Mesoamerican history, had a population of 5 million to 6 million persons in 1519. The earlier empires of Tula and Teotihuacán must have had populations well in excess of 1 million. Even in periods of political fragmentation states like those of Late Classic Cholula and Xochicalco, or thirteenth-century Acolhuacan and fourteenth-century Azcaputzalco had populations exceeding 100,000 inhabitants. We have previously noted the strong tendency toward the evolution of these unusually large polities in Central Mexico.

In our discussion of the societal size for the various levels of social structure we noted a considerable overlap in the range of minimal and maximal size for each level. This overlap of range, we feel, can be explained in terms of the impact of large societies on small ones. In the Intermediate Area the Highland Chibcha chiefdoms were the largest organized society. Their size is probably at or near the maximum for chiefdom social structure: The important point is that it was within the range; there were no larger societies, and all other chiefdoms were considerably smaller. Therefore the stimulus to the evolution of the state was absent. This of course contrasts sharply with Mesoamerica.

The Late Classic and Postclassic political history of Mesoamerica provides ample and dramatic documentation for the theses we have advanced. Both of the Mesoamerican macrostates—the pan-Mesoamerican empires of Tula and Tenochtitlán, plus smaller regional states of Cholula and Xochicalco—were based in Central Mexico. Still another successful example of state organization, that of Oaxaca, was also based in a geographical zone similar in many ways to the Central Plateau. The extent of control of the Oaxacan civilization is not known in detail, although it does not appear to have possessed the tendencies to imperialistic expansion that characterized the states of Central Mexico.

If the evolution of the state level of development can, as we have demonstrated, be related to ecological factors on the local and regional levels, the appearance of macro-states and empires cannot be completely explained by reference to these factors alone. However, once the state appears on a local level in response to the stimuli of population pressure, hydraulic agriculture, and the symbiotic patterns, it tends to generate further pressures—economic, military, political—with strong repercussions in surrounding areas. A process which we have analyzed on lower levels, that of competition, comes into play on the higher level; here the competing units comprise entire polities. As we have mentioned previously, the organization of the state gives it competitive advantages. A stronger state will tend to absorb and incorporate a weaker. The result is an empire or supraregional superstate.

This does not imply that the centers of such macro-states could have depended for support upon a sustaining area composed of their entire tributary territories and populations. Paradoxically enough, sustaining areas remained local; the organization of the state became one of overlapping hierarchies of increasingly inclusive centers. These local areas, the most tightly integrated parts of the macro-states, tended to be stable units even with the breakup of the macro-state of which they formed component subunits. The Aztec tribute lists and the history of their conquests indicate that the collection of food surplus was restricted to a radius of some 200 km. from Tenochtitlán. Where transportation is by foot alone and when loads must be carried on the backs of men, who must be fed en route, there is a practical effective limit on the size of territory that can be drawn upon economically for bulky and basic subsistence goods like grain. Tribute from more peripheral areas consisted almost entirely of exotic foods—particularly cacao which was nonperishable and which was sufficiently valuable in even small quantities to defray the costs of import—and such other products as feathers, honey, skins, jade, metals, all consumed exclusively by the elite classes. Much of the long-distance trade of the pochteca was of this character (Chapman 1957).

Yet the motivation for expansion by the macro-state was, we feel, economic. In fact, the Aztec Empire at the time of the Conquest was generally considered a thoroughly rapacious institution, an opinion that won for the Spaniards large numbers of native allies. The ceremonial and prestige functions of warfare were important aspects of Aztec ideology but we do not see these as fundamental causes. When examined anthropologically, Aztec militarism is seen to possess considerable economic and demographic functions: means of population control in a pressure situation, a means of internal social integration, control of access to strategic resources, and doubtless others as well.

Part THREE

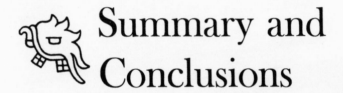 Summary and
Conclusions

IX / CULTURAL ECOLOGY AND CULTURAL EVOLUTION

The ecological approach offers what we feel to be a significant tool for the scientific treatment and analysis of cultural phenomena. One assumption underlying our methodology has been that of uniformitarianism, that the principles observed to operate in the present can be safely projected into the past as well; we are therefore justified theoretically in considering both past and present as amenable to discussion within the same explanatory framework. This view in no sense implies a static conception of cultural ecological processes, that "there is nothing new under the sun." The evidence we have adduced to the contrary in preceding sections should be ample to obviate such an accusation. What this view does imply, however, is that clear empirical evidence of cultural changes of various kinds and different degrees of significance can and must be analyzed according to a second assumption corollary to our first: that cultural evolution is a regular process, subject to law and therefore analyzable by scientific methods.

If culture is regarded as, in one sense, comprising an analytical level of its own and subject to laws germane to that level, it still remains to discover and describe the operation of such laws (cf. White 1949). Paradoxically, it is precisely by the removal of culture from this august and autonomous philosophical pedestal and regarding it rather as one subsystem functioning inevitably as part of a larger and more inclusive system—the ecosystem —that we feel such laws can best be formulated. The superorganic is, for some purposes, a highly productive concept; yet too strict an adherence to it leads ultimately to an overly restrictive view of cultural processes and a corresponding limitation on their explanation. White's treatment of culture as an energy-capturing system renders true, a priori, his statement that culture evolves with the increased harnessing of energy. We are not advocating reductionism, however, of the geographical-determinist, or the culture-and-personality varieties. Both such positions are reductionist in that to a greater or lesser degree they altogether eliminate the factor of culture as an independent variable from the equation; the former by treating what we consider cultural patterns as simply the effects of geography, direct and unmediated, upon human behavior; the latter by considering culture as the product of individual personalities and behavior alone. At the same time, however, we avoid the opposite pitfall, that of viewing culture as self-determining and therefore tautologous in its splendid isolation. Human responses are overwhelmingly cultural ones, in our view, and culture remains for us in a sense an autonomous level on this basis. Yet we cannot consider these responses to occur in a vacuum or as part of a conceptually circular framework and still hope to elucidate or explain the regularities of these responses.

We regard culture, rather, as the specifically human mechanism of adaptation to environment, enabling man to compete successfully with other animals—including his fellows—with plants, and with the elements. A measure of the success of this adaptation is population density, and by this criterion man is an exceptionally, strikingly successful creature; his numbers and the extension of his geographical range are virtually unparalleled in the organic world. The means by which he has accomplished this has been his culture. Culture to man is, on one level, a specialization broadly analogous to the long neck of the giraffe, or the heavy coat of the woolly mammoth, or the social behavior of infra-human primates. Unlike these examples, however, culture comprises a different analytical order of phenomena, nonorganic in its means of transmission and spread and in the laws to which it is subject. Although rooted in what are undoubtedly innate, organic capacities, it can be analyzed without reference to this basis, which can be taken, for our purposes, as a constant and a given.

Because of the broadly organic analogy in the function of culture to its possessor, we can justify its treatment under a similar theoretical rubric, that of evolution. This is not to say that the mechanisms of cultural change are those of biological evolution. Rather, the basic principles underlying cultural evolution—those of variation, adaptation, selection—are considered applicable as well to the higher analytical level, the superorganic. The units involved and, accordingly, the laws relevant to them will be different in terms of mechanism and function from level to level.

The process of cultural evolution, like that of organic evolution, must be regarded as essentially nonorthogenetic, that is, without immanent direction or "purpose." This view does not mean that these processes are random, idiosyncratic, or without regularity. Variations in both organic and superorganic realms may arise unpredictably and "spontaneously," but once in existence their survival and perpetuation must be considered as anything but random. An innovation that increases the efficiency of its possessor will be strongly favored by the operation of selection. A mutation that makes the individual more successful in competition with his fellows will tend to spread through a population; a population possessing it may in turn be enabled to drive out other populations competing with it for the same resources. On the cultural level a more efficient tool or mode of social organization will tend to displace less efficient ways of doing the same thing; a group with the "new improved model," so to speak, will similarly survive at the expense of its competitors. This is in effect Tylor's explanation of the incest taboo among human groups.

The conditions and means which are responsible for biological transmission of innovations follow different laws from those which operate at the cultural level, a self-evident fact which does not negate the similarity in principle of the evolutionary process on these two levels. No cultural trait is innate; culture traits, transmitted by learning, can therefore be adopted rapidly by groups not initially possessing them by means of a process called diffusion. As we have observed, however, this is not a mechanical process. In evolutionary terms, the potential of diffusion is in the speeding-up of the evolutionary process; evolution and diffusion are not, in other words, mutually exclusive or opposed concepts. It is instead advantageous to consider them in the same analytical framework. In this way the conclusions reached are, we feel, worth the effort, though some may consider them radical.

According to evolutionary theory, innovations and variations are constantly arising, and each is subject to selective pressures which govern its survival and spread. These selective pressures, at the superorganic level, operate on all culture traits regardless of their origins, whether independently invented or borrowed from someone else. In other words, the same principles, those of adaptation and selection, determine the fate of any innovation. What was responsible for the survival of the innovation in the first place is precisely what is responsible for its diffusion. In the course of time, it is highly probable that a needed invention will ultimately be made. The operation of diffusion reduces the requirement of time, and thus accelerates the evolutionary process—it is often faster to borrow a trait than to invent it. But it will be neither borrowed nor invented—nor would it survive the selective screen—unless it is of superior efficiency in a given cultural context. In the analysis of any cultural system, therefore, the origins of the component traits become immaterial and, for our purposes, essentially irrelevant. We consider the dichotomy a false one, based on too simplistic a view of both evolution and diffusion and on a misunderstanding of what constitutes explanation. What is adapted, no matter what its source, will be adopted. Or, as Paul Collins puts it (personal communication), an adaptive trait is one which facilitates its own reproduction.

We have referred earlier to Romer's Rule, which emphasizes the essential conservatism of innovation, the initial effect of which is to preserve an old way of life under changed conditions, or to increase its efficiency. In the long run, of course, such an innovation may permit or even necessitate a radically changed adaptive system (Hockett and Ascher 1964). On the organic level Romer's example is that of the Devonian lungfish whose strengthened fins and primitive lung permitted it to get back to water under conditions of dessication. The invasion of the land as a new ecological niche was a consequence of, but not responsible for, the perpetuation of this innovation (Romer 1959). The origin and survival of food-producing, Childe's Neolithic Revolution, can be seen in a similar light. A population dependent on hunting and gathering of potential domesticates and closely associated with them would in all probability take the next step, that of domestication, not to gain control of the breeding of these creatures—the effect—but initially to preserve and subsequently render less precarious an existing way of life by making them available to be hunted and gathered when the need arose.

In our discussion of cultural evolution in Mesoamerica we have been concerned with changes of both line and grade (Coon 1962), or, in the terminology of Sahlins and Service (1960), with both specific and general evolution and particularly with the relationship between these two aspects of the evolutionary process. Line, or specific evolution, is essentially a ramifying process of change within a single sequence; grade involves changes in principle in levels of organization. We have dealt primarily with a single historical line, a single group of related cultures. Within this line, however, our emphasis has been on describing the changes of grade and on specifying the causal factors responsible for each such change. The two aspects, specific and general evolution, may for some purposes be considered separable in that changes of line need not involve changes of grade (we have cited examples of this) and vice versa. However, the question we have asked and attempted to answer is: Under what circumstances does specific evolution lead also to general evolution?

A significant advantage of the ecological approach to the problem of cultural evolution lies in its potential for evaluating "efficiency." Although it is, of course, possible to measure mathematically and by experimentation the absolute efficiency of a device or institution, we prefer a more relative concept: efficiency vis-à-vis what? Given our view of culture as man's principal adaptive mechanism, we can and must consider it within the functional context of such adaptation, as one member of a more inclusive ecosystem, in interaction with other components of that ecosystem. What is efficient, or adaptive, in one context is not necessarily so in another—and for our purposes therefore, evaluation of absolute efficiency becomes by itself meaningless. Harris (1966) has shown, for example, that the undersized cattle of India are more efficient within the setting of Indian agriculture than would be larger breeds which would make more "efficient" use of fodder than the smaller cattle, because such larger breeds could not survive within the present ecosystem without actually competing with man. Human needs, as Childe (1951) observed, are not fixed quantities. They depend upon environment and upon culture, neither of which is fixed or static.

As cultures change so too do their effective environments. A resource does not become a resource until it is so recognized and exploited by a culture. Environment is always perceived and mediated by culture. Put another way, a potential resource may comprise part of the environment according to the evaluation of a geographer, but unless the culture has a need for it, and, concomitantly, means for putting it to use—or unless it impinges in some way, perhaps negatively as a limiting factor—it does not become part of the ecosystem. Arable land is a resource only to an agricultural people; an oil well is a resource to a culture with an industrial technology which requires oil and provides, at the same time, the means of getting it out of the ground into the refinery. It is this point which Hawkes (1954) appears to misunderstand when he observed that despite the utility of the ecological approach in some respects, he sees nothing in North American ecology to compel the institutions of either the Iroquois or modern New York State. Although the environment has not changed drastically, the ecosystem has in fact done so.

The essence of cultural ecology is in its interactive approach —its consideration of habitat, biome, and culture as functionally interrelated, mutually interdependent aspects of a single wider system. Changes in one aspect produce corresponding changes in reaction in the other parts, their extent being a matter for empirical determination. This sounds in effect very like the functionalism of British social anthropology; yet the two approaches differ in several significant ways. One principal difference is that in the ecological method not all functions are considered equally important for all purposes. There is a hierarchy of functions in cultural ecology, with some recognized as having more widespread and pervasive repercussions throughout the system. Some variables are best considered independent, others dependent. Since we are treating culture as an adaptive mechanism, some aspects of culture are empirically seen as being more important than are others in promoting that adaptation.

White (1949) distinguishes three levels of culture—technology, sociology, ideology—and his view is one of technological-economic determinism. It is the efficiency of technology that governs the institutions of the sociological and, if more indirectly, the ideological levels. Although he admits the process of mutual influence on all levels, he argues that the effective direction is overwhelmingly from technology to the other two: It is technology that is largely responsible for the harnessing of energy. Steward's concept of the hierarchy of function in culture in a sense complements that of White and is considerably less doctrinaire. He distinguishes core features—those most closely connected with subsistence activities—from superstructural ones, which are less closely determined and more variable.

It is these core features, from any level of the "layer cake" which exhibit regularity and which are therefore amenable to scientific treatment. We conceive of core features, somewhat more broadly than the original definition, as those which affect most strongly the success of adaptation of a population to its physical, biotic, and sociocultural environment. Superstructural features would be, in evolutionary terms, adaptively neutral, or certainly more so than core ones. The advantage to us of the method and theory of cultural ecology lies in its greater and more inclusive explanatory power as compared to economic or technological determinism. The ecological approach can and must take into account a greater multiplicity of factors and interrelations among them than the other two theories, which are more simplistic and can in fact be seen as merely special instances of the broader theory, in much the way that Newtonian physics is a special case of relativity physics.

Another substantial difference of cultural ecology from the functionalism of social anthropology is the requirement of the former for time depth in its data, and the explicit rejection on the part of the latter of any but synchronic data. The difference provides the methodological control necessary to substantiate the previous argument regarding the hierarchy of function. On a strictly synchronic level it would be difficult to determine with reliability which aspects of a system, composed by definition of mutually interrelated parts, were more important: Synchronic data alone will not distinguish the independent variable from the dependent, nor cause from effect. In a sense we are dealing with what is very nearly a tautology: What is adaptive is what survives. All that is, however, is not necessarily of importance. Archaeological data provide the record of change and in so doing elucidate the operation of cause; such information is not irrelevant but essential to the building of a more general theory of culture. Selection will in the course of time favor the survival of the more efficient over the less so; a more favorable variant—in any ecological niche—will be perpetuated at the expense of less well-adapted competitors. The control provided by archaeological data enables us to evaluate relative efficiency and importance of traits in a hierarchy in a way that can be done only arbitrarily on the purely synchronic level.

The other side of the relationship between archaeology and ethnology has often been stressed in a way which the points made in the preceding paragraph have not been. Braidwood's statement that archaeology is "the total anthropology of extinct cultures" (1959), Phillips' "archaeology is anthropology or it is nothing" (1955), and other statements resembling these suggest that it is ethnological evidence, obtained in the present, that enables us to interpret cultures of the past that are no longer directly observable. Without such inference, of greater or lesser reliability, archaeology could consist of very little more than catalogues of preserved artifacts and chronological charts. Archaeological inference is not, at its best, sheer rank speculation, although at its worst it may all too frequently approach this level. Nor is it a practice of projecting, uncritically and in the understandably naïve fashion of the nineteenth century, any and all practices observed among contemporary peoples of the lower cultural levels back into the past. The conditions under which this can be done and the level of reliability must be stated, and this is one of the tasks of theory. The broad justification for archaeological inference is, in effect, the principle of uniformitarianism; but taken alone its explanatory and predictive-retrodictive powers are limited.

Both Vogt (1956) and Hawkes (1954) feel that sound

archaeological inferences must be based on a situation in which the living groups are the cultural descendants of the group represented archaeologically. In some instances, such as the case of the tropical forest tribes of the Amazon Basin, this is often feasible in practice. It is altogether likely that at least some of the modern inhabitants of this area are descended from at least some of its past occupants. But this is not, to us, the crucial variable. The inhabitants of Tenochtitlán were clearly the cultural descendants of the inhabitants of, say, Early Zacatenco, and at least some of those in modern Mexico City descendants of both. Yet changes of line (historical changes) have led to changes of grade, that is, of level of cultural development. Meaningful comparisons and reliable inferences are possible only within such levels.

Cultural ecology is of considerable assistance in the formulation of the regularities that provide theoretical justification for archaeological inference. At least not, however, on the basis of the simplistic equation of same environment, and therefore same culture. As we have previously observed, there is usually more than one possible way to exploit any given environment— although of these some are more efficient, more successful, than others. The similarities that form the basis for legitimate comparison are those of ecological adaptation, and therefore, of cultural core. Just as there may be many ways of exploiting a given environment, so too may widely different kinds of environments pose approximately similar kinds of challenge to human exploitation. Our argument has been that similar causes produce similar effects, independently of historical or lineal relationships of cultures. The cultural descendants of a common ancestor may be similar to that ancestor and to each other—but whether they in fact are is a matter for empirical investigation. Conversely, greater similarities may obtain between the end products of widely separated historical traditions than between these and their own historical ancestors: Aztec is more like Inca than it is like Early Zacatenco. Convergence is not only possible, but, given certain specified conditions, extremely probable.

We have considered in detail the kinds of conditions we feel to be responsible for changes in structural type, that is, in evolutionary grade. Following Service's classification, we have distinguished four such evolutionary levels: band, tribe, chiefdom, and civilization or state. Archaeological evidence from Mesoamerica has confirmed the appearance of each of these progressive levels in the chronological order of their ascending structural complexity. Elsewhere in this section we will return to the general implications of our data for the method and theory of cultural evolution.

At this point, however, we shall answer still another criticism of the ecological approach, that is, that while ecological determination of cultural institutions is universally considered evident and admissible on the lower levels of cultural development, these factors wane in importance on the higher levels. This argument contends that where the level of civilization is reached and the state appears, the ecological determinants are no longer operative. As the preceding evidence suggests, we do not subscribe to this view. Causation is simpler and more easily observed in simpler societies and is more complex in both theory and practical application at the higher levels, where greater numbers of factors and more complex feedbacks among them must be taken into account. This fact does not, in our view, suggest that different general principles must be used for the analysis of the higher levels. Nor, moreover, does it imply that there are no new properties emergent on the levels of the more advanced structural types. There are such properties, but analysis of these is in principle the same.

In support of the criticisms of applying the ecological model to the higher levels of cultural evolution the suggestion is often made that such advance depends upon man's increasing control of his environment. Agriculture, animal domestication, irrigation, and industrialization free him from natural limitations of supplies of food, water, and other resources. But increased control does not mean emancipation; even were the control in theory complete, there would still remain something there to control, and the consequent need remains for structuring and institutionalizing that control. In practice, of course, control is never so complete, and it would seem that the apparent solution of one set of problems serves to raise others equally thorny. This essentially is the heart of Toynbee's concept of challenge and response. In a different sense, human modification of an environment involves the development of new resources, the distribution of which may be very different from that of the old, and the management requirements of which pose new problems which must be solved if the cultural system is to continue to operate. Cultural innovation accordingly changes the effective environment, the ecosystem as a whole. Permissive and limiting factors continue to operate, and although these factors may be very different ones empirically from those under former conditions (for example, absence of game is not a limiting factor to exploitation of an area by an agricultural or industrial culture) their operation is in principle the same. The agricultural potential of a region, Meggers (1954) to the contrary, is directly dependent upon technological development. Even with a theoretically omnipotent technology some areas would still have greater potential with fewer restrictions upon the utilization of that technology than would others.

X / THE ORIGINS OF CIVILIZATION

Of Childe's criteria for civilization (1950) we have rejected some, modified others, and accepted still others. We do not feel, for example, that the invention of writing is a necessary criterion of civilization. Although on empirical grounds there is a correlation of written language with civilization and the state, the generalization does not apply uniformly. Writing was not, for example, characteristic of the Central Andean civilizations. It is true that Morgan held this trait as diagnostic of civilization, and there is some theoretical as well as empirical justification, with reservation, for its inclusion, in some cases, as an important characteristic of this evolutionary level. Along with the development of a certain level of social complexity, a level of sociocultural integration involving a demographic base in the tens of thousands with marked specialization of function within a large-scale economic system and a concomitant social stratification, there is a corresponding requirement of social and economic control. Writing is a device facilitating such control. The increased complexity of a large sociopolitical system would render the reliance upon human memory, for, say, tax collections, relatively less efficient. Yet complex civilizations have in fact been maintained in the absence of writing.

The presence of true cities implies the existence of the social complexity, scale of cultural integration, and demographic base that are indicative of civilization. Their absence, however, does not imply that the functions which cities carry out within the wider context were also absent. Coe (1961a) as well as the present authors have cited the presence of what we would on other grounds consider state organization, in which the functions of large-scale territorial organizations were localized and patterned in different ways. Social stratification, specialization of function, and monumental public works, however, were present. We have suggested that the "civilizations without cities" may represent a response to pressures emanating from nearby truly urban states, as the former areas entered into various kinds of relationships with more complex neighbors—diplomatic, commercial, political—relationships from which it is likely that at least a veiled threat of force was never wholly absent. These generalizations seem applicable to at least the two examples used by Coe, the Classic Maya and the Khmer of Indochina: the Classic Maya, in a partly symbiotic, partly exploited relationship with Teotihuacán, and the Khmer, sandwiched between India and China and receiving influences from both. The problem of the origin of cities, then, is to us quite distinct from that of the origin of civilization. The two processes, civilization and urbanization, are often correlative; we have attempted to demonstrate the circumstances in which they occur together, and those in which they do not. Urban and nonurban civilizations are two subtypes of a single class of phenomena; while urbanism implies civilization, the reverse is not true.

A principal characteristic of civilization, to Childe and to us as well, is the presence of monumental architecture, not only for its fortunate—and gratifying—ease of recognition and likelihood of preservation in the archaeological record, but because of what we consider its clear sociological implications and prerequisites. These prerequisites are in fact precisely those of civilization, and the presence of such remains enables us to infer with great reliability the social structure of the culture which produced them. The construction of such buildings requires not merely a large, but also a diversified labor force. Tasks are both skilled and unskilled, and specialists to control, coordinate, and in some sense pay, the actual participants in the labor are required. Recompense may involve simply the fact that the workmen are paying off their taxes in this fashion; it may, as in the case of Mesopotamia, include reallocation of centrally stored food to the workers during the construction. In addition to the unskilled labor, the services of architects, masons, sculptors, painters, often even astronomers would generally be needed—usually full-time professional craftsmen who must be paid from the surplus produced by others.

Civilized society is above all stratified society. This implies differential access to the strategic resources of the society—a group of wealthy and a larger group of poor, a group in control of power and one which is dominated. The more general implications of this fact are several. The first is that social class rather than kinship is the principal means of social integration. While this does not suggest that the kinship system, including even the existence of corporate kin groups, atrophies, it does necessarily imply a change of function for such groups. Where in a smaller, less complicated overall structure, these groups represent the only means of integration and control, in a stratified context their functions become reduced and their importance modified accordingly, as the direct result of their incorporation within a larger social system. Structural changes of various sorts may accompany this process. The history of the Roman gens and probably also of the Attic deme provide examples of this; so too very likely, would that of the Aztec calpulli.

We feel that the ecological approach can best explain the dynamics and origin of civilizations, their development out of structurally simpler social systems, and their function with respect to their physical and social environments. Although the developmental changes themselves may be gradual and continuous, essentially quantitative, our analysis has depended upon an assumption that at various points in the continuum there is a threshold effect which can be viewed as qualitative. Empirically, the juncture at which such a threshold makes its appearance will vary, depending upon a number of mutually interacting, dynamic aspects of habitat, biome, and culture. These factors will act in specified ways to mitigate, nullify, or reinforce each other. The resulting thresholds are our levels of development—bands, tribes, chiefdoms, and civilizations—and each represents, in anthropomorphic terms, a process of choice among several available alternatives. The achievement of each such level, furthermore, effects new organizational and ecological concomitants and requisites germane to it.

As we have regarded function as a concept requiring hierarchical treatment on the grounds that some of the discernible functions in a system are more important and far-reaching than others, so too do we consider the concept of a series of alternative choices. First, at any given time and within the context of a given cultural-ecological system, some responses will be more likely to occur than others. Previous "choices" act to limit future ones. Second, of the possible alternatives, selective pressures may favor one over another; one may be more adaptive than another. Third, important for analytical purposes, is the fact that any change inevitably occurs within the dynamic equilibrium of a feedback system; given a response in one area its very occurrence may require, permit, or preclude particular directions of compensatory response in other areas. The concept of hierarchy is significant here in that we consider some kinds of initial response in some aspects of the system as providing wider, more inclusive stimuli for responses elsewhere in the system; some will involve greater or lesser degrees of freedom than will others.

If we can use population size as a measure of the efficiency of a productive system, it is more than this alone. Most of the institutional changes we have discussed in the preceding sections have been mediated directly or indirectly by demographic changes. These must be viewed therefore as a dynamic factor in the analysis of any ecosystem. A culture must, in a sense, adapt on the institutional level to its own numbers. Although we have considered the figure of 10,000 persons within a single large social system as the minimum requisite for the level of civilization, the empirical threshold is probably a variable one, its level determined in each instance by a multiplicity of factors. The principle, however, of a minimal population size, is, we feel, a valid one, although the critical size may vary from instance to instance. Our use of this concept resembles, in broad analogy, the concept of critical mass as used in nuclear physics. A larger population would both require and be able to afford social institutions that smaller numbers could neither need nor support: a larger army needs more generals, and more levels of generals, than does a small one; whereas an army with more officers than men is both inefficient and absurd.

Given a population of our suggested 10,000, the means of kinship and ceremonial ties used with great efficiency to integrate smaller absolute numbers would become too diffuse to carry out the integrative functions adequately. Other means must be developed, and the result is the social-economic-political hierarchy characteristic of civilization. The hallmark of civilization is the existence of social communities in a hierarchy of overlapping levels of inclusiveness, some subordinate to and at the same time dominant over others within a single network. The greater the territory and population subordinate to any such center, the higher the relative status and power of the community at that center. There is an approximately conical model, with an apparent *minimum* of three such levels in a civilization, two (center and hinterland) in a chiefdom. Within such an overall network the function and structure of each point in the network would be modified by the relative position within the network as a whole.

The institutions of civilization represent, in our view, one highly adaptive solution to certain kinds of sociocultural-ecological problems. It is not the only alternative, and, in the series of choices leading to it, other alternatives may be possible. Reduction of population is equally feasible—by emigration, by warfare, or by famine. Such responses are conceivable but, by definition, represent limited evolutionary potential. The relevant factors tipping the balance, so to speak, are many, and the complexity of their interrelations so great and involving so many "if . . . then" statements that it is difficult to represent them in simple cause and effect schemata. Causality is far from simple, and theory cannot as a result be simplistic. In many cases the chain of cause and effect is self-intensifying, with a cause producing an effect which in turn exacerbates the original causal constellation. It is often not easy to determine which is which. In addition, the functional interdependence of the multiple factors comprising the ecosystem means that the priorities, chronological or analytical, may not be ascertainable with precision. Sometimes this need not trouble us unduly: Is productive, permanent, intensive agriculture a cause or an effect of population growth? The processes are clearly concomitant and mutually reinforcing. A factor may in one analytical context be considered a cause; in another context, an effect. The complexity of alternatives at each critical point must also be taken into account. The production of a surplus may be an impetus to population differentiation or may, alternatively be channeled into demographic expansion, or both.

A principal mechanism fundamental to the origin of the state is that of population growth, leading ultimately to competition within a society and between societies. We have further suggested that there is in some circumstances strong selective pressure in favor of cooperation as a response to competition. We are dealing with factors that must be evaluated not only absolutely, but in relation to each other and to a particular ecosystem as a whole. Density, although it can be calculated absolutely as a measure of people to land, acts as though it were a relative factor. It is based upon not only distribution of people and productive potential of the land under any given regime of exploitation, but is also dependent on technology and even on social organization. A variable related to population density is population pressure. Depending directly upon natural limiting factors in the physical environment, a hunting-and-gathering group may experience severe population pressure with a density of one person per square mile or even less. A more favorable environment, under the same productive system, may be capable of supporting many more people without pressure. Changes in technology may expand the theoretical carrying capacity of an area, and represent therefore a possible response to increased density and pressure; a new cycle of demographic filling in will result. Another often more economical response to over-population is, of course, emigration, the feasibility of which is a product of both geographical and social environments in combination with the technological means available for coping adequately with these challenges.

Competition, therefore, can arise at any social level and is dealt with by means appropriate to that level. Kinship groups and sodalities function efficiently in its regulation, but are mechanisms of limited extensibility. Fragmentation and emigration may be possible. Warfare among groups and feuding within the group may occur. This can lead to the expropriation of the weaker by the stronger; more important, occasional warfare may be a means of controlling the demographic expansion that originally gave rise to the competitive situation, thus alleviating it temporarily. Technological change may act to reduce competition. Yet it has long been noted that populations tend to outgrow their food supplies, and ultimately, all things being equal, the problem will reemerge and an adjustment, often at a higher level, becomes necessary once more. The result is a social institution capable of regulating conflict and turning it to cooperation.

All civilizations are based on the artificial production of staple foodstuffs. There are examples of chiefdoms, such as that of the Kwakiutl, based on gathering in an exceptionally productive natural environment. In the case of the acorn-gatherers of California, maize agriculture with a neolithic technology may actually be less productive and reliable, capable of supporting fewer people, than acorn-gathering. Such an economic base does not, however, produce civilizations even when it does permit sedentary life, one of civilization's necessary, but not sufficient, preconditions. The sociological implications of hunting and gathering generally preclude differential access to strategic resources. Food-production gives man a certain amount of control over his food supply and brings into focus different kinds of ecological limiting factors. The potential for the production of surplus over and above subsistence needs continues to evolve, as it usually cannot with an economy based exclusively on wild food resources. Land and water do not merely permit the strategic resource—game—to flourish, but become in themselves strategic resources, the means of production; in this fact lies the basis of social stratification.

A result of increased population, surplus production, and competition for strategic resources is the specialization of occupation characteristic of civilization and, to a lesser degree, of the more complex chiefdoms. If surplus is channeled into population growth, this would ultimately provide the stimulus for social control, which would in turn alter the pattern of disposing of surplus and produce still increased demand for production of surplus. The specialization of function is in a sense self-intensifying once under way. Part of this is of course definitional: food production becomes a full-time speciality too when other occupations have become professionalized, if only by contrast. More substantive processes are, however, also operative. As the diversification of economic interest becomes greater, the greater is the need for centralized regulation to reconcile these interests. Specialists in control of men and of resources—political specialists—are increasingly required and can be supported from the increased production. As such authorities acquire more functions, they become more indispensable to the society as a whole, and their position is accordingly strengthened.

In the ecological analysis of specialization and population differentiation by occupation and status, permissive, limiting, and forcing situations are involved. Distribution of resources and a level of productivity sufficient to assure reliable and ample surpluses for exchange may act as permissive and limiting factors in any given instance. Analysis of these problems must take into account both geographical and cultural data and the relation between them. Another requisite would be a sufficiently large and specialized population to assure need for and dependence on exchange. Forcing situations are somewhat different—those in which the man-land ratio becomes too high for the support of the population by any means other than specialization. There comes a point which Geertz (1963) terms involution, when the investment of additional labor in the land leads to no further increase in total production; the cost of keeping surplus population on the land becomes, in other words, too high. Occupational specialization and the resultant increased social complexity become adaptive solutions.

Increasing intensiveness of agriculture has been noted as a feature of the Mesoamerican developmental sequence. One subtype of intensive permanent agriculture, the hydraulic, has been considered as of critical importance in the dynamics of civilization. A means of dealing technologically with the problem of feeding large numbers of people in relatively small areas, its very productivity results in further population growth. It has, however, sociological effects in addition to those resulting from increased production. First, specialists in management and control are necessitated if the irrigation system of considerable size is to continue to function efficiently. The construction, cleaning, and maintenance of such works require continual and substantial investment of labor, and such a labor force must be regulated. Second, its existence virtually assures true stratification. Intensive agriculture of any type involves often substantial modification and improvements of lands, and its permanence generally assures continuity of tenure and often private ownership of a kind relatively impractical in most swidden systems. Irrigation, furthermore, induces other significant differentials: those between irrigated and unirrigated land and between upstream and downstream users. On the one hand, the process of stratification is greatly intensified and accelerated; on the other, new cycles of competition are initiated.

An irrigation system of any size necessarily involves the linkage of more than a single local group into a larger network. Conflicts over resources are more frequent, and it falls to a central authority to control such conflicts. Without such regulation the whole system is likely to break down. This acts to strengthen the economic and political power of the central authority, and the result is the classical Oriental Despotism described by Wittfogel.

In the instances cited of the development of civilizations, the foregoing processes occur interdependently and act to reinforce each other in specified ways. These characteristics are, in our view, responsible for the evolution of the state. Large populations, relatively large and variable territorial areas, and generally a productive and distributive system that requires centralized control for continued efficiency are all essential factors in the process leading to civilization. The area controlled in each instance is limited effectively by available means of transportation and communication; without these means, the extension of close social integration and control are restricted. As the effectively controllable area becomes smaller, the population density required to support state institutions would necessarily be higher. At the initial stages of the development of the state, small territorial extent, particularly that of a circumscribed, non-open environment, would actually seem to be an accelerative factor, all else being equal. The process of pristine state formation is viewed as essentially a local process based on the dynamics of a local ecosystem.

Once the state comes into existence, the kinds of institutions it possesses act to modify that ecosystem still further. A new and more complex equilibrium results. By the nature of its structural characteristics, the state is adapted to expansion, both by its planned intensification of the processes which brought it into being (it functions as a virtually monopolistic entrepreneur), and by the incorporation of adjacent territories and populations which its institutions, unlike those of tribes or bands, are capable of integrating and absorbing. Non-state-organized neighbors cannot compete effectively with the state in economics, politics, or warfare. The formation of empires and macro-states involves processes occurring above the level of the local ecosystem. The formation of secondary states can be explained in two ways. First, surrounding areas develop state institutions in order to withstand the competitive pressure of an existing state; or, alternatively, they develop such organization by being absorbed. This first model, in contrast to the second, is essentially a synchronic one; the second is at least in part diachronic, as illustrated by the cyclical-conquest empires, in which the institutions of later powers are modeled upon those of their predecessors in time, with historical continuity of institutions from one to another. Ecological and geopolitical factors on the supra-local level are inevitably involved; even within macro-states there will be some areas more closely integrated with the center than others, either because of their proximity or because of their strategic importance.

The problem of urbanism is distinct from that of the state. While urbanized societies are invariably states, not all states are urban. We have accordingly defined two subclasses of our civilization level. In addition, then, to describing the processes underlying civilization as a whole, we must next turn to a summary of those which determine urbanism. These latter include increases of population size and density, differentiation of function on the basis of occupational specialization and social stratification, and nucleated settlement. Although any of these may occur in the absence of the others, only when they occur together do we have an overall process that can be called urbanization. An urban community is one with a large, dense permanent population, composed primarily of non-food-producers who are specialists in crafts, economics, government, religion; as a community, it is accordingly dependent upon the surplus produce of the sustaining area for food, and, ideally, the population of the hinterland must obtain needed goods and services from the city. The existence of cities, therefore, necessarily implies the presence of a large social system, integrated in the way that Durkheim terms "organic solidarity."

The economic and social implications of the city are, therefore, that regular, patterned means exist not only for the production of surplus, but for distributing it to feed a settlement of people who themselves are not primary producers. In other words, it is insufficient for the peasantry to produce a surplus; there must also be some incentive for them to spend it in this particular way. In the case of civilizations there are generally two types of incentive. The first, of course, characterizing all types of state, urban or no, is force. Surplus is channeled into the city (or, in the case of nonurban civilizations, to the elite) in the form of taxation, tributes, tithes, and rents; and effective sanctions exist to assure payment. Considered by itself, the class exacting these payments tends to be parasitic, unless, as we have pointed out, it has some function which is essential to the primary producers. In the urban setting, there is an additional incentive: The concentration of craft and other professionals in the city and the function of the city as the locus of market exchange transform a parasitic situation into a more clearly symbiotic one. Directly or indirectly, much of peasant technology is either manufactured in or distributed through the city; fair exchange is no robbery. In addition, the integration, both horizontal and vertical, of the society as a whole is immeasurably reinforced and strengthened.

Within the matrix of civilization, the city is at once a product of intense symbiosis among various local and regional components of an overall framework and an intensifier of that symbiosis. Specialization of regions and of people becomes greater and more indispensable to all the diverse segments of the society. Coe (1961a) attributes the absence of cities in the tropical lowlands to an absence of local symbiosis and therefore lack of reliance upon commerce in procuring subsistence staples. In turn, such absence is based upon an overall relative geographical uniformity, in which most land usable at all is usable for the same things, and no significant differences obtain in harvest times or in local distribution of other essential resources. Sanders (1957) makes the same observation, and, as noted elsewhere in this volume, we cite the existence of additional factors related to the requirements of the productive system, reinforcing this already decided tendency to the ceremonial center-hamlet pattern, an alternative site-stratification pattern characteristic of nonurban civilizations.

In the Maya area the economy was based upon swidden cultivation rather than on intensive, permanent agriculture. A correspondingly larger area is required per family to allow for the rotation cycle of slash-and-burn. Limitations of transport militate against large nucleated settlements of any type under such conditions. Factors promoting such settlement in the Highlands include the generally smaller holding requirements per family, the superior efficiency of cooperative labor in exploiting the environment, and the greater ease of distribution of surpluses within the framework of a well-developed market system. All these facilitative advantages are lost in the Maya Lowlands, where nucleated settlement becomes uneconomical. When we consider the function of such a settlement in the collection and redistribution of surplus, its size and complexity may be seen as correlated with market volume and degree of specialization among both the suppliers and consumers. Larger urban settlements would tend to correlate with large and specialized rural populations within a radius whose effective length is a function of transport. In the Petén, we are dealing with a smaller and sparser rural population, probably less sedentary than the Highland peasantry owing to the exigencies of swidden agriculture and, in effect, within a territorial unit as circumscribed in size as the Highland one. In turn, these peasants were more generalized producers than their Highland counterparts, less dependent upon the market systems that are an important *raison d'être* of the city. As nucleated settlement of any kind is costly, so especially is the city.

The evolution of the city is a product of the interaction of both the geographical characteristics of the habitat, and of the utilization of these factors by especially the technological and economic subsystems of culture. Besides the essentially local and autochthonous factors causally underlying the development of the city, other factors of supra-local nature must be considered in the origin and function of cities. These latter factors are directly dependent on the macroecological dynamics of macrostates. We have suggested a possible model for this intensification in the Maya area as a result of its relationship with another state. What we would call true cities remain absent; nonetheless, site stratification appears intensified as a result of foreign contacts. The entire socioeconomic network of the Maya area was expanded and complicated, increasing the need for centralized control. In a modern instance, such expansion appears to be more complex still; in contemporary Lowland Tabasco and Veracruz, it has resulted in the formation of small urban communities. Modern transport and communication have linked cash-crop production of bananas, sugar cane, and cacao in this area directly to an international market system, for which the urban communities serve as collection and redistributive centers. Technological change has made the enterprise profitable. As the relationship of an area to other areas changes, so too will the purely local dynamics be affected.

We have stressed the restricted distribution of pre-Iron Age civilization, and discussed the advantages and disadvantages of civilization to individuals and to communities. From a broad evolutionary perspective it seems evident that the advantages outweigh the disadvantages; one could argue that the achievement of civilization on a worldwide basis was and is inevitable. The interrelated dynamic processes we have emphasized as stimuli of social evolution—growth of population size and density, competition, and cooperation—are universal. Hence the universality of civilization. What this study really attempts to explain, therefore, is precocity and retardation. Why were early civilizations restricted to certain culture areas? Why, within these culture areas, were some sectors more precocious than others during the various phases of societal evolution? We hold, with Steward, that the observed regularities in the development of these early civilizations are due to similarities of ecological systems, systems of unique type whose significant components are microgeographic adaptation and hydraulic agriculture.

Civilization, in our view, is a regularity, a successful adaptive response to certain kinds of pressures which we have delimited. So too is the special subtype of civilization which we call urbanism. As a response to certain kinds of stimuli favored by selection, it can be regarded as in effect inevitable where these circumstances occur. Migration and diffusion as responsible factors become unnecessary as explanatory devices in themselves; rather, these factors themselves demand clarification and explanation, without which invoking them is merely to beg the question. By "inevitable" we mean that the constellation of features we have analyzed will arise in certain kinds of areas, with high probability in the course of time; when they do, there will be strong selective pressure in their favor to assure the perpetuation and intensification of these forms.

Bibliography

ADAMS, ROBERT M.
  1960a "The origin of cities," *Scientific American*, Vol. 203, No. 3.
  1960b "Early civilization, subsistence and environment," in *City Invincible*. Chicago: Oriental Institute, Special Publication.
  1962a *A Synopsis of the Historical Demography and Ecology of the Diyala River Basin, Central Iraq*. University of Utah, Civilizations in Arid Lands, Anthropological Paper 62.
  1962b "Agriculture and urban life in early southwestern Iran," *Science*, Vol. 136, No. 3511.
  1966 *The Evolution of Urban Society: Early Mesopotamia and Prehispanic Mexico*. Chicago: Aldine Publishing Company.
ALLAN, WILLIAM
  1965 *The African Husbandman*. New York: Barnes and Noble.
ANDREWS, E. WYLLYS
  1965 "Archaeology and prehistory in the northern Maya Lowlands," in *Handbook of Middle American Indians*, Robert Wauchope, gen. ed. Vol. 2. Austin: University of Texas Press.
ARMILLAS, PEDRO
  1948 "A sequence of cultural development in Mesoamerica,"

in *A Reappraisal of Peruvian Archaeology*, W. C. Bennett, ed. Menasha, Wisconsin: Society for American Archaeology, Memoir No. 4.

1949   *Notas Sobre los Sistémas de Cultívo en Mesoamerica.* Mexico, D. F.: Instituto Nacional de Antropología e Historia, Anales, No. 3.

1950   "Teotihuacán, Tuly y los Toltecas." Buenos Aires: *Runa*, Vol. III.

1964a   "Condiciónes Ambientales y Movimientos de Pueblos en la Frontera Septentrional de Mesoamerica," *Homenaje a Fernando Marquez Miranda*. Madrid: Publicaciones del Seminario de Estudios Americanistas y el Seminario de Antropología Americana.

1964b   "Northern Mesoamerica," in *Prehistoric Man in the New World*, J. D. Jennings and E. Norbeck, eds. Chicago: University of Chicago Press.

AVELEYRA ARROYO DE ANDA, LUIS

1965   "The pleistocene carved bone from Tequixquiac, Mexico: a reappraisal," *American Antiquity*, Vol. 30, No. 3.

BANDELIER, ADOLPH

1880   *On the Social Organization and Mode of Government of the Ancient Mexicans.* Peabody Museum of American Archaeology and Ethnology, Annual Reports, Vol. XII, No. 2.

BENNETT, WENDELL C.

1946   "The archaeology of the Central Andes," in *Handbook of South American Indians*, Vol. 2 (The Andean Civilizations). Washington, D.C.: Smithsonian Institution, Bureau of American Ethnology, Bulletin 143.

1948   *A Reappraisal of Peruvian Archaeology*, W. C. Bennett, ed. Menasha, Wisconsin: Society for American Archaeology, Memoir No. 4.

BENNYHOFF, J. A., and R. F. HEIZER

1965   "Neutron activation analysis of some Cuicuilco and Teotihuacán pottery: archaeological interpretation of some results," *American Antiquity*, Vol. 30, No. 1.

BORAH, WOODROW, and SHERBURNE F. COOK

1960   "The population of Central Mexico in 1548," *Ibero-Americana*, Vol. 43.

1963   "The aboriginal population of Central Mexico on the eve of the Spanish conquest," *Ibero-Americana*, Vol. 45.

BORHEGYI, STEPHAN F. DE

1965a   "Archaeological synthesis of the Guatemala highlands," in *Handbook of Middle American Indians*, Robert Wauchope, gen. ed. Vol. 2. Austin: University of Texas Press.

1965*b*   "Settlement patterns of the Guatemala highlands," in *Handbook of Middle American Indians*, Robert Wauchope, gen. ed. Vol. 2. Austin: University of Texas Press.

BRAIDWOOD, ROBERT J.

1959   "Archaeology and the evolutionary theory," in *Evolution and Anthropology, a Centennial Appraisal*. Washington, D.C.: Anthropological Society of Washington.

————, and CHARLES REED

1957   "The achievement and early consequences of food production," *Cold Spring Harbor Symposia on Quantitative Biology*, Vol. XXII.

BRONSON, BENNET

1966   "Roots and the subsistence of the ancient Maya," *Southwestern Journal of Anthropology*, Vol. 22, No. 3.

BUCHANAN, K. M., and J. C. PUGH

1966   *Land and People in Nigeria*. London: University of London Press.

BULLARD, WILLIAM R., JR.

1960   "Maya settlement patterns in northwestern Peten, Guatemala," *American Antiquity*, Vol. XXV, No. 3, 355–372.

1962   "Settlement Pattern and Social Structure in the Southern Maya Lowlands During the Classic Period." Mexico: XXXV Congreso Internacional de Americanistas, *Actas y Memorias*.

BURGESS, E. W.

1925   "The growth of the city," in *The City*, R. E. Park and E. W. Burgess, eds. Chicago: University of Chicago Press.

CALNEK, EDWARD

1966   *The Aztec Imperial Bureaucracy*. Paper presented at the 65th annual meeting of the American Anthropological Association, Pittsburgh, Pennsylvania.

CARNEIRO, ROBERT

1961   "Slash and burn cultivation among the Kuikuru and its implications for cultural development in the Amazon Basin," *Antropológica*, No. 10.

CARR, ROBERT F., and JAMES E. HAZARD

1961   *Map of the Ruins of Tikal, El Petén, Guatemala*. Tikal Report No. 11, University Museum, University of Pennsylvania, Philadelphia.

CARRASCO, PEDRO

1961   "El barrio y la regulación del matrimonio en un pueblo en el Valle de México en el siglo XVI," *Revista Mexicana de Estudios Antropológicos*, Vol. 17.

1964   "Family structure of sixteenth century Tepoztlan," in *Process and Pattern in Culture*, Robert A. Manners, ed. Chicago: Aldine Publishing Company.

CASO, ALFONSO
    1959 "La tenencía de la tierra entre los antiguos Mexicanos,"
    Memorias del Colegio Nacional, Vol. IV, No. 2.
CHAPMAN, ANNE C.
    1957 "Port of trade enclaves in Aztec and Maya civilization,"
    in *Trade and Market in the Early Empires*, Karl Polanyi,
    Conrad M. Arensberg, and Harry W. Pearson, eds. New
    York: The Free Press.
CHILDE, V. GORDON
    1950 "The urban revolution," *Town Planning Review*, 21.
    1951 *Social Evolution*. New York: Henry Schuman.
    1957 *New Light on the Most Ancient East*. New York:
    Grove Press.
COE, MICHAEL D.
    1961a "Social typology and tropical forest civilizations,"
    Comparative Studies in Society and History, Vol. IV, No. 1.
    1961b *La Victoria*. Papers of the Peabody Museum of
    Archaeology and Ethnology, Harvard University, Vol. LIII.
    1962 *Mexico*. New York: Praeger, Ancient Peoples and
    Places Series.
    1963 "Olmec and Chavin: rejoinder to Lanning," *American
    Antiquity*, Vol. 29, No. 1.
    1965a *The Jaguar's Children: Pre-Classic Central Mexico*.
    New York Museum of Primitive Art.
    1965b "Archaeological synthesis of southern Veracruz and
    Tabasco," in *Handbook of Middle American Indians*, Robert
    Wauchope, gen. ed. Vol. 3. Austin: University of Texas
    Press.
    1965c "The Olmec style and its distribution," in *Handbook
    of Middle American Indians*, Robert Wauchope, gen. ed.
    Vol. 3. Austin: University of Texas Press.
    1966 *The Maya*. New York: Praeger, Ancient Peoples and
    Places Series.
    ———, and KENT V. FLANNERY
    1964 "Microenvironments and Mesoamerican prehistory,"
    Science, Vol. 143, No. 3607.
    1967 *Early Cultures and Human Ecology in South Coastal
    Guatemala*. Washington, D.C.: Smithsonian Contributions
    to Anthropology, Vol. 3.
    ———, RICHARD DIEHL, and M. STUIVER
    1967 "Olmec civilization, Veracruz, Mexico: dating of the
    San Lorenzo phase," *Science*, Vol. 155, No. 3768.
COE, WILLIAM R.
    1965 "Tikal: ten years of study of a Maya ruin in the low-
    lands of Guatemala," *Expedition*, Vol. 8, No. 1.

COLLIER, JOHN
  1955 "Development of civilization in the coast of Peru," in
  Irrigation Civilizations: A Comparative Study, Julian H.
  Steward, ed. Washington, D.C.: Pan American Union,
  Social Science Monographs I.

COOK, SHERBURNE F., and WOODROW BORAH
  1960 "The Indian population of Central Mexico, 1531–
  1610," *Ibero-Americana*, Vol. 44.

——, and LESLEY BYRD SIMPSON
  1948 "The population of central Mexico in the 16th century," *Ibero-Americana*, Vol. 31.

COON, CARLETON S.
  1948 *A Reader in General Anthropology*. New York: Henry
  Holt and Company.
  1962 *The Origin of Races*. New York: Alfred A. Knopf.

COVARRUBIAS, MIGUEL
  1957 *Indian Art of Mexico and Central America*. New York:
  Alfred A. Knopf.

DIXON, KEITH A.
  1959 *Ceramics From Two Preclassic Periods at Chiapa de
  Corzo, Chiapas, Mexico*. Papers of the New World Archaeological Foundation, No. 5, Orinda, California.

DIXON, ROLAND B.
  1928 *The Building of Cultures*. New York: Charles Scrib-
  ner's Sons.

DOBYNS, HENRY F.
  1966 "Estimating aboriginal American population," *Current
  Anthropology*, Vol. 7, No. 4.

DRUCKER, PHILIP A.
  1952 *La Venta, Tabasco: A Study of Olmec Ceramics and
  Art*. Washington, D.C.: Smithsonian Institution, Bureau of
  American Ethnology, Bulletin 153.

——, ROBERT F. HEIZER, and ROBERT J. SQUIER
  1959 *Excavations at La Venta, Tabasco*. Washington, D.C.:
  Smithsonian Institution, Bureau of American Ethnology,
  Bulletin 170.

DUMOND, D. E.
  1965 "Population growth and cultural change," *Southwestern Journal of Anthropology*, Vol. 21, No. 4.

DURKHEIM, EMILE
  1933 *The Division of Labor in Society*, trans. by George
  Simpson. New York: Macmillan Company.

EKHOLM, GORDON F.
  1962 "The Possible Chinese Origin of Teotihuacán Cylindrical Tripod Pottery and Certain Related Traits." Mexico:

XXXV Congreso Internacional de Americanistas, *Actas y Memorias.*

1964 "Transpacific contacts," in *Prehistoric Man in the New World*, D. J. Jennings and E. Norbeck, eds. Chicago: University of Chicago Press.

ERASMUS, CHARLES J.

1965 "Monument building: some field experiments," *Southwestern Journal of Anthropology*, Vol. 21, No. 4.

ESTRADA, EMILIO, and CLIFFORD EVANS

1963 "Cultural development in Ecuador," in *Aboriginal Cultural Development in Latin America: An Interpretative Review*, B. J. Meggers and C. Evans, eds. Washington, D.C.: Smithsonian Institution, Miscellaneous Collections, Vol. 146, No. 1.

FALLERS, LLOYD

1965 *Bantu Bureaucracy.* Chicago: University of Chicago Press, Phoenix Books.

FLANNERY, KENT V.

1967 *The Agricultural Revolution in the Valley of Oaxaca and its Consequences.* Paper presented at the 32nd annual meeting of the Society for American Archaeology, Ann Arbor, Michigan.

FORTES, M., and E. E. EVANS-PRICHARD, eds.

1940 *African Political Systems.* Oxford and New York: Oxford University Press.

FOSTER, GEORGE M.

1960 *Culture and Conquest.* Chicago: Quadrangle Books.

1965 "Peasant society and the image of limited good," *American Anthropologist*, Vol. 67, No. 2.

FOWLER, MELVIN L.

1966 *The Temple Town Community: Cahokia and Amalucan Compared.* Paper presented at the XXXVII International Congress of Americanists, Mar del Plata, Argentina.

FRANKFORT, HENRI

1951 *The Birth of Civilization in the Near East.* Bloomington: Indiana University Press.

FRIED, MORTON H.

1960 "On the evolution of social stratification and the state," in *Culture in History: Essays in Honor of Paul Radin*, Stanley Diamond, ed. New York: Columbia University Press.

GARCÍA-PAYÓN, J.

1950 *Restos de una Cultura Prehistórica encontrados en la region de Zempoala, Veracruz*, Vol. II. Jalapa: Universidad Veracruzana.

GEERTZ, CLIFFORD

1963 *Agricultural Involution: The Process of Ecological*

Change in Indonesia. Berkeley: University of California Press.

GROVE, DAVID C.
1967   The Preclassic Olmec in Central Mexico: Site Distribution and Inferences. Paper presented at the 66th annual meeting of the American Anthropological Association, Washington, D.C.

HARRIS, MARVIN
1964   Patterns of Race in the Americas. New York: Walker and Company.
1966   "The cultural ecology of India's sacred cattle," *Current Anthropology*, Vol. 7, No. 1.

HAVILAND, WILLIAM A.
1967   "Stature at Tikal, Guatemala: implications for ancient Maya demography and social organization," *American Antiquity*, Vol. 32, No. 3.

HAWKES, CHRISTOPHER
1954   "Archaeological theory and method: some suggestions from the Old World," *American Anthropologist*, Vol. 56, No. 1.

HOCKETT, CHARLES F., and ROBERT ASCHER
1964   "The human revolution," *Current Anthropology*, Vol. 5, No. 3.

HORKHEIMER, HANS
1964   "La arqueología Peruana en marcha," *Suplemento Especial de Fanal*, Vol. XIX, No. 69.

INCAP-ICNND
1961   Food Composition Table for Use in Latin America. Bethesda: National Institutes of Health, June.

JENNINGS, JESSE D., and EDWARD NORBECK, eds.
1964   Prehistoric Man in the New World. Chicago: University of Chicago Press.

KAPLAN, DAVID
1963   "Men, monuments and political systems," *Southwestern Journal of Anthropology*, Vol. 19, No. 4.

KIDDER, ALFRED V., II, LUIS A. LUMBRERAS, and DAVID B. SMITH
1963   "Cultural development in the Central Andes—Peru and Bolivia," in *Aboriginal Development in Latin America: An Interpretative Review*, B. J. Meggers and C. Evans, eds. Washington, D.C.: Smithsonian Institution, Miscellaneous Collections, Vol. 146, No. 1.

KIRCHOFF, PAUL
1943   "Mesoamerica," *Acta Americana*, Vol. I.
1959   "The principles of clanship in human society," in *Readings in Anthropology*, Vol. 2, Morton H. Fried, ed. New York: Thomas Crowell and Company.

KOSOK, PAUL
  1965   *Life, Land and Water in Ancient Peru.* New York: Long Island University Press.
KRIEGER, ALEX D.
  1953   "New World culture history: Anglo-America," in *Anthropology Today*, Alfred L. Kroeber, ed. Chicago: University of Chicago Press.
KROEBER, ALFRED L.
  1947   *Cultural and Natural Areas of Native North America.* Berkeley: University of California Press.
  1948   *Anthropology.* New York: Harcourt, Brace and World.
KUBLER, GEORGE
  1948   *Mexican Architecture of the Sixteenth Century*, 2 vols. New Haven: Yale University Press.
LANNING, EDWARD P.
  1965   "Early man in Peru," *Scientific American*, Vol. 213, No. 4.
LEWIS, OSCAR
  1951   *Life in a Mexican Village: Tepoztlán Restudied.* Urbana: University of Illinois Press.
LORENZO, JOSÉ LUIS
  1960   "Aspectos físicos del Valle de Oaxaca," *Revista Mexicana de Estudios Antropologicos*, Vol. XVI (Mesa Redonda sobre Oaxaca).
LOWE, GARETH
  1959   *Archaeological Exploration of the Upper Grijalva River, Chiapas, Mexico.* Papers of the New World Archaeological Foundation, No. 2, Orinda, California.
MCBRYDE, FELIX W.
  1947   *Cultural and Historical Geography of Southwest Guatemala.* Smithsonian Institution, Institute of Social Anthropology, Publication No. 4.
MACNEISH, RICHARD S.
  1954   "An early archaeological site near Panuco, Veracruz," *Transactions of the American Philosophical Society*, New Series, Vol. 44, Part 5.
  1958   "Preliminary archaeological investigations in the Sierra de Tamaulipas, Mexico," *Transactions of the American Philosophical Society*, New Series, Vol. 48, Part 6.
  1964   "Ancient Mesoamerican civilization," *Science*, Vol. 143, No. 3606.
MANGELSDORF, P. C., R. S. MACNEISH, and W. C. GALINOT
  1964   "Domestication of corn," *Science*, Vol. 143, No. 3606.
MARTYR, PETER
  1912   *De Orbe Novo*, translated by Francis Augustus MacNutt. London and New York: G. P. Putnam and Sons.

MASON, J. ALDEN
  1957   *The Ancient Civilizations of Peru.* Baltimore: Pelican Books.
MAY, JACQUES M.
  1965   *The Ecology of Malnutrition in Middle Africa.* Studies in Medical Geography, Vol. 5. New York and London: Hafner Publishing Company.
MAZESS, R. B., and P. T. BAKER
  1964   "Diet of Quechua Indians living at high altitudes: Nuñoa, Peru," *American Journal of Clinical Nutrition,* Vol. 15, December.
MEAD, MARGARET
  1930   *Social Organization of Manua.* Honolulu: Bernice P. Bishop Museum, Bulletin 76.
MEGGERS, BETTY J.
  1954   "Environmental limitation in the development of culture," *American Anthropologist,* Vol. 56, No. 5.
  1963   "Cultural development in Latin America: an interpretative review," *Aboriginal Cultural Development in Latin America: An Interpretative Review,* B. J. Meggers and C. Evans, eds. Washington, D.C.: Smithsonian Institution, Miscellaneous Collections, Vol. 146, No. 1.
  1964   "North and South American cultural connections and convergences," in *Prehistoric Man in the New World,* J. D. Jennings and E. Norbeck, eds. Chicago: University of Chicago Press.
———, and CLIFFORD EVANS
  1957   *Archaeological Investigation at the Mouth of the Amazon.* Washington, D.C.: Smithsonian Institution, Bureau of American Ethnology, Bulletin 167.
———, CLIFFORD EVANS, and EMILIO ESTRADA
  1965   *Early Formative Period of Coastal Ecuador: The Valdivia and Machalilla Phases.* Washington, D.C.: Smithsonian Contributions to Anthropology, Vol. 1.
MILLON, RENÉ
  1954   "Irrigation at Teotihuacan," *American Antiquity,* Vol. 20, No. 2.
  1957   "Irrigation systems in the Valley of Teotihuacan," *American Antiquity,* Vol. 23, No. 2.
  1960   "The beginnings of Teotihuacan," *American Antiquity,* Vol. 26, No. 1.
  1962   *Variations in Response to the Practice of Irrigation Agriculture.* University of Utah, Cultivation in Arid Lands, Anthropological Papers, No. 62.
  1964   "Teotihuacan mapping project," *American Antiquity,* Vol. 30, No. 3.

1966a   Urbanization at Teotihuacán. Paper presented at the XXXVII International Congress of Americanists, Mar del Plata, Argentina.
1966b   Extensión y Población de la ciudad de Teotihuacán en sus Diferentes Periódos: Un Calculo Provisional. Paper presented at the Eleventh Mesa Redonda de la Sociedad Mexicana de Antropología, Mexico, D.F.
1967   "Teotihuacán," Scientific American, Vol. 216, No. 6.
————, CLARA HALL, and MAY DIAZ
1962   "Conflict in the modern Teotihuacán irrigation system," Comparative Studies in Society and History, Vol. IV, No. 4.
MONZON, ARTURO
1946   "La organización social de los Aztecas," in Mexico Prehispanico. Mexico, D.F.: Instituto Nacional de Antropología e Historia.
MORENO, MANUEL M.
1931   La Organización Política y Social de los Aztecas. Mexico, D.F.: Universidad Nacional Autonóma.
MORGAN, LEWIS HENRY
1877   Ancient Society. Chicago: Charles H. Kerr and Company.
MURDOCK, GEORGE P.
1949   Social Structure. New York: Macmillan Company.
NEELY, JAMES A.
1967   Formative, Classic and Post-Classic Water Control and Irrigation Systems in the Valley of Oaxaca. Paper presented at the 32nd annual meeting of the Society for American Archaeology, Ann Arbor, Michigan.
OLIVER, DOUGLAS L.
1955   A Solomon Island Society. Cambridge, Mass.: Harvard University Press.
ORLANDINI, RICHARD J.
1967   A Formative Well from the Valley of Oaxaca. Paper presented at the 32nd annual meeting of the Society for American Archaeology, Ann Arbor, Michigan.
PALERM, ANGEL
1952-3   "Etnografía antigua totonaca en el Oriente de Mexico," in Huastecos, Totonacos y Sus Vecinos, Vol. XIII of the Revista Mexicana de Estudios Antropologicos. Mexico, D.F.: Sociedad Mexicana de Antropología e Historia.
1955   "The agricultural base of urban civilization in Mesoamerica," in Irrigation Civilizations: A Comparative Study, Julian H. Steward, ed. Washington, D.C.: Pan American Union, Social Science Monographs I.
————, and ERIC WOLF
1961   "La agricultura y el desarrollo de la civilización en

Mesoamerica," *Revista Interamericana de Ciencias Sociales*, 2nd epoca, Vol. 1.

PELZER, KARL J.
   1945   *Pioneer Settlement in the Asiatic Tropics.* New York: American Geographical Society, Special Publications, No. 29.

PHILLIPS, PHILIP
   1955   "American archaeology and general anthropological theory," *Southwestern Journal of Anthropology*, Vol. 11, No. 3, 246–258.

PIÑA CHAN, ROMÁN
   1955   *Chalcatzingo, Morelos.* Mexico, D.F.: Dirección de Monumentos Prehispanicos.
   1958   *Tlatilco.* Mexico, D.F.: Instituto Nacional de Antropología e Historia.
   1960   *Mesoamerica.* Mexico, D.F.: Instituto Nacional de Antropología e Historia, Memorias VI.

RANDS, ROBERT
   1961   "Elaboration and invention in ceramic tradition," *American Antiquity*, Vol. 26, No. 3, Part I.

REICHEL-DOLMATOFF, GERARDO
   1965   *Colombia.* New York: Praeger, Ancient Peoples and Places Series.

ROMER, A. J.
   1959   *The Vertebrate Story.* Chicago: University of Chicago Press.

ROWE, JOHN H.
   1946   "Inca culture at the time of the conquest," in *Handbook of South American Indians*, Vol. 2. Washington, D.C.: Smithsonian Institution, Bureau of American Ethnology, Bulletin 143.
   1962   "Stages and periods in archaeological interpretation," *Southwestern Journal of Anthropology*, Vol. 18, No. 1.
   1963   "Urban settlement in ancient Peru," *Ñawpa Pacha.* Berkeley: Institute of Andean Studies.
   1966   "Diffusionism and archaeology," *American Antiquity*, Vol. 31, No. 3.

ROYS, RALPH L.
   1943   *The Indian Background of Colonial Yucatan.* Washington, D.C.: Carnegie Institution, Publication 548.
   1957   *Political Geography of the Yucatan Peninsula.* Washington, D.C.: Carnegie Institution, Publication 613.

SAHAGÚN, FRAY BERNARDINO DE
   1959   *General History of the Things of New Spain.* Florentine Codex, trans. by Charles E. Dibble and Arthur J. O. Anderson in Thirteen Parts. Part X, Book 9, *The Mer-*

chants. Published by The School of American Research and the University of Utah.

SAHLINS, MARSHALL D.
1958   *Social Stratification in Polynesia.* Seattle: University of Washington Press.
————, and ELMAN R. SERVICE
1960   *Evolution and Culture.* Ann Arbor: University of Michigan Press.

SANDERS, WILLIAM T.
1956   "The central Mexican symbiotic region," in *Prehistoric Settlement Patterns in the New World,* Gordon R. Willey, ed. New York: Viking Fund Publications in Anthropology, No. 23.
1957   *Tierra y Agua.* Ph.D. dissertation, Harvard University.
1962   "Cultural ecology of nuclear Mesoamerica," *American Anthropologist,* Vol. 64, No. 1, Part 1.
1962–3   "Cultural ecology of the Maya lowlands" (Two parts), *Estudios de Cultura Maya,* Vols. II, III. Mexico, D.F.: Universidad Nacional Autonóma de Mexico.
1965   *Cultural Ecology of the Teotihuacán Valley.* Pennsylvania State University, Department of Sociology and Anthropology.

SAUL, FRANK P.
1967   *Osteobiology and the Interpretation of Maya History.* Paper presented at the 66th annual meeting of the American Anthropological Association, Washington, D.C.

SERVICE, ELMAN R.
1962   *Primitive Social Organization: An Evolutionary Perspective.* New York: Random House.
1966   *The Hunters.* Englewood Cliffs: Prentice-Hall, Foundations of Modern Anthropology Series.

SMITH, ROBERT E.
1955   *Ceramic Sequence at Uaxactun, Guatemala.* New Orleans: Middle American Research Institute, Tulane University.

SORENSON, JOHN L.
1955   "A chronological ordering of the Mesoamerican preclassic," *Middle American Research Records,* Vol. II, No. 3.

SPINDEN, H. J.
1928   *Civilizations of Mexico and Central America.* New York: American Museum of Natural History, Handbook Series No. 3.

STADELMAN, RAYMOND
1940   *Maize Cultivation in Northwestern Guatemala.* Contribution to American Anthropology and History, No. 33.

Washington, D.C.: Carnegie Institution, Publication No. 523.

STEGGERDA, MORRIS
1941 *Maya Indians of Yucatan.* Washington, D.C.: Carnegie Institution, Publication No. 531.

STEWARD, JULIAN H.
1938 *Basin Plateau Aboriginal Sociopolitical Groups.* Washington, D.C.: Smithsonian Institution, Bureau of American Ethnology, Bulletin 120.
1948 "A functional-development classification of American high cultures," in *A Reappraisal of Peruvian Archaeology*, Wendell Bennett, ed. Menasha, Wisconsin: Society for American Archaeology, Memoir No. 4.
1949 "Cultural causality and law," *American Anthropologist*, Vol. 51.
1955a *Theory of Culture Change.* Urbana: University of Illinois Press.
1955b "Some implications of the symposium," in *Irrigation Civilizations: A Comparative Study*, Julian H. Steward, ed. Washington, D.C.: Pan American Union, Social Science Monographs I.
———, and L. C. FARON
1959 *Native Peoples of South America.* New York: McGraw-Hill.

STIRLING, MATTHEW W.
1955 *Stone Monuments of the Rio Chiquito, Veracruz, Mexico.* Washington, D.C.: Smithsonian Institution, Bureau of American Ethnology, Bulletin 157.

STRONG, WILLIAM DUNCAN
1948 "Cultural epochs and refuse stragigraphy in Peruvian archaeology," in *A Reappraisal of Peruvian Archaeology*, Wendell Bennett, ed. Menasha, Wisconsin: Society for American Archaeology, Memoir No. 4.

SUGGS, ROBERT C.
1960 *The Island Civilizations of Polynesia.* New York: New American Library, Mentor Books.

TOYNBEE, ARNOLD
1947 *A Study of History* (Abridgement of Vols. I–V). Oxford and New York: Oxford University Press.

VAILLANT, GEORGE C.
1930 *Excavations at Zacatenco.* Anthropological Papers of the American Museum of Natural History, New York, Vol. XXXII, Part 1.
1934 *Excavations at Gualupita.* Anthropological Papers of the American Museum of Natural History, New York, Vol. XXXV, Part 1.

1941 *Aztecs of Mexico*. New York: Doubleday, Doran and Company.

VAYDA, ANDREW P.

1961 "Expansion and warfare among swidden agriculturalists," *American Anthropologist*, Vol. 63, No. 2.

VOGT, EVON Z.

1956 "An appraisal of 'Prehistoric Settlement Patterns in the New World,'" in *Prehistoric Settlement Patterns in the New World*, Gordon R. Willey, ed. New York: Viking Fund Publications in Anthropology, No. 23.

1961 "Some aspects of Zinacantan settlement patterns and ceremonial organization," *Estudios de Cultura Maya*, Vol. 1. Mexico, D.F.: Universidad Nacional Autonóma de Mexico, pp. 131–146.

1964 "The genetic model and Maya cultural development," in *Desarrollo Cultural de los Mayas*, Evon Z. Vogt and Alberto Ruz L., eds. Mexico, D.F.: Universidad Nacional Autonóma de Mexico.

WAUCHOPE, ROBERT

1950 "A tentative sequence of preclassic ceramics in Middle America," *Middle American Research Records*, Vol. 1, No. 14.

WEST, ROBERT, and PEDRO ARMILLAS

1950 "Las chinampas de Mexico," *Cuadernos Americanos*, Vol. L, pp. 165–182.

WHITE, LESLIE A.

1949 *The Science of Culture*. New York: Grove Press.

WILLEY, GORDON R.

1953 *Prehistoric Settlement Patterns in the Virú Valley, Peru*. Washington, D.C.: Smithsonian Institution, Bureau of American Ethnology, Bulletin No. 155.

1964 "An archaeological frame of reference for Maya culture history," in *Desarrollo Cultural de los Mayas*, Evon Z. Vogt and Alberto Ruz L., eds. Mexico, D.F.: Universidad Nacional Autonóma de Mexico.

——, and WILLIAM R. BULLARD, JR.

1965 "Prehistoric settlement patterns in the Maya lowlands," in *Handbook of Middle American Indians*, Robert Wauchope, gen. ed. Vol. 2. Austin: University of Texas Press.

1966 *An Introduction to American Archaeology*, Vol. One: *North and Middle America*. Englewood Cliffs, N.J.: Prentice-Hall.

——, WILLIAM R. BULLARD JR., JOHN B. GLASS, and JAMES C. GIFFORD

1965 *Prehistoric Maya Settlements in the Belize Valley*. Papers of the Peabody Museum of Archaeology and Ethnology, Vol. LIV.

————, and PHILIP PHILLIPS

1958   *Method and Theory in American Archaeology*. Chicago: University of Chicago Press.

WITTFOGEL, KARL A.

1955   "Developmental aspects of hydraulic societies," in *Irrigation Civilizations: A Comparative Study*, Julian Steward, ed. Washington, D.C.: Pan American Union, Social Science Monographs I.

1957   *Oriental Despotism: A Comparative Study of Total Power*. New Haven: Yale University Press.

WOLF, ERIC R.

1959   *Sons of the Shaking Earth*. Chicago: University of Chicago Press.

1966   *Peasants*. Englewood Cliffs: Prentice-Hall, Foundations of Modern Anthropology Series.

ZAIDE, GREGORIO F.

1963   *Philippine Political and Cultural History*. Manila: Philippine Education Company.

ZORITA, ALONZO DE

1942   *Breve y Sumaria Relación de los Señores de la Nueva España*. Mexico, D.F.: Ediciones de la Universidad Nacional Autonóma de Mexico.

CONVERSION TABLE

Weights

1 gram = .0353 ounce
1 kilogram = 2.2046 pounds

Linear Measures

1 millimeter = .0394 inch
1 meter = 1.0936 yards
1 kilometer = .6214 mile

Square Measures

1 square kilometer = .3861 square mile
1 hectare = 2.471 acres

(1 square mile = 2.59 square kilometers)

Index

Abejas (Tehuacán), 107, 108
Adams, R., xv, 183–86
Adaptation, ix, x, 73, 96–97, 214
Agriculture, and geography, 10, 60, 101ff., 123, 129, 133; and population density, 9, 10, 85ff., 91, 93, 124, 130, 197–98; and sedentarism, 112ff.; and social evolution, 86, 106, 200–01, 233; crops, 9, 87, 91, 92fn., 109ff.; evolution of, 24, 29, 96, 107ff., 119, 133; labor in, 87–88, 96, 141, 145–46, 177, 190–91, 234. *See also* Calmil, Chinampas, Economic specialization, Infield-outfield, Irrigation, Swidden, Tlacolol
Aguilár (Huasteca), 111
Ajalpan (Tehuacán), 111
Altitude zones, 104–05
Amacusac, 119
Amazon Basin, 129, 130
Amelucan, 125fn.
Anasazi, 46, 62, 75
Andrews, E. W., 144, 160
Archaeology, and ethnology, 221; techniques, 46–47, 53, 115–16, 139–40
Archaic, 21, 23–24, 25
Architecture, diffusion of, 33, 166;

monumental, 30, 37, 53–57, 127, 140, 165–66, 226
Arévalo (Kaminaljuyú), 111
Armillas, P., xiv, 7, 33, 148, 151, 179, 180
Art style, convergence and divergence in, 60–62; diffusion, 68, 117ff., 167; inference from, 19, 30, 63–64, 119–21, 166
Atlihuayan, 118, 121
Azcaputzalco, 208
Aztec, vii, 26, 32, 34, 126; and Inca, 167–68; and Maya, 161ff.; and Olmec, 126; economy, 152, 161, 168, 209–10. *See also* Calpulli, Empire, Social stratification, Political structure, Population

Balsas Basin, 108, 123, 133
Bands, 41–42; archaeological recognition of, 52; distribution, 49, 59, 106ff.; economy, 80–81, 109; population, 79–80, 130. *See also* Hunting and gathering
Barrio, *see* Calpulli
Belén-Santamaria (Argentina), 63
Bennett, W., 7, 17, 120, 166
Borah, W., 147, 184fn.